ADMIRAL LORD
ST VINCENT –
SAINT OR TYRANT?

James A.S. Danikar

ADMIRAL LORD ST VINCENT – SAINT OR TYRANT?

The Life of Sir John Jervis,
Nelson's Patron

by

James D.G. Davidson

Pen & Sword
MARITIME

First published in Great Britain in 2006 by
Pen & Sword Maritime
an imprint of
Pen & Sword Books Ltd
47 Church Street
Barnsley
South Yorkshire
S70 2AS

ISBN 1 84415 386 x
978 1 84415 386 2

A CIP catalogue record for this book is
available from the British Library.

Typeset in 11/13 Sabon by
Phoenix Typesetting, Auldgirth, Dumfriesshire

Printed and bound in England by
CPI UK

Pen & Sword Books Ltd incorporates the imprints of Pen & Sword
Aviation, Pen & Sword Maritime, Pen & Sword Military, Wharncliffe
Local History, Pen & Sword Select, Pen & Sword Military Classics
and Leo Cooper.

For a complete list of Pen & Sword titles please contact
PEN & SWORD BOOKS LIMITED
47 Church Street, Barnsley, South Yorkshire, S70 2AS, England
E-mail: enquiries@pen-and-sword.co.uk
Website: www.pen-and-sword.co.uk

To all those whose courage and hard work
have enabled others to prosper or even
to achieve celebrity.

Contents

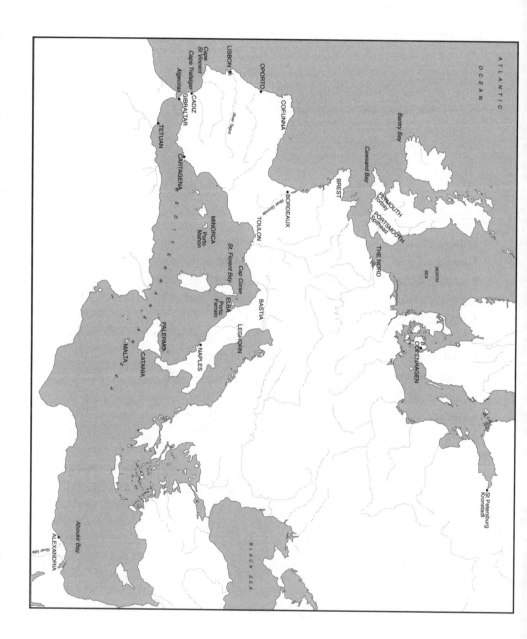

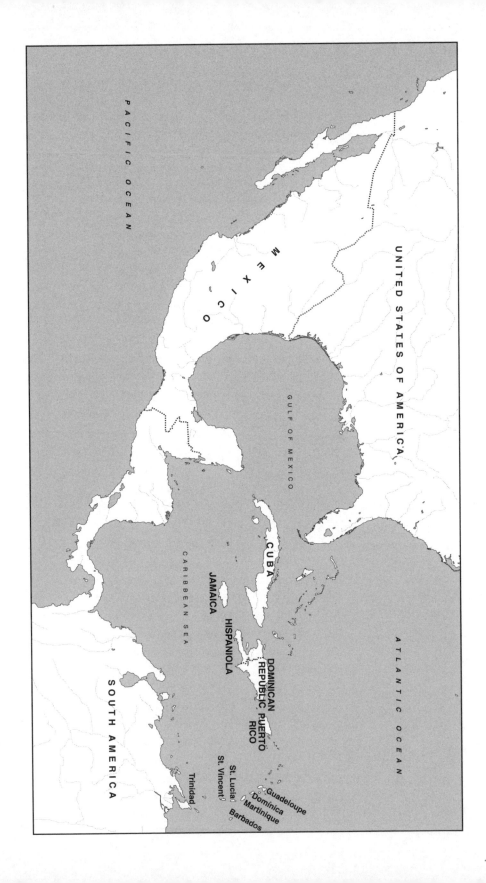

Introduction

It would be difficult to find a greater contrast between two men, successful in the same chosen profession, than between Admiral of the Fleet Lord St Vincent (1735–1823) and Vice Admiral Lord Nelson (1758–1805). Both were men of outstanding courage, professional competence and endurance, but there the similarity ends. The former was stocky, tough, unemotional, but capable of both explosive temper and wry humour; the latter slim, wiry, charismatic, but vain and mercurial. Their relationship at the professional level was almost symbiotic: St Vincent, the master strategist and ruthless reformer; Nelson, the brilliant tactician and polished diplomat. Their personal relationship was more like that between father and a favourite but wayward son than between flag officers – senior and subordinate – in the Royal Navy.

Neither St Vincent nor Nelson grew up in naval families, although both had naval relatives on the maternal side. Horatio Nelson was the son of a Norfolk parson. St Vincent was born John Jervis on 20 January 1735 at Meaford in the English shire of Stafford, the second son of Swynfen and Elizabeth Jervis. In later life he liked to claim that his youth was spent in straitened circumstances, and that he rose to eminence without family influence or any hint of nepotism. However, without detracting from his outstanding qualities, the facts would indicate otherwise. The Jervis family had long been established in Staffordshire and were known as the Jervis's of Stone. Stone is a market town on the River Trent, 7 miles north of Stafford. It is distinguished by a priory

1

and has a history of manufacturing ceramics, glass and footwear, and of brewing beer. The canal which links the Trent with the Mersey and Grand Union canals skirts the brewery walls. The canal was once important commercially but in the twenty-first century it is now mainly used by pleasure craft.

Meaford, the property of Swynfen Jervis, was a small country estate situated in the fertile, well-wooded, arable countryside to the north-east of the town. The manor house of Meaford Hall had substantial outbuildings to house coaches, horses and the other appurtenances of a small landowner. John Jervis may have grown up in a climate of thrift and economy, but not of poverty and hardship. However, the habit of thrift and economy, and an aversion to waste, remained with him throughout life.

John Jervis' father was a successful barrister as well as a small-scale landowner. His mother, Elizabeth, was daughter of George Parker of Park Hall in the same county, and sister of Thomas, who was to be knighted as Lord Chief Baron of the Exchequer. Elizabeth was a careful housewife with social ambitions for her two sons and two daughters. She was a cousin of the renowned circumnavigator of the world, Admiral Lord Anson who also hailed from the area.

It is not clear why John was sent for his early education to the grammar school in Burton on Trent, 25 miles away. Grammar schools provided arguably the best education in England, and one had been established in Stone itself for nearly 200 years. Perhaps the Jervis family did not respect the head teacher of the Stone grammar school, or perhaps, as the most promising of four children and destined for the legal profession, his parents decided it was worth the expense of boarding young John in Burton on Trent to enable him to attend a better school; it was certainly too far away for daily travel. This decision must have affected the youngster profoundly. Residence as a weekly boarder at some distance from home may well have inured the boy to homesickness, while simultaneously encouraging independence and self-sufficiency at the expense of sensitivity and tolerance. It also left him open to the radical influence of the family's coachman, Pinkthorne, during the long weekend drives back and forth between Burton on Trent and Stone. It is on record that

Pinkthorne considered all lawyers to be rogues and all sailors to be heroes.

It is perhaps significant that John Jervis was attending the grammar school in Burton on Trent at the time of the Jacobite uprising in 1745. At the beginning of December, when the army of Prince Charles Edward Stuart reached Derby, there must have been consternation in the nearby towns and villages, including Burton on Trent just 10 miles down the road south-west of Derby; there was near panic in London, 130 miles away. The atmosphere in the school must have been apprehensive, to say the least, for the Highlanders had been depicted as wild savages. Many, perhaps most, English people, regarded the Jacobites as a Scottish army attacking England and overlooked the reality: that it was an army comprised mainly of Catholics and Episcopalians from the Highlands and the North-East, with some Irish and a few English, opposed by Protestants, both English and Scots. Luckily for the residents of Burton on Trent and other nearby towns and villages, Prince Charlie's general, Lord George Murray, decided to retreat. Nevertheless, the events of December 1745 must have left a deep impression on a ten-year-old boy, cut off from his family at a school 25 miles from his home.

However, life was about to change dramatically for John Jervis. When he was twelve years old his father was appointed an Admiralty solicitor, and Treasurer of that prestigious naval establishment, Greenwich Hospital, once a royal palace and favourite residence of King Henry VIII, but adapted to accommodate naval pensioners at the time of Swynfen Jervis' appointment. The boy was moved to a private school in Greenwich, Swindell's Academy, the same school attended by James Wolfe who, twelve years later, would command the troops which would storm the Heights of Abraham and defeat the French on the Plains of Quebec. James Wolfe was eight years older than John Jervis so they could hardly have met at school, but they were to be closely associated in Canada. The fascinating career of the future Lord St Vincent would take him to both sides of the Atlantic, and from the Mediterranean to the Caribbean, but he would never see the other half of the world – west of North America and east of the Adriatic – he was destined to play a leading role in the wars to curb the ambitions of Napoleon.

3

John Jervis left no legitimate issue. It is from his nephew Edward who married twice, first to a Mary Turner and second to his cousin Mary Anne Parker, that the present representatives of his family are descended.

Chapter One

John Jervis joins the Navy

Situated on the south bank of the Thames, within sight and sound of ships from all over the world plying the river, the atmosphere of Greenwich borough was overwhelmingly nautical. The intention that John should follow his father's footsteps into the legal profession sank without trace. Under the maritime influence, perhaps reinforced by the opinions of Pinkthorne and the fame of his mother's cousin, Lord Anson, he decided to go to sea. The intensity of this urge resulted in an escapade which gave his family three days of serious worry. Accompanied by a school friend, he stowed away for three days and nights on a ship docked at Woolwich until, overcome by hunger and guilt, he returned home to inform his family that he wished to become a sailor.

In his old age, Lord St Vincent described this defining moment in his life to his relative, Captain Edward P. Brenton, author of two volumes published in 1838 entitled *Life and Correspondence of John Earl of St Vincent*. John Jervis formed a friendship at Swindell's Academy with a boy who was the son of a Dr Strachan in Greenwich and grandson of an admiral:

> He told me such stories of the happiness of a sea life, into which he had lately been initiated, that he easily persuaded me to quit the school and go with him. We set out accordingly, and concealed ourselves on board of a ship at Woolwich. My father was at that time absent on the northern circuit. My mother and sisters were in a state of distraction at learning our

absence from school fearing that some disaster had happened to us. But after keeping them for three days in the utmost anxiety, and suffering ourselves much privation and misery, we thought it best to return home. I went in at night and made myself known to my sisters who remonstrated with me rather warmly on the impropriety of my conduct and assured me that Mr Swinton would chastise me severely for it; to which I replied that he certainly would not, for that I did not intend to go to school anymore, and that I was resolved to be a sailor.

The next day my mother spoke to me on the subject, and I still repeated that I would be a sailor. This threw her into much perplexity; and, in the absence of her husband, she made known her grief, in a flood of tears, to Lady Archibald Hamilton, mother of the late Sir William Hamilton, and wife of the Governor of Greenwich Hospital. Her ladyship said she did not see the matter in the same light as my mother did – that she would undertake to procure me a situation in some ship of war.

In the mean time, my mother sent for her brother, Mr John Parker, who, on being made acquainted with my determination, expostulated with me, but to no purpose. I was resolved I would not be a lawyer, and that I would be a sailor.

Whether Admiral Lord Anson's influence was brought to bear at this stage is not recorded. Lord Anson survived until John Jervis was aged twenty-seven and had been promoted to captain. For most of that time Anson was First Lord of the Admiralty and in a position to influence appointments and promotions. It seems highly unlikely that in those days of flagrant nepotism Lord Anson had no effect on his young relative's early career, even if it was no more than to ensure that John Jervis served under captains of good repute and was not overlooked when he became eligible for a commission or for promotion. Yet Jervis seems to have been so embarrassed by his influential connections that he developed a prejudice against anybody to whom clung a whiff of nepotism, who bore a title, or had links with the aristocracy – at least until he himself was raised to the peerage.

Nepotism was widespread in the Royal Navy of the eighteenth and nineteenth centuries, although that did not prevent some men of outstanding merit from rising to the higher ranks from humble beginnings. To give two examples from among John Jervis' contemporaries: John Campbell, born in 1720 into a working-class family in south-west Scotland, was apprenticed at an early age to the Master of a coasting vessel where he learned his seamanship and navigation. He entered the Royal Navy by offering himself in exchange for the press-ganged Mate of a warship, the Mate being the assistant to the Master, who was the ship's navigator. A large ship would have had both a Captain and a Master, but in smaller ships the Master might also be the Captain. In 1740 John Campbell sailed in HMS *Centurion* as Captain George Anson's navigator on his voyage round the world. Subsequently, after commanding two frigates and two ships of the line, he was Admiral Hawke's Flag Captain at the Battle of Quiberon Bay in 1759. Having turned down a knighthood he was eventually appointed Commander-in-Chief and Governor of Newfoundland with the rank of Vice Admiral in 1782.

Perhaps the outstanding example of a naval officer's rise to fame from humble beginnings is that of Captain James Cook, whose three voyages of exploration between 1768 and 1779 opened up the Pacific and the Antipodes to the world at large. James Cook, who was born in 1728 in North Yorkshire on a farm out of sight and sound of the sea, was the son of a Scottish farm worker who had migrated there, married a local girl and risen to be farm bailiff. James was apprenticed to a local haberdasher at the age of twelve, but following a dispute with his employer he went to sea as a collier's apprentice, and by sheer ability rose eventually to the rank of captain in the Royal Navy, becoming one of the greatest navigators and explorers of all time.

Examples of men who reached flag rank in the Royal Navy of the eighteenth and nineteenth centuries because of who, rather than what, they knew, would not be hard to find, but it must be said that the majority of them seem to have been men of both experience and some competence. Whether or not John Jervis entered the Royal Navy backed by influence, there is no question mark over his professional skill, integrity, courage and commitment. Some people, both during his lifetime and since, have questioned his wisdom, imagination, humanity and judgement. The only way to reach a verdict is to take a close look at his life, his letters, his opinions and, not least, his achievements. Most of those who do so will reach a favourable verdict.

Shortly after John Jervis' escapade in the ship moored at Woolwich, Lady Archibald Hamilton, future mother-in-law of Emma, introduced the twelve-year-old John to Lady Burlington, and she to Commodore George Townshend who was on the point of departure in HMS *Gloucester* to take over as C-in-C in the West Indies, based in Jamaica. Lady Burlington requested that the Commodore take young John on his quarterdeck and he readily consented. The boy was entered on the books of HMS *Gloucester* as an able seaman on 4 January 1748, sixteen days before his thirteenth birthday. The ship's Captain was Lord Colville who, no doubt, was asked to keep a paternal eye on the boy.

In maturity, Jervis described how he joined the Navy to Captain Brenton:

> My equipment was what would now be called rather grotesque. My coat was made for me to grow up to; it reached down to my heels and was full large in the sleeves. I had a dirk and a gold-laced hat; and in this costume my uncle caused me to be introduced to my patroness, Lady Burlington. Here I acquitted myself but badly. I lagged behind my uncle and held by the skirt of his coat. Her ladyship, however, insisted on my coming forward, shook hands with me and told me I had chosen a very honourable profession. She then gave Mr Parker a note to Commodore George Townshend, who lived in one of the small houses in Charles Street, Berkeley Square, desiring that we should call there early the next morning. This we did; and after waiting some time, the commodore made his appearance in his night-cap and slippers, and in a very rough and uncouth voice asked me how soon I would be ready to join my ship? I replied 'directly'. 'Then you may go tomorrow morning,' said he, 'and I will give you a letter to the first lieutenant.' My uncle, Mr Parker, however, replied that I could not be ready quite so soon, and we quitted the commodore.

They took with them a letter to Lieutenant Maurice Suckling, First Lieutenant of the *Gloucester*, who was a relative of Horatio Nelson and would be the first captain Nelson served under twenty-two years later. John Jervis continued:

In a few days after this we set off; and my uncle took me to Mr Blanchard, the master-attendant, or the boatswain, of the dockyard, I forget which, and by him I was taken on board the hulk, or receiving ship, the next morning; the *Gloucester* being in dock at the time. As soon as the ship was ready for sea we proceeded to Jamaica and, as I was always fond of an active life, I volunteered to go into small vessels and saw a good deal of what was going on.

Jervis served as an Able Seaman in this ship of the line from 1748 to 25 June 1752, when he was rated midshipman and transferred to the *Severn*, another ship of the line, commanded by Captain Henry Dennis. During these four years he would have learned the basics of seamanship, the handling of sails and rigging and something of navigation, gunnery and organization. There is little on record describing how he spent this important period of apprenticeship, but in retirement years later he told Captain Brenton:

My father had a very large family with limited means. He gave me twenty pounds at starting and that was all he ever gave me. After I had been a considerable time on the station I drew for twenty more, but the Bill came back protested. I was mortified at this rebuke and made a promise, which I have ever kept, that I would never draw another bill without a certainty of it being paid . . . I immediately changed my mode of living; quitted my mess, lived alone and took up the ship's allowance which I found quite sufficient; washed and mended my own clothes; made a pair of trousers out of the ticking of my bed and having by these means saved as much money as would redeem my honour, took up my bill . . . and from that time to this I have taken care to keep within my means.

Uniforms had been introduced in April 1748 for naval officers, but the rule was confined to executive officers, including midshipmen. It would not have affected an able seaman. This lesson in economy was so deeply imprinted in the mind of John Jervis that it became an integral part of his character and personality. In later years, when he was in a position to influence expenditure in dockyards and at the Admiralty, it governed his outlook to an extent that it became more than a loathing of waste and extravagance and verged on false economy. When he became First Lord of the Admiralty in the years before Trafalgar and the coasts of France and Spain were under blockade by the British fleet for long periods, the ships were constantly short of stores and desperately in need of refitting. In 1810 he would write to Lord Elliot, whom he had come to know and respect as Vice-Regent of Corsica during the British occupation of that island:

> Having fought my way up to where I now stand, without the smallest pecuniary aid from any one, even when I was a mid, I cannot possibly entertain an opinion that officers of this day, whose half-pay is considerably more than formerly, cannot practise the same necessary economy which marked the character of, My dear Sir, your very sincere and obedient servant, St Vincent.

The apprentice seaman's preoccupation with economy is reflected in a letter written to his sister from the West Indies, and gives some indication of how he passed the time during these important years under training: 'There are many entertainments and public assemblies here but they are rather above my sphere, many inconveniencies and expenses attending them, so that my chief employ, when from my duty, is reading, studying navigation and perusing my old letters.'

When John Jervis became a midshipman in the *Severn* he took on real responsibility. It was his opportunity to distinguish himself with a view to being commissioned as a lieutenant. Midshipmen understudied the ship's Master to gain maximum experience in navigation. They were usually allocated the duty of leading parties to board other ships – either in attack or to investigate them for

10

contraband or other reasons. They might then be put in charge if the ship boarded was taken as a prize or otherwise taken into custody. In the distribution of prize money midshipmen were entitled to more shares than other members of a ship's company except the Captain, the lieutenants, the Master and the Master's Mate, which is an indication of their importance and status in a ship's hierarchy, but if they did not pass the examination for lieutenant they could remain as a midshipman indefinitely.

John Jervis matured early. By the time he became a midshipman at the age of seventeen one can assume that his appearance was not unlike the portraits painted in later life, because his features differ little between a painting of him in middle age by J. Keenan and another of him in his eighties by Carbonier. That is a tribute to both portrait painters and confirmation that the man wore well and that there was little change over the years in his character and personality. He was as formidable looking at nearly ninety as he had been at half that age. The eyes which dominate his face are wide-set under heavy brows. They are blue, penetrating, quizzical with the ghost of a sense of humour lurking somewhere, emphasized by creases at the corners of a straight, hard mouth. One of his humorous customs as an admiral was to summon the chaplains of the fleet for a conclave when the weather was particularly rough, either to check their ability to calm the waters, or to see if they were immune to seasickness. His long, pointed, aquiline nose might have been designed to cleave through the wind and waves, the firm jaw to clamp on an enemy's shrouds – or even his throat.

Jervis was not a big man but what he lacked in size was compensated for by his compact vitality. In looks and personality he was very different from his protégé, Horatio Nelson, whose gentle, almost delicate exterior hid a core of steel and a brilliant, imaginative mind.

During the six years which John Jervis spent in the Caribbean (1748–54) Great Britain was not officially at war with France. At sea they were relatively uneventful years although there was intense rivalry between the two colonial powers in areas from North America to India, and from the Caribbean to the Mediterranean. In North America the French were firmly based in Quebec, but in 1755 they were expelled from their settlements. Midshipman

Jervis, having spent two further years in the *Severn*, had left the Caribbean. Captain Henry Dennis, having found the young man promising and reliable, had taken him to the *Sphinx* when posted to that ship on 30 June 1754 to sail her home to England. This gave the nineteen-year-old midshipman an opportunity to become a commissioned officer. He had just two months left to complete the six years service necessary before he would be eligible to sit the examination for the rank of lieutenant. He spent one month in the brig *Seaford* and another in the yacht *Mary*, then on 22 January 1755 he successfully passed the exam, was promoted lieutenant and appointed to the *Royal George*. Within a month he was transferred to a ship of the line, the *Nottingham*, as part of a squadron about to be sent to North America under Vice Admiral Sir Edward Boscawen, nicknamed 'Old Dreadnought'. Rivalry between Great Britain and France was rapidly deteriorating into warfare.

The Duke of Newcastle, by most accounts a corrupt and untrustworthy political schemer, had become Prime Minister of Great Britain. He ordered Boscawen to follow a large French squadron which had sailed from Brest and to attack it if its purpose was to reinforce French forces in North America, but not to attack it 'unless he thought it worth while'. Admiral Lord Anson, by this time First Lord of the Admiralty, protested at the irresponsible wording of the order, but it was nevertheless approved by Newcastle's council. The French Ambassador responded by announcing that 'the King, his master, would consider the first gun fired on the sea in a hostile manner to be a declaration of war.'

Boscawen's squadron, comprising eleven ships of the line, with two regiments on board, sailed from Spithead on 27 April 1755. Shortly afterwards a further six sail were sent to join him. The two British squadrons joined forces on 21 June off the Newfoundland Banks, but not before Boscawen's eleven ships had fallen in with a superior French squadron on 6 June. Despite the disparity, Boscawen gave chase but lost contact in a thick fog. Two days later he fell in with three of the French ships and captured two of them, the third escaping in the fog. The rest of the French fleet gained the estuary of the St Lawrence and eventually reached Quebec.

A 'putrid jail fever' broke out in the British ships and Boscawen was forced to put into Halifax, Nova Scotia, for fresh supplies and to land the sick. Lieutenant Jervis was fortunate not to be infected. Meanwhile, on 13 July, a 1,500-strong column of British and Virginian troops was ambushed on its way to attack the French garrison of Fort Duquesne which guarded the Ohio Valley; two-thirds of them were killed or wounded. By November, when the French were expelled from their colony of Arcadia in Nova Scotia, Boscawen's squadron had been so debilitated by disease that he had been forced to take the ships back to England. They reached Spithead on 14 November having lost more than 2,000 men through sickness. John Jervis was lucky to escape.

On 31 March 1756, Lieutenant John Jervis was appointed to the *Devonshire*, but three months later transferred to another ship of the line, the *Prince*, which was fitting out in Chatham as the flag-ship for Admiral Lord Anson, should he decide to move from the admiralty to an active sea command. The Captain of the *Prince* was the man who had been Anson's First Lieutenant during his circum-navigation of the world eight years previously, Captain Charles Saunders.

Although war against France was not formally declared until 17 May 1756 – the start of the Seven Years' War – the French had been threatening the island of Minorca since the beginning of the year; Port Mahon, the island's capital, was then Britain's only Mediterrranean base east of Gibraltar. Admiral John Byng was sent out from England with a small fleet of ill-manned and indifferently equipped ships to beat the French blockade and save the island. On 30 May he encountered a French fleet which was numerically equal, better armed and equipped, and competently commanded. As a consequence of poor communications and questionable tactics, inhibited by the Royal Navy's obsolescent Permanent Instructions, Admiral Byng failed to engage the enemy effectively before turning and retreating to Gibraltar, leaving Minorca at the mercy of the French. As is well known, Byng was later court-martialled and executed by firing squad on the quarterdeck of his own ship – as the French put it, '*pour encourager les autres*'.

When Jervis sailed for the Mediterranean on board *Prince* on completion of her refit soon after this infamous action, he would have been acutely aware of the severe blow to British morale and to that of the Navy in particular. In due course he would learn the details of the court martial and its pitiless verdict and this would influence his attitude to command throughout his future career. He would never need encouragement to do whatever he considered to be his immediate duty, although it would be left to Horatio Nelson and others to risk using imagination, break with convention, ignore Permanent Instructions, and even disobey an admiral's orders in the interest of achieving decisive victory.

Chapter Two

The Years of Waiting

The early influence of Lord Anson is apparent in the appointment of John Jervis as Third Lieutenant of *Prince* in June 1756 to serve under the Admiral's protégé, Captain Saunders, later Admiral Sir Charles Saunders. Not only had Saunders been Anson's First Lieutenant on his voyage round the world, but Anson had been responsible for sponsoring Charles Saunders as Member of Parliament for the borough of Heydon, and maintained a close friendship with him. Many examples can be found of captains and admirals in the eighteenth and nineteenth centuries who became Members of Parliament to fill in time between wars, or to occupy themselves in retirement. Elections were often just a formality – sometimes an expensive one with success achieved by bribery, or sometimes simply by the power brokers' nomination.

Prince was an elite ship of the line and was visited by many people of influence, which did nothing to harm the prospects of young Lieutenant Jervis. Saunders was sent to the Mediterranean mainly to redress the shortcomings of the unfortunate Admiral Byng, but in October 1756 he was promoted to rear admiral and appointed by William Pitt the Elder to the naval command of an expedition to capture Quebec from the French. He took Jervis with him on the *Culloden* as second lieutenant when he transferred his flag to that ship of the line the following month. Saunders was only forty-five years old and the military commander, General James Wolfe, only thirty-two.

In January 1757, Saunders demonstrated his confidence in Jervis when he gave him command of the sloop *Experiment*, whose commander had fallen ill and had to be replaced at short notice. Jervis attracted the attention of his superiors by successfully defending a convoy of merchantmen off Cape Gata on 16 March, against a French privateer superior in both armament and speed to his own vessel. He returned to the *Culloden* soon afterwards but went with Saunders to the *St George* when the Admiral again transferred his flag in June.

In 1758 Lieutenant Jervis was given command of the *Foudroyant*, a prize which had been taken from the French in a fiercely contested action, in order to sail her to England. However, Saunders was sufficiently impressed with Jervis to demand his return as first lieutenant on board the *Neptune* in which the Admiral sailed for North America in January 1759, arriving at Louisberg in Nova Scotia on 21 April. There, General Wolfe was a guest in the flagship and Lieutenant Jervis was able to make his acquaintance with his former fellow pupil. There was only an eight year age gap between them.

The powerful currents and navigational hazards of the St Lawrence River had given the great river an awesome reputation among ships' masters and navigators. Their reluctance to negotiate its waters was one obstacle to General Wolfe's plan for the capture of Quebec; another was the wall of cliffs, the Heights of Abraham, which rose from the river to the plains above. The French pilots, who treated the river with great respect, thought that a British fleet would be unable to navigate the Traverse, a particularly tricky section downriver from Quebec, but James Cook – already recognized as an outstanding navigator – spent three days taking soundings and declared himself 'satisfied with being acquainted with the channel'. The Master of one of the troop transports, distrusting his French pilot, had also taken over and established the channel by observing the colour of the water and the surface ripples. In later years, John Jervis suggested that the French had deliberately kept the British in ignorance of 'the easy navigation of the Gulf of the River St Lawrence'. With the confidence of hindsight he declared: 'I believe Sir Charles Saunders would have turned his back upon it, even after Admiral Durrell got up the Traverse, if I had not been his first lieutenant and virtually his captain.'

On 4 July 1759 Saunders appointed Jervis acting commander of the sloop *Porcupine*, detaching him to guide the troop transports up the river through the shoals and rapids to Quebec. Amongst the troops were Highlanders of the 77th and 78th regiments, Montgomery's and Frazer's, some of whom had been involved on one side or the other in the Jacobite rising of the previous decade. Wolfe and Jervis, the first with his experience of serving as a lieutenant in Cumberland's army at Culloden, and the latter with his boyhood memories of the Highland army approaching his school at Burton on Trent, must have reflected on the turn of history which now had Highlanders fighting for King George against the French. Wolfe used them as scouts and shock troops in advance of his main force.

The French general, Montcalm, did not believe it possible for troops to attack by way of the Heights of Abraham. Nevertheless, on the night of 12 September 1759, guided by the *Porcupine*, troops were landed at the foot of the cliffs and scaled them in the dark, led by Highland scouts. In the morning light of the 13th, the French discovered the British army drawn up along the cliff top. At 10.00 am the French charged; they were met by repeated volleys of musket fire and lost 650 men. The British losses were less than a tenth of that number. Quebec was taken, but Wolfe had been killed. Five weeks later, Admiral Hawke virtually destroyed the French fleet at the Battle of Quiberon Bay off the coast of Brittany, and soon afterwards Canada became British.

It is reputed that John Jervis took General Wolfe's last letter to his fiancée back to England, together with personal mementos, including a miniature which had hung around his neck. Wolfe had ample opportunity to ask him to undertake this personal favour, in the event of his death, while *Porcupine* was escorting the troops upriver prior to the assault.

Following the capture of Quebec, Jervis was appointed to the command of the frigate *Scorpion* whose captain had died and on 25 September he was sent home to Portsmouth with dispatches. Within a few weeks he was ordered to return to the North American station with dispatches to General Jeffrey Amhurst, the Commander-in-Chief of the British forces there. On passage down Channel from Portsmouth the *Scorpion* sprung a serious leak and put in to Plymouth. There the Port Commodore gave him command of the *Albany* and ordered him to sail for the West Indies – the reason is not recorded. The ship sailed on 13 January 1760, reaching its destination five weeks later.

Jervis returned to England in the *Albany* in May of that year and for five months was attached to the Channel fleet under Rear Admiral George Rodney, who commanded a small squadron of line-of-battle ships, frigates and bomb vessels, deployed to prevent any French vessels from crossing the Channel and to intercept coastal trade. Rodney's ships had already bombarded Le Havre and destroyed a flotilla of flat-bottomed craft destined for the invasion of England. On 13 October Jervis was posted to the 44-gun frigate *Gosport* and confirmed in the rank of captain at the age of twenty-five – a reward for his valuable service on the St Lawrence, and proof that friendly eyes in the Admiralty were watching over him and responding to complimentary dispatches from Rear Admiral Saunders.

Gosport was attached to the Channel fleet and sometimes deployed in the North Sea, but Jervis was in charge of a convoy of merchant ships to North America in May 1762, accompanied by Captain Joshua Rowley in the *Superb*, when they fell in with a superior French squadron en route to attempt to reinforce their troops in Newfoundland, and successfully repelled it. In September *Gosport* joined the squadron of Admiral Lord Colville, which recovered Newfoundland from the French.

Gosport returned to England before the Treaty of Paris was signed on 10 February 1763, and, along with many other ships of the Royal Navy, the crew were paid off and the officers put on half pay. The Treaty brought to an end the Seven Years' War with France, and British colonial power was confirmed in Canada, Louisiana, Florida and lands east of the Mississippi, islands in the Caribbean and disputed territory in Africa and India. Most importantly for the future of Mediterranean strategy and its effect upon John Jervis' career, the Balearic island of Minorca, with its valuable Port Mahon, was ceded to Britain.

The end of the Seven Years' War meant a break in Jervis' successful career and six years of pinching and scraping on half pay.

By 1763 John Jervis was already taking an interest in politics and

18

was a confirmed Whig supporter, evidently striking up a friendship with John Wilkes, who had entered Parliament in 1757 and founded the radical publication *The North Briton* in 1762. Jervis was a reformer by nature and was drawn to Wilkes's radical agenda, although being young, unemployed and living at the family home, Meaford Hall, no doubt he enjoyed himself within the limits of his restricted income. At that stage of his life he had no interest in marriage, not having the means and considering it a major obstacle to a successful naval career – he knew it was only a matter of time before war broke out again.

It is not known when Jervis first met John Wilkes, but years later he referred in a letter to Nelson to 'my old friend Wilkes'. Any time which he gave to politics during those six years on half pay was interspersed with country pursuits. 'For the recovery of my finances', he explained, he kept a low profile, taking an interest in poultry breeding and dogs, hunting and shooting. He bought a horse for thirteen guineas but described himself as 'the most blood-less of all shooters'. He played cards with his father, visited neighbours and travelled around the countryside with his brother Billy.

John Jervis enjoyed arguing and employing his incisive wit and sharp tongue. In one letter home he wrote: 'I was never in better spirits or in a truer mood for cutting to pieces the vulgars about me, and indeed I have not spared them.'

He described a lady he met in a hotel in Buxton as 'the least polished of any women who ever had such advantages' and flirted with three ladies described as 'the genteelest people there'.

He and his brother went riding and played cards, danced and drank, but had to cut short that particular social venture in Buxton because of Billy's health. On the return journey they visited Manchester, went to see the Bridgewater Canal and went to the theatre. Billy collapsed at about three in the morning and then had 'fainting cold sweats' at breakfast time – evidence, perhaps, of a severe hangover. His brother 'lugged him upstairs' and put him to bed with an emetic which, John said, 'I am morally certain saved his life.'

On their way home they called at a friend's house where, John said, 'By talking lightly of the Sabbath and spilling coffee over Mrs

Hatsell's new garter blue gown, I have lost her good opinion for ever.'

A week or two after spoiling the unfortunate Mrs Hatsell's dress, John went to a 'water party' at the Anson family's home in Shugborough. He recounted in a letter to his sister how:

> When tea was over we went on the water. Captain Wolseley and myself rowed one boat with the choicest beauties, Whitworth and George Barker in the other. The ladies sung duets, and very clever it was – nothing wanting but the French horns. The moment the sun got below the hills we assembled to dance, Mr Anson is fond of minuets and every one of the Ladys danced a minuet which exposed your poor brother sadly. However, I put on a good face and got through it as well as I could. We continued dancing till eleven and then sat down with our partners to a cold collation.

Towards the end of his six years on half pay John Jervis was involved in the campaign to have his friend John Wilkes re-elected to Parliament as the Member for Middlesex. In 1764 Wilkes, then MP for Aylesbury, had caused a furore by using *The North Briton* to criticize the terms of the Treaty of Paris and to accuse King George III and the then Prime Minister, Lord Bute, of telling lies. Eight months later he also published an allegedly obscene satirical poem, *Essay on Women*. Summoned for seditious libel he escaped to France and stayed abroad until 1768. On his return he was elected MP for Middlesex by a large majority before being expelled in 1769 for the alleged libel. Sentenced to twenty-two months in prison and fined £1,300, his supporters ran riot in London, chanting 'damn the king, damn the government and damn the justice'.

High prices, low wages and poor working conditions triggered riots all over the city with six rioters being shot dead and fifteen wounded. Three times John Wilkes was returned for Middlesex by huge majorities but was prevented from taking his seat at Westminster.

In February 1769, as Parliament voted to expel Wilkes for his criticism of the slaughter of rioters outside King's Bench prison the previous May, Captain John Jervis was appointed to command the 32-gun frigate *Alarm*. Though smaller than his last command *Gosport*, she was one of the first of a new type of frigate with a copper-sheathed hull. Probably the exploration vessel *Dolphin* had been the first in the Royal Navy, but the French had been using this method of preserving hulls – which gave an added advantage by enhancing speed – for several years. Command of the *Alarm* was a clear acknowledgement that Captain John Jervis' ability was recognized. Perhaps it was no coincidence that the Whigs had come to power and that Charles James Fox, who became one of John Jervis' dearest friends, was a lord of the Admiralty.

In May 1769, the *Alarm* sailed for the Mediterranean. Although it was still officially peacetime, the clouds of war were accumulating on the horizon. Spain, the colonial power in Argentina, was threatening to expel British colonists from the Falkland Islands, while a lack of understanding of the North American colonists' objections to taxation and trade restrictions, imposed by the London government, was pushing them towards independence – with the opportunist support of the French.

On 7 September *Alarm* arrived off Genoa with a freight of 200,000 Spanish dollars assigned to merchants of the city for exported goods. On 9 September, at anchor off the city, a boat was sent inshore. When alongside a wharf in the harbour two Turkish slaves jumped into the boat, wrapped themselves in the Union Flag and declared that they were now free. The slave-owner sent guards who boarded the boat and dragged the slaves out, tearing the flag in the course of a scuffle. When Captain Jervis heard about the incident, he was furious, remonstrating through the British consul and insisting on 'the two slaves immediately being delivered up and exemplary punishment inflicted on the persons who had thus dared to insult the British flag.'

The following day Jervis, through the British consul, informed the doge and senate that if ample satisfaction was not made in the course of the next day, he would consider himself in a state of hostility with the republic and act accordingly.

On 11 September the slaves were delivered to *Alarm* and the Genoese government expressed disapproval of the action of boarding the boat from the *Alarm* and subsequently arrested the guards responsible. This was an early example of Jervis' radical sentiments being put into practice.

On 3 March 1770, *Alarm* was shipwrecked. At anchor off Marseilles, she parted her cables in a violent gale and was driven onto the rocks; her copper-sheathed bottom was ripped open and without skilful seamanship she would have been a total loss. With French help, her bottom was temporarily repaired, she was dragged off and towed into the harbour. Over a period of three months of intense effort by the ship's crew, and by French shipwrights, *Alarm* was completely repaired for the relatively insignificant sum of £1,415. The Harbour Master of Marseilles was presented with a piece of silver plate in recognition of his help, and when Jervis was not reprimanded by the Admiralty but congratulated, his reputation was enhanced. He wrote to his father: 'A glorious action in the midst of a war could not be more applauded than the gallantry of the officers and crew.' Others in that situation might have faced a court martial for anchoring a ship in a vulnerable position.

When *Alarm* returned safely to England in the spring of the following year, Captain John Jervis was almost immediately paid another compliment. His friendship with John Wilkes was overlooked and the son of King George III, Prince Henry, Duke of Gloucester, was entrusted to his charge. The prince suffered from poor health and a Mediterranean cruise was prescribed. John Jervis, the hard man, suffered from a bout of servility. He was even reduced to tears by an encounter with the young prince. He wrote to his sister:

> I cannot convey a higher idea of this amiable Prince to you than by reciting his last words to me, which have made an indelible impression. 'Jervis, your acquaintance and mine has been very short. I lament it has not been longer, that I might have confer'd some mark of the favour and esteem I have for you', pressing my hand upon his heart during the declaration. I cannot describe to you the flow of passionate gratitude that took place in my heart. I was happy to make my retreat, lest I betrayed marks of distress that might have affected His Royal Highness, tho' he was possessed of a magnanimity far superior to anything I ever saw or heard.

In the weeks that followed Captain Jervis trailed around the courts of the small Italian monarchies, attached to the prince's retinue, Naples and Rome among them. There he was introduced to glamorous and attractive women, including Lady Mary Cornwallis whom he described as 'a yummy thing', and a Miss Scott who won his superlatives. He may even have fallen in love, but a serious obstacle – part thrift, part ambition, part Puritanism – came between him and his desires. He wrote to his sister: 'To be virtuous is here the most contemptible of all characters. This as a bachelor one might find convenient, but the indelicacies of the French are too bad to relate.'

Throughout this royal cruise, Prince Henry, Duke of Gloucester, lived mainly on board the ship and John Jervis got to know him intimately. This did no harm to his future career, although he must have been aware of a certain inconsistency between his friendship with the prince on the one hand, and with John Wilkes on the other. Following this cruise, *Alarm* sailed to England to pay off in May 1772. Once again Captain Jervis found himself forced to live on half pay.

Chapter Three

The Years of Preparation

John Jervis used his three years on half pay, from 1772 to 1775, to take stock of the nation's potential enemies; to observe their national characteristics and customs; to study the architecture of their ships, ports, harbours and civic buildings; and, in the case of the French, their language. He deduced that the rivers and canals of Western Europe produced 'a hardy and numerous race of men for the occasional service of their fleets which, joined to the extensive fisheries on their coasts, is a capital resource in that department not well understood in England.'

Despite holding this view, he formed the somewhat biased and insular opinion that the French were not naturally a seafaring nation. Yet it must have been apparent to his seaman's eye that the French built better ships than those built in England, where most yards were riddled with corruption. French ships outsailed and outlasted their English equivalents. Captain Edward Brenton himself, both a relative of Jervis and author/editor of his *Life and Correspondence*, wrote in 1838: 'in the art of constructing ships of war the French were a full century ahead of us.'

Jervis was aware, however, that France was by far the most likely antagonist in a future war. Five months after paying off the *Alarm* he set out on a tour of the country, starting with a sightseeing visit to Paris, which lasted for three weeks. He travelled on to Lyons, and from there toured the manufacturing towns, learning a great deal about the country and its people – and acquiring good, if not fluent, French. At this point, he had already decided to marry his first

24

cousin, Martha Parker, when circumstances and finances permitted, but it was never going to be anything more than a convenient relationship of affection and respect. Judging by his interest in and attitude to women, he may well have taken advantage in France of his bachelor status and distance from home influence. He returned to England in November 1773, satisfied with his understanding of and ability to speak the language of the potential enemy.

Jervis' closest friend in the Navy was a captain some six years older, Samuel Barrington, who would reach flag rank six years before him. Having paid off the *Venus* in 1772 he, too, was languishing on half pay. Barrington was the son of Lord Barrington, a friend and associate of Lord Anson and it is probable that they knew one another socially before their paths crossed professionally while Jervis was a lieutenant in the *Culloden* under Rear Admiral Saunders, and Barrington was a captain serving with Commodore Keppel on the North American station.

Early in 1773 the two captains pooled their resources and took passage by merchant ship to Kronstadt, the Russian naval base in the Gulf of Finland. This was the Russian Empire's only outlet to the Baltic for merchant shipping, pursuing a valuable trade in timber and flax exports and manufactured imports from the West. Russian manufacturing industry barely existed. In summer the golden spires and cupolas of the imperial city of St Petersburg caught the eye to the east, glinting in summer sunshine. In winter they would have been coated with snow and the Gulf of Finland ice covered and impassable. Kronstadt had been created as a naval base seventy years previously by Tsar Peter the Great, who had spent several years working incognito as a shipwright in the yards of Amsterdam and in Deptford, west of Greenwich. John Jervis made detailed pilotage notes and corrections on his own charts on their voyage to Kronstadt, because those available proved to be dangerously inaccurate.

In St Petersburg the two friends mixed social activity with a thorough investigation of the ships, installations, arsenals and ship-building facilities at the naval base. Jervis was unimpressed, perhaps failing to realize the extraordinary achievement of Peter the Great in creating a navy and a supporting base from virtually nothing. The English captain not only conceived a profound contempt for the Russian Navy, but made sweeping and derogatory assumptions about the Russian character. However, succumbing to his weakness for royalty, he was favourably impressed by the Empress Catherine. Among those who adversely affected his opinion of Russians was a Monsieur de Stahlin – certainly not an ancestor of the twentieth century tyrant, whose real family name and origin were Georgian. Jervis wrote of de Stahlin as 'a very considerable member of the Academy of Sciences and looked up to as the most capital figure in the Empire of that class. Found him a vain, empty, ignorant body who could not have imposed himself on any other country beyond the character of an almanac maker.' Perhaps some of the Russians he met found him opinionated and intolerant, but he was reputedly a good diplomat and able to hide his reactions.

There is no record of the two men encountering Rear Admiral Samuel Greig, a Scot who had entered the Russian service when, as a lieutenant in the Royal Navy, he also found himself unemployed at the end of the Seven Years' War in 1763. Greig had learned his seamanship and navigation in the merchant ships belonging to his shipowner father, who worked from Inverkeithing on the Firth of Forth. He had served under Admiral Hawke as a master's mate during the blockade of Brest and the Battle of Quiberon Bay, and was present at the capture of Havana. Given rapid promotion to captain in the Russian Imperial Navy, he commanded a division in the Mediterranean, then distinguished himself at the defeat of the Turkish fleet in 1770, which earned him promotion to rear admiral. At the time of Jervis' visit to Kronstadt, he was probably still in the Mediterranean, where he commanded a division which defeated a superior squadron of ten Turkish warships and was promoted to vice admiral. That winter, as Jervis and Barrington were leaving Russia, Greig was appointed Grand Admiral and Governor of Kronstadt, and spent the next fourteen years working to improve the discipline, training and organization of the Russian Navy. He was much decorated and highly regarded, recruiting many British, and particularly Scottish, officers into the Imperial Navy. When he died he was accorded a state funeral in October 1788, just two months after Great Britain had entered into the short-lived Triple Alliance with Prussia and the Netherlands against France, the Holy

Roman Empire and Russia. He never had to face the dilemma of taking action against his own country.

Barrington and Jervis were much more impressed with their visits to Stockholm and Karlskrona in Sweden and, particularly, Copenhagen. Their investigation of the port facilities of the Danish capital would prove useful to Jervis as an admiral during the Napoleonic war. They returned to England via Lubeck, Hamburg and Holland's North Sea ports, loaded with copious notes and amended charts.

In 1774 the pair chartered a yacht and undertook a voyage south along the French coast, taking in Cherbourg, Brest, Lorient, Quiberon Bay, Rochefort and the River Gironde up to Bordeaux. Although they examined the Brest roadstead, they did not look at the port closely enough to enable Jervis to plan an effective blockade in later years, when in command of the Channel fleet. He was to comment: 'If Captain Jervis had known what he was about in 1774, Lord St Vincent would have been saved anxiety at Brest in 1800.'

He did not restrict himself entirely to preparing for war against the French, for he also studied philosophy, the works of John Locke, the English philosopher, being part of his personal library. Locke's view that experience is the only original source of knowledge, his advocacy of absolute freedom of religious thought and his doctrine of the ultimate sovereignty of the governed, profoundly affected both Jervis' political outlook and his views on leadership and man management.

Early in 1774 Captain Jervis was appointed to the *Kent*, although this was only temporary. On 1 September 1775 he was appointed to the command of the 80-gun *Foudroyant*, the former French line-of-battle ship, now the largest two-decker in the Royal Navy, and the same ship that he had been ordered to take back to England from the Mediterranean as a prize after her capture in 1758. Two years before that, in 1756, she had been involved in the fiasco off Minorca which culminated in the execution of Admiral John Byng by firing squad on his own quarterdeck. Early one morning in 1758, a squadron of British ships of the line had encountered an inferior French squadron, including the *Foudroyant*, off Cartagena – inferior in numbers but mostly superior in speed. The French squadron declined action and ran before the wind, pursued by the British. Only one British ship was capable of outsailing the French – the 64-gun *Monmouth* commanded by Captain Arthur Gardiner, who had been Admiral Byng's flag captain off Minorca in 1756. Captain Gardiner still suffered from the humiliation of that action, although he bore none of the blame. Late in the evening *Monmouth* came up alone with the *Foudroyant* which turned to engage her. Captain Gardiner cleared decks and briefly addressed his ship's company: 'That ship must be taken. She appears above our match but Englishmen are not to mind that, nor will I quit her while this ship can swim or I have a soul left alive!'

In the heat of the moment he overlooked the fact that – on the evidence of the make-up of the ship's company of *Implacable* at the time of Trafalgar – only about half of the crew would have been English; the other half in descending numerical order would have been Irish, Scots, Welsh, North American, western Europeans, West Indians and a handful from elsewhere.

The ship-to-ship action continued for five hours into the gathering darkness. More than a hundred of the crew of the *Monmouth* were killed or wounded; Arthur Gardiner himself was wounded twice but refused to leave the quarterdeck. The ship's sails were torn, her masts splintered, her rigging tattered, but the *Foudroyant* was so badly damaged that she became unmanageable. By midnight, when two more British ships had caught up, Captain Gardiner had already died of his wounds. The French commander knew he would have to surrender but would only strike his flag to the gallant *Monmouth*. He finally handed his sword to her First Lieutenant, Lieutenant Carkett, and the French 80-gun ship of the line became a prize of the Royal Navy. Twenty-seven years later, John Jervis became her captain and would remain in command of her for nearly eight years.

Chapter Four

Captain of the *Foudroyant*

John Jervis' progress to flag rank and the peerage was not an easy one. He had to overcome opposing currents of professional jealousy, corrupt practices, political bias, government parsimony, habitual procrastination, endemic nepotism, mutinous resentment and, sometimes, ill health. In doing so he demonstrated almost superhuman moral courage, determination and integrity. His service as Captain of the *Foudroyant* was the time when he first raised his head above his contemporaries and established a reputation at a level high enough to carry him over these obstacles.

The first three years of his command passed uneventfully. The 80-gun line-of-battle ship was attached to the Channel Fleet as guardship at Plymouth, carrying out routine duties, but in 1778 everything changed. Following their opportunistic support of the American colonists at the time of their Declaration of Independence, the French declared war again on 17 June of that year. Admiral the Hon Augustus Keppel was appointed to the command of the Channel Fleet. He was told by the Admiralty that thirty-five ships were ready for action and another twelve in course of final preparation, but on arrival in Portsmouth he found only six ships fully manned and in commission.

Frederick North, second Earl of Guildford, was Prime Minister and largely responsible for the policies which resulted in the break with the American colonists. Jervis wrote to his sister: 'What will become of us now Lord Chatham is gone? The very name of Pitt actually kept the House of Bourbon in awe. This wretched pitiful scoundrel North will act his underpart to our destruction.'

Eventually Keppel sailed from St Helens on 13 June with a fleet of twenty ships of the line, including *Foudroyant*. When he learned that the French had twelve more vessels than he had and a dozen frigates in Brest, he returned to port and demanded reinforcements. North's government was slow to respond but on 9 July he sailed again with ten more ships. His van (the Red division) was commanded by Vice Admiral Sir Robert Harland, and the rear (the Blue) by Rear Admiral Sir Hugh Palliser. John Jervis' station in the *Foudroyant* was immediately astern of Admiral Keppel's flagship *Victory* (later Nelson's flagship at Trafalgar) in the centre division (the White).

In the third week of July, the main French fleet under l'Amiral Le Comte d'Orvilliers emerged from Brest and reached west into the Atlantic. The fleet was first sighted by the British Channel Fleet off Ushant, 25 miles further west, and 10 miles off the coast, on 23 July. Keppel gave chase but it was not until 27 July that the French, reluctant to give battle, turned onto a reciprocal course, probably intending to return to Brest. While it is difficult to reconstruct exactly what happened, it appears that they swung north, then east, skirting to windward of the British fleet in a ragged line ahead. Admiral Keppel hoisted the signal for battle.

Jervis reported during the subsequent court martial that at this time, about the middle of the forenoon watch, Rear Admiral Palliser, in his flagship *Formidable*, was about 3½ miles distant on his starboard bow. It seems therefore that, initially, the three divisions of the British fleet were loosely deployed abreast, with each division in line ahead. The French manoeuvre brought them into close action with Palliser's rear division and part of the centre, while the van was hardly in action at all.

During this brief but close action both fleets sustained damage – the British mainly to their masts and rigging, the French mostly below the waterline. Keppel's attempt to renew the engagement after the fleets had passed on opposite tacks was inhibited by the severe damage to the rigging of several of the ships in the rear division, which made tacking difficult, and their failure to respond to his signals. Keppel therefore wore his fleet (stern through the wind), which was less demanding on their damaged rigging than tacking, to try to get into a position to renew the engagement. Some of the ships of the rear division had drifted to leeward and were in danger of becoming isolated. Palliser either misunderstood or failed to interpret Keppel's intentions correctly and did not wear his division simultaneously with the rest, thus obliging Keppel to delay. Keppel continued to signal and even sent a frigate to summon Palliser, but eventually the Commander-in-Chief had to signal each ship of Palliser's division individually to return to him. By then it was too late to catch the French who made no attempt to renew the action, despite their advantage in numbers, but headed north-east towards Brest.

Accounts of this skirmish – it was little more, although substantial damage was sustained by both fleets – are as confused as the action itself. John Jervis, as captain of the ship of the line next astern of the flagship in the centre division, had a better opportunity than most officers present to observe the whole action objectively and to form an unbiased opinion of the way it had been conducted. His evidence not only proved vital in the ensuing courts martial but illustrated his clarity of thought, his powers of observation and his professional competence.

Four days after the action, John Jervis told George Jackson, Second Secretary to the Admiralty, by letter that the French would not have joined battle but for a sudden change in the direction of the wind and that they had escaped as soon as they could. In his opinion the British rear under Palliser had, in any case, been too badly damaged to renew the action.

On 9 August he wrote again to George Jackson:

I do not believe the attack could have been renewed to any effect the evening of the 27th. It was certainly intended by Admiral Keppel who when he found the Vice [Palliser] and his division did not form the line agreeably to the signal, sent Sir Hugh a message by a frigate to the effect – tell him I only wait for his division to renew the attack. Neither the signal nor message was obeyed in any degree till it was too late, and the *Formidable* did not in my view bear down at all. I conclude she was so disabled she could not – in that event ought not the flag to have been shifted? All this is a chimaera of my own perhaps – for I have heard it from no one.

The public and political assessment of the action off Ushant was that an opportunity had been lost to achieve an important victory over the French. Palliser, though junior to Keppel in naval rank, was a member of the Board of Admiralty and determined to cast all the blame for the failure onto his Commander-in-Chief. He demanded a court martial and had charges prepared intended to put his superior in the wrong: he alleged that Keppel had deserted his badly damaged rear division, hauled down the battle flag in the middle of the action (which indeed he had, to supersede it with a signal to Palliser to reform the line of battle) and then by wearing and altering course, had been running away from the enemy. Although the two flag officers were not on good terms, Keppel had been scrupulously fair in his report of the battle. He had praised both Palliser and Harland, and had made no reference to the former's disregard of his signals. Although Palliser's charges were maliciously contrived, there was sufficient evidence of uncertainty to make a court martial necessary to clear Keppel's name.

In October Palliser was anonymously attacked in the press. He responded by openly attacking Keppel. Jervis in turn responded by writing to Keppel that he had read

> with a mixture of contempt and indignation, the publication in the *Morning Post*, signed H. Palliser. It is replete with vanity, art and falsehood, and though I agree with the rest of your friends that it would be unbecoming your exalted character and station to write in a newspaper, I am clearly of an opinion the public should be undeceived somehow. . . Upon the whole, my conclusion is that though his courage is indisputable and I can even acquit him of treachery to you, in that day's business, a more direct disobedience of signals and orders, and a grosser negligence in not doing his utmost to support and enable the Commander-in-Chief to renew the attack on the enemy was never proved against any man in the record of naval transactions than, to the best of my judgment and knowledge, could be proved against him; and without knowing the cause, I ascribe it to the confusion and disorder created by the direful effects of the explosion.

Some might see Jervis' intervention as an attempt to curry favour with his commander-in-chief, but in fact Keppel was by now out of favour with both the government and the Admiralty, whereas Palliser was a Lord of the Admiralty. Captain Jervis hardly knew Admiral Keppel at this time, not having served under him previously. He was acting in character, as a man who put truth and discipline at the top of his list of virtues.

In November, the controversy was discussed in Parliament and the possibility of an official inquiry was raised in both Houses. On 9 December, with government support, Palliser publicly brought charges of misconduct and neglect of duty against Keppel and demanded a court martial. The Admiralty under its Tory Lord Commissioner and First Lord, Lord Sandwich, who had already acquired a reputation for poor administration and neglect of the Navy, readily acceded. The King was disgusted that 'the strange managed dispute' should be aired in Parliament and wanted to dismiss Sandwich, but the Prime Minister persuaded him not to. Parliament did, however, allow the court martial to be held ashore – not in Keppel's flagship – and the accused travelled to Portsmouth accompanied by a retinue of influential members of society.

The court assembled in January 1779 in Government House in Portsmouth. Its outcome was to have far-reaching effects throughout the Royal Navy, in areas as disparate as tactics, communications, discipline and command structure, as well as affecting the future careers of the officers involved. The trials and the details of the action off Ushant became the subject of frequent discussion and argument amongst naval officers for years.

Keppel and Palliser were both Members of Parliament, but of opposing political persuasions, Keppel being a Whig and Palliser a Tory. There was some suspicion that Palliser had been appointed by the Admiralty as subordinate to Keppel in order to spy on him.

The court martial became a political affair with the Tories and government aligned behind Palliser. The Whigs, independents and most of the Navy and general public were behind Keppel. Lord Sandwich personally produced an 'order of merit' of the officers involved. In it he described the Captain of the *Foudroyant* as 'a good officer but turbulent and busy and violent as a politician attached to Mr Keppel'.

33

At the same time, a memorial to the King was drawn up and signed by a group of senior admirals, including Lord Hawke, victor in actions against the French off Finisterre and in Quiberon Bay, and himself formerly First Lord of the Admiralty. They emphasized the danger of appointing officers such as Palliser who 'are at once in high civil office and in subordinate military command'.

John Jervis helped both to draw up the line of defence for Keppel and acted as chief witness for it. It throws light on his character and competence and helped to establish his reputation. Keppel was acquitted – a verdict popular with most of the general public and with the Navy. Palliser was seriously criticized for failing to let Keppel know that his ship was too badly damaged to obey the order to reform the line, but he escaped a verdict of guilty. The King wanted to have him dismissed, but Sandwich wished to retain him.

Jervis took the risk of active involvement in canvassing a memorial for signature by the captains of the fleet, petitioning the King to remove Palliser from employment both as a Lord of the Admiralty and as a flag officer. The King took no action, but public opinion finally forced Palliser to resign and the door was finally closed on that indecisive action off Ushant.

Following the court martial of Admiral Keppel, the *Foudroyant* remained attached to the Channel Fleet where morale was low under the command of a succession of tired and uninspired admirals. In a letter to his sister Jervis wrote: 'Crimes multiply and courts martial continue.' To his friend at the Admiralty, George Jackson, he wrote: 'You seem not to know how to employ your fleet or why let us lie here to shout forth discontent, faction and mutiny which are the never failing productions of inactivity in military establishments.' And again to his sister:

> If eight or ten of our captains (who are so stupid, lazy and ignorant they will not try to execute our new evolutions) were ashore I should not have a bad opinion of the fleet . . . Lord North, was always contemptible in my eye, now represents the last stage of prostitution and strongly resembles an old harlot at the back of the point of Portsmouth, bloated with gin, infamy and disease, yet capable of corrupting intemperate youth by flashes of wit and semblance of candour. He has

been the greatest curse this country has felt since the revolution and yet will I fear die in his bed.

Lord North did not, in fact die until 1792, but he only held office as Prime Minister until 1782.

Early in 1779, after Spain had joined France in an alliance against Great Britain, a combined French and Spanish fleet of sixty-six ships appeared off Plymouth. A British fleet of thirty-five ships of the line, commanded by Admiral Sir Charles Hardy, the *Foudroyant* among them, sighted them, but retreated ignominiously. Had Jervis been a Cochrane or a Nelson, he might have ignored his Commander-in-Chief and attacked alone, obliging his fellow captains to come to his aid, but despite his unquestionable courage, he lacked imagination and had too much respect for authority to act independently. After the encounter he wrote: 'I am in the most humbled state of mind I ever experienced from the retreat before the combined fleets all yesterday and this morning.'

In March 1782 Lord North resigned and was succeeded as Prime Minister by a Whig, Lord Rockingham, who although not much better, appointed two of Jervis' friends as Lords of the Admiralty – Keppel and Harland. Many senior naval officers who had refused to serve under North's unpopular administration approached the Admiralty to re-offer their services, among them the distinguished Admiral Howe.

The Admiralty now decided that an attack should be made on the French fleet which was at Brest, apparently preparing for an expedition to the East Indies. Jervis' old friend, Samuel Barrington, now a vice admiral, was given command of a special squadron with orders to intercept the French expeditionary force. Captain Jervis was delighted when the *Foudroyant* was detached from the Channel Fleet to form part of Vice Admiral Barrington's squadron of twelve ships of the line, which sailed from Spithead on 13 April 1782. Jervis was about to achieve one notable victory at sea which would win him a knighthood and enough prize money to enable him to embark on the long-contemplated marriage to his first cousin, Martha Parker.

On the afternoon of 20 April, the enemy fleet, consisting of a large convoy of merchantmen escorted by six ships of the line, was sighted south of Ushant. Barrington immediately made the signal for a general chase. This suited Captain Jervis because the French-built *Foudroyant* was the fastest line-of-battle ship in the British squadron and soon outsailed the others. At sunset the *Foudroyant* came up with the sternmost of the escorting French warships but found that the convoy had been ordered to disperse. Captain Jervis could see only half of the convoy and three line-of-battle ships. Accounts differ but according to one, *Foudroyant* found herself on the port quarter of the 74-gun *Pégase* which put her helm up in order to cross the bows of the *Foudroyant,* intending to rake her with a broadside – a favourite tactic because the chasing ship could only reply to a full broadside with a single bow-chaser.

Jervis' first intention was to follow suit, presenting *Foudroyant*'s starboard broadside to the port or larboard beam of the *Pégase.* However, a Midshipman Bowen, who was acting as the Captain's 'doggy' or aide-de-camp, had the nerve to suggest the opposite helm, which would enable *Foudroyant* to pass under the stern of *Pégase* and rake her with a broadside without retaliation. His captain had the sense to accept the youngster's suggestion, with devastating effect, and the *Pégase* never recovered from that lethal broadside, the action continuing for three-quarters of an hour. The French, outgunned and devastated by that first broadside, had eighty men killed or wounded; the British only five slightly wounded, John Jervis among them. Then the *Foudroyant* was laid on board the larboard quarter of the *Pégase* and the French captain struck his colours. It was blowing half a gale and Jervis had difficulty in taking possession of the badly damaged prize. When the rest of Barrington's squadron caught up, the Vice Admiral ordered the *Queen* to take charge of the *Pégase,* but nobody could take the credit from Captain Jervis.

Many years later, describing the action to Captain Edward Brenton, Jervis said:

> On our way into port, the French captain showed me the copy of a letter which he had written to the Minister of the Marine, giving an account of his capture and asking my opinion of it. I read it and returned it to him, saying I had but one objection, namely, that not one word of it was true . . . 'Mais

comment! Pas vrai!' repeated the Frenchman. 'No sir, not one word of it is true,' I repeated, 'but you can send it if you please.' He did send it; and, when he was tried for the loss of his ship, the letter was produced: he was dismissed the service, and had his sword broken over his head.

Being the first victorious action of a newly declared war, its significance was exaggerated by the government. The fact that the French convoy was successfully defended and got away with the loss of one warship which had fought gallantly against a more heavily armed opponent was conveniently overlooked. It became known later that the *Pégase* had been newly commissioned, was poorly manned and short of officers. In the circumstances, it would have cost John Jervis nothing to have endorsed the French captain's letter, unless it deliberately misrepresented the actions of the *Foudroyant*.

In his report, Admiral Barrington wrote:

My pen is not equal to the praise that is due to the good conduct, bravery and discipline of Captain Jervis, his officers and seamen on this occasion. Let his own modest narrative speak for itself. It is as follows:

At sunset I was near enough to discover that the enemy consisted of three or four ships of war, two of them of the line, and seventeen or eighteen sail under convoy, and that the latter dispersed by signal. At half-past nine, I observed the smallest of the ships of war to speak with the headmost, and then bear away; at a quarter past ten, the stern-most line-of-battle ship, perceiving that we came up with her very fast, bore up also. I pursued her; and, at forty-seven minutes past twelve, brought her to close action, which continued three quarters of an hour when, having laid her on board on the larboard quarter, the French ship of war, *Le Pégase* of seventy-four guns and seven hundred men, commanded by the Chevalier de Cillart, surrendered.

I am happy to inform you that only two or three people, with myself, are slightly wounded but I learn from the Chevalier de Cillart that *Le Pégase* suffered very materially in masts and yards, her fore and mizzen topmasts having gone away soon after the action.

Not surprisingly, Jervis made no reference to the contribution of Midshipman Bowen, but equally he did not boast that he was 'the first officer who ever set royals on all three masts'. According to a certain Admiral Tomlinson, this was the feat of seamanship which guaranteed that the French-built *Foudroyant* achieved the maximum speeds she was capable of and was able to overtake a French convoy.

Jervis had not been actively involved in the war on the far side of the Atlantic where French support helped to ensure the success of the American colonies' bid for independence, but this notable victory won him a knighthood and enough prize money to enable him to plan for his long-contemplated marriage. He was invested with the red ribbon of the Order of the Bath – the equivalent of today's KBE – and received a handsome share of the prize value of the *Pégase*. He acquired a coat of arms with the motto *Thus* – apparently inspired by the customary order given to a helmsman to keep a ship's head on an indicated point of the compass when, for instance, chasing an enemy. The shield or escutcheon above the motto commemorated both ships involved in the action: an eagle grasping a thunderbolt for the *Foudroyant* and a winged horse for the *Pégase*.

On the same day that Jervis took his French prize, Admiral Howe was raised to the peerage and simultaneously hoisted his flag in the *Victory*. Vice Admiral Barrington became Lord Howe's second in command and in September his squadron took part in the relief of Gibraltar, threatened by Spain and France. The fleet comprised thirty-four ships of the line, *Foudroyant* amongst them, with a convoy of frigates, transports and smaller vessels numbering 183 sail altogether. In addition to stores and ammunition, two regiments had been embarked to reinforce the garrison. The huge convoy sailed from St Helens on 11 September but it took a month to reach the straits of Gibraltar. When off Cape St Vincent Lord Howe learned that a powerful combined French and Spanish fleet lay in Algeciras Bay just west of the Rock. Despite an appalling muddle, which took all the transports and store ships past Algeciras

Bay and beyond the Rock to the east, the superior enemy fleet disdained the opportunity to attack the British convoy and its escort. A fortuitous change of wind enabled all but one of Howe's ships to retrace their course against the current and eventually to anchor safely under the guns of Gibraltar. The troops, stores and ammunition were successfully disembarked and the main purpose of the expedition was achieved – more by luck than good management. No doubt Captain Sir John Jervis made critical observations and learned invaluable lessons about communications and the handling of a fleet.

When the Channel Fleet made its return voyage through the straits, the combined French and Spanish fleet was sighted off Cape Spartel on the African side, but the enemy, despite having both a numerical advantage and the windward position, failed to accept a golden opportunity to attack. Lord Howe was fortunate to return to England with his fleet undamaged and his reputation untarnished – and seemingly enhanced, for in January of the following year he was appointed First Lord of the Admiralty. Meantime *Foudroyant* had been paid off.

Captain Sir John Jervis at last considered himself sufficiently well established, both financially and in his naval career, to marry and to think about entering Parliament. He wanted to establish a domestic base in the countryside within easy reach of Westminster and Whitehall, where he hoped to pursue his urge for reform. He therefore consulted his close friend Sam Barrington, now not only married, but also a flag officer and Lord of the Admiralty, and eminently placed to offer him guidance both personal and professional. Jervis had certainly given a lot of thought to the question of marrying his cousin, Martha Parker, the idea having apparently been first mooted a decade earlier. All the available evidence qualifies the marriage as one of convenience and, possibly, affection, but not of total commitment or passion.

Martha was a person of strong moral and religious convictions, not noted for her beauty. However the marriage was at last celebrated in the summer of 1782. If the long wait had made either of them suffer any degree of frustration, there is no record of it. Jervis is recorded as saying, 'The honour of an officer may be compared to the chastity of a woman, and when once wounded can never be recovered.' Whereas chastity is definable, honour is not, so readers must draw their own conclusions.

Jervis needed a home base more convenient than the parental home in Staffordshire, and for professional reasons he needed a hostess of respectable and affluent background, preferably with some influence in the upper reaches of society and the establishment. Marriage to Martha would kill more than one bird with one stone: he would have a physical partner when convenient; a wealthy wife with social position and aristocratic connections to serve as a hostess and chatelaine when required; the attractive small estate of Rochetts, at South Weald in Essex, on the road to Chipping Ongar – inherited by Martha in 1784 through her mother, Lady Parker – for rest and recreation, a convenient base within 20 miles of London; and congenial neighbours in the Tower family who had owned the big estate of South Weald and Weald Hall since 1750, former monastery lands which had associations with royalty. One day in the future, an Admiral Tower of Weald Hall, who had been captain of the Royal Navy guardship at Elba in 1813, would present a sculpted head of Napoleon Bonaparte by Canova to his neighbour, Lord St Vincent. It was returned to the Tower family after his death.

John and Martha Jervis produced no children, though one individual, resident in Portugal, recently claimed direct descent from Sir John. The latter enjoyed the company of women and gave his eyes considerable license to rove. He never publicly expressed disapproval of Nelson's flagrant infidelity to his wife, or of his love affair with the promiscuous Lady Hamilton, although Nelson's relationship did encroach upon his duties and, at times, his judgement. Jervis preferred that his subordinates follow their sexual predilections rather than contract a marriage which might interfere with naval duties or efficiency. There is no reason to doubt that he himself adhered to this precept, having first established a respectable domestic background. He had no inhibitions on religious grounds and his code of morality was entirely centred round professional duty and integrity. In Lisbon in later years he would have ample opportunity for self-indulgence without detracting from his naval responsibilities or diplomatic duties.

Despite his own marriage, Jervis still considered marriage to be a disadvantage for a naval officer, at least until he was well established. To one young lieutenant who requested a favour from him in later years when he was a senior officer of flag rank he wrote: 'Sir, you having thought fit to take to yourself a wife are to look for no further attentions from, Your humble servant.'

When duty or efficiency were at stake – for example when he became Commander-in-Chief of the Channel Fleet – Jervis did not hesitate to forbid officers to sleep ashore when in harbour. This made him extremely unpopular with many of them. One furious wife offered a toast to him at a public dinner, which may not have helped her husband's career: 'May his next glass of wine choke the wretch!'

Jervis had been interested in politics, as a convinced Whig and reformer, ever since his first meeting with John Wilkes. This was an era when naval and army officers had no inhibitions about active participation in politics whilst simultaneously pursuing a naval or military career. In some cases it was no doubt a matter of choosing the political complexion which was most likely to enhance the career, but Jervis was already acutely aware of corruption in the Admiralty and dockyards and wished to make reforms.

Jervis gained the patronage of the Prime Minister, Lord Shelburne, and stood for election as Whig member for Launceston in Cornwall, some 26 miles from Plymouth, in 1783. As he did not conduct any sort of election campaign, we can safely assume that Launceston was a pocket borough. Lord Shelburne, who later became the first Marquess of Lansdowne, had distinguished himself as a soldier during the Seven Years' War before entering Parliament in 1760. He became closely associated with William Pitt the Elder. His views did not entirely coincide with those of Jervis, and he had supported the expulsion of Wilkes from Parliament, but this was outweighed by Shelburne's opposition to the government's short-sighted policies towards the American colonies.

John Jervis voted consistently with the Whigs but seldom spoke on the floor of the House, confining his parliamentary work to naval problems. Lord Shelburne was soon replaced as leader of the country by a coalition between Lord North and the great reformer, Charles James Fox. As we have seen, Jervis strongly disliked North, whereas Fox became one of his close friends. William Pitt the

Younger took over the reins after the Fox/North coalition had been defeated on the India Bill, the occasion of Jervis' first recorded vote in the Commons. He had supported Charles Fox's proposal to transfer the authority of the East India Company – the aggressive monopoly which controlled all British trade with the East – to seven commissioners nominated by Parliament with a term of office of up to four years, after which any vacancies would be filled by the Crown. Although the Bill was passed by the Commons, the House of Lords, on the directive of George III, threw it out.

The arrival of William Pitt the Younger might have made little difference to Jervis but for the fact that the new Prime Minster did not have his father's understanding of military and naval affairs. Threatened with invasion by Napoleon's armies, he took the view that the vital naval bases of Plymouth, Portsmouth and Sheerness should be defended by heavy shore fortifications, rather than relying on the Navy to defeat any invasion force at sea. This would be an expensive policy and was anathema to Jervis and to most naval officers, who considered it insulting to the Navy, and likely to divert badly needed expenditure from the ships to the shore. Fortunately the King supported the latter view.

At the 1784 election, Sir John Jervis became the member for North Yarmouth, a place much closer to the centre of his interests. Concerned about the costs of Pitt's proposed shore defensive works, Parliament decided to set up a Royal Commission on naval defences. Sir John was among those appointed to it and this stimulated him to greater parliamentary activity. Not surprisingly, he took the view that the shore defences visualized would only be necessary if the British fleet had first been defeated at sea – or become non-existent through negligence. He made this opinion known in a sarcastic report to the King, condemning Pitt's arguments. His view was carried in the House of Commons by the casting vote of the Speaker – a defeat not easily forgotten by William Pitt and his supporters. This was probably the beginning of the powerful opposition, mostly right-wing, which Jervis was to meet in his later attempts to introduce naval reforms when at the Admiralty.

Sir John spoke for the first time in a debate on 31 May 1785. One of the Lords of the Admiralty had moved for 26,000 seamen to be employed in the Royal Navy that year, which provided an opportunity for a general debate on naval affairs. It was broadened to include criticism of the poor state of discipline in the Navy and the custom of promoting youngsters to the rank of lieutenant without the requisite length of service at sea, despite their being incompetent to take a watch. Instances were given of children who had achieved their rank by nepotism. Sir John Jervis' subject was the poor state of HM ships deployed to apprehend smugglers. He drew attention to the unproductive competition for prizes between naval vessels and revenue cutters, both vying to capture smugglers for profit. Sir John's somewhat one-sided solution was to guarantee the Royal Navy a higher proportion of the seizures as an incentive to make them more efficient and alert.

On 22 March 1786, Sir John supported a Captain McBride in condemning the uneconomic practice of repairing old and dilapidated Third or Fourth Rate ships of the line, warships of 50 to 80 guns, at a cost which often exceeded their original cost of construction. It was customary at the time to remove the copper sheathing from warships when they were laid up in reserve because it was believed that copper corroded the iron bolts. Sir John Jervis was in favour of this precaution until it became the practice to construct new ships using copper bolts which overcame the problem of corrosion and had the added advantage of not affecting the magnetic compass.

Perhaps surprisingly for a Whig with a full armoury of reforming zeal, Sir John did not support the movement to abolish slavery. It appears that he was more influenced by the economics of trade than by moral, philosophical or religious considerations, although he must have been well aware of the views of Wilkes, Fox and Wilberforce. Possibly he considered that such a matter was not within the remit of a professional naval officer.

The Treaty of Versailles in 1783 had concluded the war with France for the time being and had recognized the independence of the United States of America. It also put an end to the commission Sir John had received to take command of the West Indies Station with the temporary rank of commodore. He had hoisted his broad pendant in the 50-gun *Salisbury* and had been ordered to proceed with a squadron of frigates to South America, with Sir John

Duckworth as his flag captain. With the signing of the Treaty, the appointment was annulled and it was not until 1787 that Jervis was promoted to Rear Admiral of the Blue, unexceptional for a man of fifty-two. The alteration in status did not offer him an immediate opportunity to distinguish himself. The term 'of the Blue' had no meaning in terms of rank by the time he was appointed. It dated from the days when a fleet was divided, as was Keppel's at Ushant, into three squadrons – Red (the van), White (the centre) and Blue (the rear) – with the Admiral or Commander-in-Chief with his flag in the centre, a vice admiral or admiral with his flag in the van, and a rear admiral with his flag in the rear. By 1787, the numbers of each rank in the Navy List had multiplied so that 'of the Blue' would only have meant the most junior rear admiral in the Navy at the time of his promotion. From the Admiralty's point of view, it was a way of informing him that he had not been forgotten and could be called upon when needed. From this point on, Jervis' progression would depend on a number of interrelated factors: luck and judgement in being in the right place at the right time – with the right government in power; avoidance of accidents – naval, tactical, diplomatic or act of God; sheer determination and the instinct for survival; and last and most important of all, an exceptional strategic sense combined with the power to impress subordinates with his consistency and integrity, which we may synthesize as trust. He would make mistakes of judgement, he would appear inhuman, but he would never let down anyone who trusted him or fail in what he conceived to be his duty.

Meantime he continued to divide his time between home and Westminster, and at the General Election in 1790, he became member for Wycombe. Later that year he hoisted his flag in the *Prince* under the Commander-in-Chief of the Channel Fleet, Admiral Howe. Spain had arrogantly claimed the whole Pacific coast of the Americas, as far north as latitude 60°, and objected to any other nation either trading or settling there. An English trader, Captain John Meares, had set up a trading post and small shipyard in Nootka Sound, an anchorage between the small Nootka Island and the west coast of the 300-mile-long Vancouver Island. The Spanish sent a 20-gun warship to Nootka and her captain seized all the British merchant ships in the Sound and built fortifications.

Captain Meares appealed to the British government which responded by mobilizing Lord Howe's fleet, among them *Prince*. The fleet cruised off the Spanish coast while diplomatic negotiations were in progress. The Spanish appealed to the French government which had come to power after the revolution of the previous year, and initially the French offered support. However, both had to back down in the face of a superior British naval force – the Spaniards not only had to withdraw from Nootka Sound but also signed a convention ceding the right to the British to trade and establish coastal settlements north of the 38th parallel. The British fleet was then paid off. Sir John Jervis would have been relieved to haul down his flag aboard *Prince* because she was a dreadful letdown after the splendid *Foudroyant*. *Prince* was notorious as one of the worst ships in the Navy in terms of sailing: slow, cumbersome and uncomfortable, she was known as 'the Haystack'.

On 17 December 1792, Sir John gave notice that he intended to introduce a motion for the relief of wounded and superannuated seamen, many of whom were destitute. He considered that every man in this category who could not be found a place in Greenwich Naval Hospital – specifically endowed for that purpose – should receive a pension. Although a seaman might be fully qualified for care there, many vacancies were occupied illegitimately by men with no naval service, put there by those who could use their power and influence to get places in the naval hospital for their own aged or infirm servants, thus relieving themselves of any obligation – and cost.

On 20 December, Sir John Jervis spoke in the House, referring to his notice:

I then declared that if the Admiralty had any measure to bring forward for the protection and preservation of those valuable men, who had spent their best days in the service of their king and country, I should not interfere; but their distressed case was so urgent and pressing, that if I did not receive satisfaction upon the subject, I should certainly feel it my duty to agitate the question on an early day ... the utmost industry has been used to misrepresent my motives, and describe them as a meditated attack on the admiralty, and thereby prejudice me in the service to which I have the honour to belong. To this I reply – that my sole object is to obtain substantial relief and support for these brave men. So much for motives. I will take up the time of the house a very few minutes longer to state the grounds of the motion I hold in my hand; in doing which I shall not enter into the history of Greenwich Hospital and its resources; suffice it to say that they failed in the year 1788 and the directors were disabled thereby from adding to the outpension list; and the principal cause of this deficiency was the profusion of expense lavished on the chapel. That preposterous jumble of the arts, which is a disgrace to the country, I do not include in this description, the fine painting of the altar, which with many other great works of the President of the Royal Academy will immortalise his fame. Nor is this the only grievance the seamen suffer from the failure of the funds. I appeal to the Right Honourable gentleman opposite [the Treasurer of the Navy, Mr Dundas, later Lord Melville] whether many of them are not kept out of their prize-money by frivolous delays and arts, to defeat their claims, and whether the salutary laws and regulations the right honourable gentleman has introduced for their protection, by which he has proved himself their best friend, or even the vigilance and activity of Mr Beddingfield, can reach the evil though, by the firmness and perseverance of that gentleman, some of those vile caitiffs, the low agents and forgers of seamen's wills, have been brought to justice, and the rest so disheartened that their wicked practices are nearly subdued. No part of this censure is applicable to another description of agents, for whom I entertain a high respect and without whose assistance, in fair and liberal terms, half the officers now called upon could not make their equipments. I understand that the right honourable gentleman intends to bring in a bill to wrestle the prize-money out of the hands it is in. I am happy to perceive by his note that I am not misinformed and he shall have my hearty support. I will not trouble the House longer than to declare that my ill state of health prevented my bringing the matter forward in the last session.

In the exchange of views which followed, there was no opposition to Sir John's bill and Henry Dundas agreed to have the matter seriously investigated. Sir John then agreed to withdraw the motion. From that time onwards, the seamen and marines in Greenwich Hospital began to receive better attention. What happened to the residents who should not have been there, or whether more places were found for those entitled but excluded, is not known.

This was the last time Jervis ever spoke in the Commons and several years were to pass before his voice would be heard in the House of Lords.

Chapter Five

Commander-in-Chief

Sir John Jervis was promoted to Vice Admiral on 1 February 1793, the day revolutionary France, which was already at war with Austria and Prussia, both of which had attacked her the previous year, declared war on Britain. Soon afterwards, and despite some opposition, Sir John was given command of the naval part of an expedition to the West Indies directed at the French-occupied islands fringing the Caribbean Sea to the east. The military commander was to be his friend, General Sir Charles Grey, their friendship guaranteeing unprecedented co-operation between the Navy and the Army, and setting an example for the future. So much depended on the personal relationship and mutual respect between army and navy commanders that their political masters should invariably have made this a priority. Often commanders-in-chief were appointed on the basis of reputation and success in their own professions – or simply their social standing and seniority. The selection of Jervis and Grey may have been no more than a happy chance, but it worked and the harmony between them was echoed down the scale and imbued the men in red tunics and blue jackets – who normally regarded one another with suspicion – with respect for each other. It seems that throughout the campaign, all decisions were made verbally, face-to-face rather than by the more usual letter. Jervis even appointed the General's son, a promising naval officer, as his flag captain in the 98-gun *Boyne*.

The squadron consisted of the *Boyne* and three other line-of-battle ships: the 74-gun *Vengeance* and the 64-gun *Veteran* and

Asia; twelve frigates of from 44 to 32 guns; and six smaller vessels – sloops and bombs. Sir John had been promised four more ships of the line, but they never materialized. Sir Charles Grey's troops, who were transported in the naval vessels rather than in transports for the sake of speed and flexibility, numbered 7,000 in three brigades, commanded by Lieutenant General Prescott, Major General Dundas and HRH Prince Edward, the Duke of Kent. They would substantially outnumber the French garrisons of the islands to be attacked.

The force sailed from England on 26 November, encountering heavy weather as they sailed south by west, stopping briefly off Madeira in late December to take on fruit and wine, before anchoring in Carlisle Bay, Barbados, on 6 January 1794.

Gunboats were constructed and preparations made for an attack on Martinique in the French-occupied Windward Islands; a mountainous, volcanic island of 185 square miles with a relatively small area of high fertility, but with numerous good harbours, Fort de France being the main French naval base in the West Indies. Despite its vulnerability to hurricanes and earthquakes, as well as to molten lava cascading down the mountainside, the island was one of the wealthiest in the Caribbean.

By the time of embarkation for the attack on Martinique yellow fever and other sickness had reduced General Grey's army to just over 6,000. The combined force sailed from Barbados on 3 February and two days later anchored off Pointe de Borguese, where the troops were disembarked into flat-bottomed barges. As they approached the shore they came under heavy fire from shore batteries which was returned with interest by Vice Admiral Jervis' squadron. The gunboats escorting the barges also gave covering fire as the soldiers leapt into the surf and waded ashore. The broadsides of the 98-gun *Boyne* and the 64-gun *Veteran* were devastating, forcing the French to abandon their fort, which was soon taken by General Grey's troops who hoisted the Union flag. The French garrison, outnumbered, retreated in disorder, setting fire to the surrounding sugar-cane fields as they went. On 6 February, 2,400 British troops under Lieutenant General Prescott were landed almost unopposed at Trois Rivières, but the French would not surrender.

On 19 March, Jervis bombarded the two forts at the entrance to the principal harbour of Fort de France, subjecting them to sustained and accurate fire. When he believed that they had been neutralized, he sent in the *Asia,* commanded by Captain John Browne, accompanied by the 16-gun sloop *Zebra*, to test whether the batteries had been silenced. The *Zebra* led the way in, possibly because she was too low in the water for the guns of the forts to be depressed to target her. *Asia* followed, but when she came under light fire from grape and round shot, she wore and came back out of range of the forts. The Admiral meanwhile had brought the rest of the fleet to a state of readiness to follow the two ships into the harbour, with topsails loosed and lying at single anchor ready to weigh and run in. When he saw *Asia* under fire from the forts, and apparently forced to wear and retreat, he assumed that either Captain Browne had been killed or the ship had been seriously damaged, so he sent George Grey, General Grey's son, in by boat to take over command of *Asia* and, if he could not get into the harbour, to run her aground under the walls of the fort. Captain Grey was soon back with the news that the ship was undamaged and had suffered no casualties. After a further unsuccessful attempt to enter by *Asia*, *Boyne* weighed anchor and, followed by the rest of the squadron, entered and took the harbour. Later that month the whole island surrendered.

Many years later, Sir John was asked by a guest at Rochetts why he had not had Captain Browne court-martialled. His reply, somewhat out of character, was, 'Madam, I thought it best to let him go home quietly.'

A garrison was established on Martinique and Jervis and Grey turned their attentions to St Lucia, some 30 miles south. It too surrendered after a combined assault and a garrison was installed there. Most of the Windward Islands were now in British possession, but four frigates were despatched, with troops on board, to take the Saintes, the tiny islands a few miles south of Guadeloupe before an assault on that island by a combined force, which sailed on 8 April.

There was fierce resistance from a chain of batteries ensconced on high ground at Palmiste, but this was overcome by a sustained naval bombardment and British troops were able to carry the highest fort. The governor sent out a flag of truce and Guadeloupe surrendered. At this point General Grey and Vice Admiral Jervis made a serious mistake by leaving a large number of French prisoners of war on the island, guarded by too few British soldiers, when they sailed first to the British-held island of St Kitts and then on to San Domingo. Although the French administrative head-quarters on San Domingo, Port au Prince, fell to a combined operation on 4 June, the French took advantage of the absence of British ships protecting Guadeloupe, where they could have provided covering fire, to land a contingent of 2,600 troops from a convoy which had escaped from Brest and Rochefort, despite Admiral Howe's blockade. They recaptured the island, assisted by the prisoners of war they had freed, and by a negro and mulatto rising spurred on by a French declaration denouncing slavery.

Attempts to take back the island proved both costly and ineffec-tive. By late June the British forces had to withdraw and return to Martinique. Throughout the previous three months yellow fever had been spreading through the ships' crews and soldiers; hundreds died. Some of the French success must be attributed to their superior diet, which protected their health more successfully than the British staples of salt meat and biscuit, too rarely augmented with fruit and vegetables. Sir John himself succumbed to the disease and had to ask to be relieved of his post. Both he and Sir Charles Grey were relieved in November, leaving their successors to face the impossible task of consolidating shrinking gains which had been based on temporary military superiority and firepower.

As the *Boyne* came within sight of the coast of southern Ireland, after crossing the Atlantic, Sir John and Sir Charles were dining with the ship's officers. It is recorded that the Vice-Admiral proposed a toast to the General:

> May the same cordial and zealous co-operation in future exist in all the united operations of our army and navy, which has been so remarkable in our late campaign, and which I attribute to a cause we both know and feel to the warm friend-ship and mutual confidence which existed between us, the commanders; a feeling which also pervaded every rank in both services!

All present drank enthusiastically to his toast.

Jervis and Grey may well have had their careers enhanced by unfair comparison with their unfortunate successors, but not all saw their campaign in the same warm afterglow. Financiers and merchants with interests in the West Indies were incensed at the proclamation, issued jointly by the two commanders after capturing Martinique, in which they levied a contribution from the proprietors of all estates on the island 'adequate to the value of the conquest'. For this purpose they had obtained a specification of all the island property and threatened to confiscate the levy by force if not paid at once. Although we must assume that the money levied was spent acceptably – perhaps on provisions for the occupying forces and to defray their unavoidable expenses – the levy had been contrary to the general usage by occupying powers and in breach of a promise of security to persons and property they had announced before the occupation.

Shortly after the squadron's arrival at Spithead on 21 January 1795, a motion of censure on both Jervis and Grey was proposed in the House of Commons. Fortunately for them it was defeated and the House instead passed a Vote of Thanks to them both for their West Indian campaign, thus putting an end to the question marks hanging over the two men. At the end of August, Jervis was promoted to Admiral and given an appointment of critical importance as Commander-in-Chief of the Mediterranean fleet.

In that era, when the quickest means of communication was almost invariably by sea – often a voyage of weeks – those in naval command were expected to fulfill a roving diplomatic role and to provide the links between embassies and outposts abroad. In years to come Nelson would find this a convenience in developing his relationship with Lady Hamilton, the wife of Britain's diplomatic representative in Naples.

Jervis understood the importance of the post he had been given and, before leaving England for Gibraltar, Britain's one naval base on the Mediterranean station, handed Lord Spencer, the First Lord of the Admiralty, a schedule of the possible political situations he might have to face, asking for guidance from the government as to how he should react. He received no advice at all, being left to use his own discretion and for the most part to take his own decisions.

This might have indicated a high degree of trust, but was probably due more to uncertainty on the part of the government. George John Spencer, the 2nd Earl Spencer of Althorp, a descendant of the Earls of Sunderland and forebear of that twentieth-century icon, Diana, Princess of Wales, had been made First Lord of the Admiralty by William Pitt in 1794, at the age of thirty-six. Both able and sensitive, he compensated for his inexperience in naval affairs by his intelligent if sometimes equivocal approach to them, and clearly recognized the ability of Sir John Jervis.

By the time Admiral Jervis left for the Mediterranean, republican France had subdued her northern enemies, occupied Holland, invaded the states of Genoa, Monaco, Nice, Savoy and Tuscany, and overrun Biscay and Catalonia. On the North African coast, she sought to dominate the independent city states of Algiers, Tripoli and Tunis. The situation Jervis was sailing into was a complex and difficult one.

Although the only established British base in the area was Gibraltar, Sir John's predecessor in the command, Admiral Lord Hood, had been active in support of the French royalists and had found himself in the position of civil commissioner in Toulon, which had adhered to the royalist cause. He had entered the port with a British fleet in 1793 in response to a pressing appeal by the royalists, and had occupied the port and its fortifications with troops and sailors. The Spaniards, who had supported him in this move, were already negotiating with the French revolutionary government.

Hood found himself with 16,000 troops under his orders, of whom just 2,000 were British and the rest a volatile mixture of Spanish, Neapolitans, Piedmontese and royalist French. In addition, knowing that the huge if ill-disciplined French republican armies were a constant threat, and realizing that he needed a base east of Gibraltar, he had made contact with insurgent Corsicans who had risen against their unpopular French masters under the leadership of General Paoli. The Corsicans responded by offering sovereignty to the British monarch. Sir Gilbert Elliot, a Scottish barrister, like Hood previously, a civil commissioner in Toulon, had been appointed in June 1794 to be Vice Regent for Corsica. Hood was then able to take over the beautiful anchorage of San Fiorenzo

Bay on the west side of the peninsula which juts out from the north end of the island less than 10 miles from the capital, Bastia.

By now Admiral Hood, nearly seventy years old, was exhausted by the demands laid on him and had asked to be relieved. He had been slighted by the Admiralty despite his conspicuous service to his country. When he had learned early in 1795 that the French had managed to collect a fleet in the Mediterranean marginally superior in numbers to his own, he asked for reinforcements but was refused. On pressing the Admiralty, he was ordered to strike his flag. Nelson was one of the many angered by this treatment, commenting, 'Oh miserable Board of Admiralty! They have forced the first officer in our service away from his command!' A few days later he wrote home: 'The fleet must regret the loss of Lord Hood, the best officer, take him altogether, that England has to boast of; equally good in all situations which an admiral can be placed in.'

Such was the situation facing Admiral Jervis, alongside the growing threat of mutiny, signs of which had already appeared. He could not wait to get his teeth into the tough assignment, yet having known about the appointment since June he was not able to hoist his flag in the 32-gun frigate *Lively* and sail for Fiorenzo Bay until November, where he arrived in a frustratingly windless calm on the 29th.

He found himself in a sheltered amphitheatre, a bay half-encircled by barren mountains, not unlike a sea loch on the north-west coast of Scotland. Most of the fleet were there. When the ship could not take her cable because of the lack of wind, Jervis impatiently took charge, signalling for boats to tow the frigate astern until her first anchor held, then to position her where he wanted before dropping a second anchor.

Jervis soon transferred his flag to the 100-gun *Victory*, destined to become the most famous ship in the British Navy. His flag captain was Robert Calder, but he had brought with him George Grey to serve as his principal staff officer. He was uneasy about discipline in the fleet. The crew of one of the ships under his command, the 74-gun *Culloden*, had mutinied in Portsmouth the previous year, though she was now commanded by the outstanding Captain Thomas Trowbridge; the crew of the 98-gun *Windsor Castle* had mutinied earlier in the year and on his arrival

Jervis heard of a mutiny in the 74-gun *Terrible*, as recently as August.

Being a student of morale and how a high level might be achieved and maintained, Jervis decided to impose the strictest discipline. In his book this applied equally to officers and men and was coupled with whatever means were possible to improve the health and living conditions of the ships' companies. He expected officers to set an example; he also believed that minute attention to detail was of paramount importance. Stores, provisions and ammunition must be meticulously accounted for; decks must be scrubbed before first light 'so that ships may seize that favourable moment to get under way, chase and fall suddenly upon the enemy'; guns must be exercised daily and manoeuvres practised at every opportunity.

To maintain good health, Sir John believed in the use of onions, lemons and other fresh fruit and vegetables as anti-scorbutics, and the distribution of fresh meat whenever available. He thought the use of lime juice overrated. Hammocks and bedding were to be regularly aired; the sick and wounded were to be treated and cared for as efficiently as was possible between the decks of a warship or vessel converted as a hospital ship, which was often the fate of two-decker frigates of the 44-gun category, to be considered poor sailers and sub-standard warships, but adequate to serve as hospital ships.

It did not take Sir John long to form clear opinions of his subordinates – those who would help him and those who would hinder. Nelson, Trowbridge, Hallowell and Fremantle he knew by reputation he could trust to follow both the letter and the spirit of his instructions, but he was less than satisfied with Rear Admiral Mann, whom he had detached with a squadron to watch the French and Spanish warships in the harbour of Cadiz. He had shown signs of weakness and indecision.

When Sir John first arrived in San Fiorenzo Bay, Nelson was captain of *Agamemnon* – which he described as 'a rotten ship' – on detached duty with a small squadron in the Gulf of Genoa. When Nelson heard that Jervis was on his way, he wrote from Leghorn to his brother:

> our new admiral is at sea. I fear he is willing to keep me with him. He had wrote me, I am sorry to say, a most flattering

55

letter and I hear I am to be offered *St George* or *Zealous* but in my present mind I shall take neither. My wish is to see England once more and I want a few weeks rest, as do everyone in my ship.

He eventually sailed for Fiorenzo Bay early in January 1796 and met Sir John on professional terms for the first time. Their first recorded, unofficial, meeting had taken place in London when they were introduced by a former Lieutenant-Governor of Greenwich Hospital, Captain Locker. They may also have met once in the Treasury corridor of the House of Commons. When Jervis had met Sir Gilbert Elliot, for whom he would develop great respect – and discussed Nelson's role in the capture of Bastia and Calvi a year earlier – he gave the Viceroy a verdict on Nelson which would only change for the better in years to come: 'He is the best fellow in the world to conduct the naval part, but his zeal does, now and then – not often – outrun his discretion.'

It is interesting to note that as a young lieutenant, Thomas Cochrane, the Sea Wolf who in an astonishing naval career unsurpassed for courage, seamanship, improvisation and adventure, briefly met Nelson when he was already famous, described him in much the same terms: 'An embodiment of dashing courage, which would not take much trouble to circumvent an enemy, but being confronted with one would regard victory so much a matter of course as hardly to deem the chance of defeat worth consideration.' The presence of Nelson as his subordinate was one of the very few shafts of light on a horizon of appalling gloom and bleakness.

Admiral Jervis' most immediate task was to blockade Toulon and Cadiz and so prevent supplies reaching the French republican armies on the Riviera and in Italy. This he had to do while facing a dearth of basic stores and a shortage of frigates, essential for communication, reconnaissance and gathering intelligence of the enemy's movements. He repeatedly reminded the Admiralty of this, but with little effect. He lacked medical supplies and fresh food while many of his men were riddled with fever, scurvy and venereal disease, and many of his ships were in desperate need of refit and repair. Pressed by British diplomats in various Italian ports to

56

provide better protection for their commerce and British residents, he reported to the Admiralty in March 1796:

> The jealousy and apprehension shown by each of His Majesty's allies in Italy of an attack from the enemy and the fears expressed by Mr Wyndham for the Tuscan territory, with the necessary attention to the preservation of this island [Corsica] places me in a very difficult situation, much increased by the unaccountable rout of the Austrian army at Vado. The intelligence from Toulon, confirmed by our own observations, does not admit of my detaching now the season approaches for opening the campaign; otherwise I should place a squadron for the protection of the west side of Corsica and Sardinia nor can I keep the sea for any length of time without the most imminent hazard of totally destroying the health of the people, among whom the scurvy breaks out after a cruise of six weeks in the most horrid shapes. Unfortunately there is not pasturage in this part of the island to maintain the Tuscan cattle, which prevents the agent victualler from providing any quantity beforehand . . . The number of officers represented as fit objects for invaliding distresses me much. I have given Dr Harness strict orders upon the subject.

In a report on naval stores he wrote:

> The rapacity of the dealers in naval stores, the failure of the lower masts, which I really believe is occasioned either by want of skill or bad workmanship . . . the very dangerous abuse which is practised by the Contractors for supplying the Navy with sailcloth . . . the disorder and confusion in the lading of the storeships . . . the condition of the *Goliath* as per enclosed statement, appears so extraordinary that I feel it my duty to lose no time in putting you in possession of it, without making any comment on the conduct of the officers and artificers of the Dockyard at Chatham where I understand this ship underwent some kind of repair and I conclude was reported fit for foreign service . . . the fleet is in the utmost distress for nails of all sorts, lead, leather, glass, oak and elm

57

planks, twine, etc; the numbers of oars was so reduced that the whole quantity in each ship will scarce complete a motley set for one boat.

The 80-gun *Ca Ira*, a prize taken from the French, caught fire in Fiorenzo Bay and was burned to a hulk. The clothing of many of the crew was destroyed; some of them were left almost naked, but there was nothing available in the ships' stores to clothe them. As for medicines, there were none in the fleet except senna, which mixed with salt water was the grand panacea under the name of a curative draught.

Ten thousand hammocks were needed and Jervis said he would have had them made except that he was obliged to use the canvas out of condemned sails for repairing others.

True to his own high standards, Sir John refused to enter into any contract which had been contrived by a British government representative to line his own pocket, and these were numerous. His efforts to protect British and friendly merchant shipping were undermined:

> I dare not trust any person in trade with the movements of His Majesty's ships. So sure as I do, it is betrayed to the enemy somehow or other while I gain no intelligence worth a *sou*. Every loss from Smyrna which has been sustained since my arrival may be justly imputed to the precipitation of the parties concerned.

Meanwhile, the fleet was 2,000 short of complement, largely due to sickness, but the only solution available to Jervis was to stop 'the rage for invaliding'. He achieved this in part by ordering the fleet doctors to be less permissive, but mainly by his efforts to keep the men healthy. Scurvy at sea could be overcome by the eating of onions and lemons, but nothing except lack of opportunity could combat venereal disease. Jervis said that there had been too much sexual latitude in Leghorn before he took command, but there was almost as much latitude on board, and Jervis took such steps as he could to clear the ships of women. It was not altogether easy because the system of taking 'wives' to sea was common and recognized by the Admiralty. Whenever he could, Jervis drove them out because, among other reasons:

> The women who still infest His Majesty's ships in great numbers, will have water to wash, that they and their reputed husbands may get drunk with the earnings and where these vermin abound, the crews are as much addicted to drinking at sea as in port and the hold is continually damp and a vapour arising from it highly pernicious to health.

Admiral Jervis appreciated that in Captain Nelson he had acquired a subordinate of exceptional talent, personality and growing reputation and spoke to him 'more as an associate than as a subordinate'. He asked Nelson whether, when he became a flag officer – which could be expected within a year or two – he would be willing to continue to serve under him. Nelson replied that he would, but that if he was not promoted he would rather return to England. Jervis, like a trainer handling a promising young racehorse, almost immediately gave Nelson a run, granting him the non-substantive rank of Commodore, and sending him with a small squadron back to the Gulf of Genoa in order to 'prevent any small number of men from making a descent upon Italy'. At that time Admiral Sir John Jervis did not have the evidence to assess the misguided military genius of the young Corsican soldier, Napoleon Bonaparte, who would shortly take over the command of the huge French republican army, come close to achieving its ominous potential, and threaten the future of Great Britain, and – at least according to France – her perfidiously acquired British Empire.

Despite all this, Jervis was able to maintain a close blockade on Toulon from the beginning of 1796, with his ships usually in two parallel lines, *Victory* on the weather bow of the weather line.

Chapter Six

Retreat from the Mediterranean

On the first day of 1796, Admiral Jervis issued the following secret order to the captains of the fleet:

> Whereas, the due performance of the plan of battle concerted between us may be essential to the success of his Majesty's arms, you are, in the event of my being slain or disabled in action with the enemy, hereby authorised and required to continue the direction of the fleet, by the signals necessary to enforce and complete such plan and evolution, lest the advantages which will probably result from a full completion thereof be lost to my king and country. But, having fulfilled the same to the best of your judgement, you are to take the first favourable opportunity of making known the accident, by signal, to the commander in the second post; and having so done, you are to repeat his signals, keeping my flag flying while in presence of the enemy.
>
> Given on board the *Victory* at sea, the 1st January 1796
> J. Jervis.

Jervis put Captain Trowbridge in command of an inshore squadron consisting of four sail of the line which kept a constant watch on the entrance to Toulon, while he himself cruised continuously off the Iles d'Hyeres, some 10 miles south-east of the port. Regardless of the weather, the blockade was unceasing, ships being detached in succession to replenish with water and whatever stores could be scraped together. Although the routine and discipline were exacting, and fresh food and vital stores sparse, health and morale remained good. To avoid exhausting the crews, they worked in three watches: one invariably resting, unless called to action stations; one on duty; and the third on standby for any emergency.

Whenever a store ship joined the fleet the ship of the line which Sir John decided was most in need of replenishment would take the store ship in tow, if possible without leaving her station in the line. Her boats would be lowered and veered astern on both sides of the store ship, loaded – returning as many times as necessary – and then the exercise would be repeated with the next ship until either requirements were met or the store ship was empty. A hospital ship was always in company to attend to the sick and injured, and was regularly inspected to ensure that the patients were getting proper attention – and that there were no malingerers.

If a ship of the line was in need of refit or repair – and most of them were in dire need – the Admiral would send the requisite number of skilled artificers and workmen from other ships to the needy one, and a refit would be carried out at sea without interrupting the blockade.

During these long weeks of tedium, Jervis had to employ every possible means to keep the ships' companies contented. Prize money had always been a prime incentive to the sailor and if the 'condemning' (which meant assessment and approval by the Admiralty Courts) of ships captured from the enemy – whether warships or merchantmen – was long delayed, or if there was a suspicion of graft or corruption in the distribution of prize money on the expected scale, then discontent simmered and morale was undermined. Almost without exception, the Admiralty Courts – dispersed wherever ships of the Royal Navy had anchorages – were notoriously corrupt. Their members and sundry port officials took their customary cuts, and delays were deliberate, creating time in which to organize misappropriation. Jervis was acutely aware of this long-standing cause of discontent. Specifically, he complained to the Admiralty of 'the extreme injury the public and several worthy individuals in this fleet have sustained by the delays and inefficiency of the temporary Admiralty Court at Corsica.'

On 1 January 1796, Sir John had sent an order to Commodore

Nelson 'to blockade the port [of Leghorn] in the closest manner; and to seize all ships and vessels attempting to enter it after the 20th inst., and send them to Bastia to be proceeded against in the Vice-Admiralty Court, and to suffer no vessel to depart from Leghorn.'

Nelson's detachment to the Gulf of Genoa met with limited success. He wrote to his new Commander-in-Chief bemoaning the lack of essentials: 'Not canvas enough to mend our sails – 10lbs of twine, no tar, not a spar. We want much and I must beg you will give me your orders to purchase stores.'

On the European continent, the opposing French and Austrian armies had been benumbed by snow and ice, which even blanketed the Riviera coast, but the French armies were expected to surge into Italy in the spring; in March Napoleon Bonaparte arrived on the Riviera to take over command of the French armies. Aged twenty-seven, he somehow inspired the half-starved and half-naked French troops. On 11 April he struck, defeating the Austrians time after time. Nelson's squadron in the Gulf of Genoa was unable to help Britain's allies directly. In weather he described as 'extraordinary' – fogs, heavy swells and gales – he succeeded in cutting out four vessels lying beneath shore batteries but this was of little help to the retreating Austrians. Losing heart, Nelson wrote to Jervis proposing that, as the service for which he had been detached – co-operation with the Austrians – was no longer possible, he should strike his commodore's broad pennant. He knew that Jervis thought highly of him, that he had asked for his further services and had already said that he could not spare him, but Nelson was weary and unwell. Concerns about his own condition were a familiar refrain whenever he was employed on mundane or repetitive duty:

> My health certainly is not bad; on the contrary, I believe a little rest and the baths of Pisa, the same nearly as those of Bath, would render me great benefit. If I could, without impediment to the service, take twenty days to fit me for another winter, I should not dislike it; and yet perhaps I shall do without it . . . do not much like what I have written.

Jervis would have read Nelson's letters with sympathy, but possibly with a touch of cynicism, although he was no stranger to ill health and hardship himself, suffering from an obscure form of dropsy. He asked Nelson to stay on station and his decision was justified when the Commodore's squadron encountered a French convoy carrying supplies for their troops in the Po valley. Despite heavy fire from shore batteries, Nelson closed and succeeded in capturing or destroying all seven ships of the convoy. He wrote to Jervis, delighted that he had captured 'the charts of Italy sent by the Directorate to Bonaparte together with three books sent to him to enhance his studies of military campaigning . . . If Bonaparte is ignorant, the Directory, it would appear, wish to instruct him; pray God he may remain ignorant.'

The *Agamemnon* was still in a very poor state of repair and Jervis appreciated that if Nelson was to continue on the station as a flag officer, when his promotion came through, he would have to be given another ship. At about this time he received a letter from Nelson, now saying that he could not bear the thought of leaving his command. Delighted that his protégé had changed his mind and was now willing to continue to serve under him in the Mediterranean, Jervis ordered Nelson to transfer to the 74-gun *Captain*. The Commodore immediately sailed for Fiorenzo Bay and on 11 June shifted his broad pendant. He then sailed for the waters south-east of Toulon where Jervis had been engaged in blockading the port for the past six weeks, but on his arrival, Jervis ordered him to return to the Gulf of Genoa and the blockade of Leghorn.

The presence of Nelson's squadron in the Gulf of Genoa had totally disrupted French trade but had inevitably had the same effect on Genoese commerce – the merchants of the city were complaining vociferously, blind to the French threat. The Genoese government objected that their neutrality was being violated while, in fact, their own merchants were trading with the French. In the same month Jervis wrote to the Admiralty from his station off Toulon: 'Nothing very material has happened in the two months that I have been in this position. The enemy bears the blockade of Toulon with Christian patience. Captain Trowbridge who commands the light squadron, never is two miles from the entrance, and I keep as near as my heavy sailing ships will enable me.' Maintaining this close blockade was exhausting for the ships' companies, for it necessitated tacking or wearing the fleet at night.

Although these manoeuvres could be executed by one watch while the other slept, this did not apply to the ship's captain and certain other officers. With a hint of irony the Admiral circulated the squadron of twelve sail of the line, informing them that he had 'too exalted an opinion of the respective captains of the squadron to doubt their being on deck when the signal was made to tack or wear in the night'. Whereas a modern warship is conned from the bridge, or even from the Operations Room, the orders necessary for a sailing ship to alter course were given from the exposed quarter-deck or raised poop aft.

Meanwhile the French armies were advancing on Leghorn, which was the British fleet's main source of essential supplies, such as fresh meat and fuel. By 15 June they were in the town. Fortunately Captain Fremantle of the *Inconstant* used his initiative and escorted some forty British and allied merchant ships away to the south-west, towards Fiorenzo Bay, taking quantities of stores and people with him. Nelson and his squadron stayed in Leghorn Roads to prevent any new arrivals from entering the port, but very soon Napoleon took possession of the town.

Among those evacuated from Leghorn was a lively and attractive young woman, Betsey Wynne, then in her late teens, who subsequently became Mrs Fremantle. Betsey's diary records her thoughts and experiences as well as passing events. One of five daughters of a wealthy Lincolnshire landowner, who had sold his estates and taken up permanent residence on the European continent, moving about at will, Betsey and her family had been living in Florence when the city was threatened by the advance of the French Army. Mr Wynne decided to move to Leghorn, for evacuation to a safer destination. When they were hustled on board the *Inconstant* (a strange name for a warship!) Captain Fremantle made an immediate impression. Following a sequence of short sea passages and transfers from one ship to another, the family found themselves ensconced in the palatial admiral's quarters of the first rate *Britannia* anchored with other ships of the fleet off Toulon.

Mrs Wynne and her daughters received a 'mighty gallant' message of welcome from Sir John on their arrival, despite his sending a terse memorandum on the same day to the women in the fleet admonishing them for wasting water and threatening to send any future offenders back to England. When *Victory* weighed anchor and passed astern of *Britannia*, he signalled for the ladies to appear on the stern gallery for his inspection. No doubt he used his telescope to advantage.

A few days later, the Admiral invited them to dinner in his flag-ship, as Betsey describes in her diary:

> The Admiral was on deck to receive us with the greatest civility and kindness. Nothing stiff or formal about him and we were not at all embarrassed as I feared we should be. He desired that we should pay the tribute that was due to him at our entering his cabin, this was to kiss him, which the ladies did very willingly.

Sir John had invited most of his captains to the dinner party. One officer who arrived after the ladies was 'abused' by the Admiral:

> For not having yet saluted us, the consequence being that we were kissed a second time . . . We were very gay, laughed much and made a monstrous noise at the table . . . Nothing can express how kind, gallant and friendly the admiral was to us, he is a fine old man, though past seventy he is as fresh and brisk as if he was only thirty.

She had overestimated his age by a decade. The partiality of Betsey and Thomas Fremantle for one another had been noted because after dinner the Admiral first persuaded Betsey and one of her sisters to sing a duet, then spoke very favourably to her parents about Thomas, saying that he approved the match. However, the party did not go on long because 'as Admiral Jervis gets up at two o'clock in the morning, he goes to bed at half past eight.'

Disgusted with Napoleon's success and the failure of the Austrians to contain him, Jervis wrote angrily to Lord Spencer that he saw 'no difficulties which may not be surmounted, my mind always mounting to the situation I happen to be placed in'.

To a military colleague he wrote: 'The French certainly do pursue their objects with steady perseverance and all the powers of Europe, except Russia, will soon be instruments in their hands against us.'

Meanwhile Spain joined France on 19 August, though she did not declare war on Britain until October.

Jervis ordered Nelson to shift his broad pennant to a frigate and to send the *Captain* to join him off Toulon, where the Admiral believed that the enemy would soon appear in strength and he would need every available line-of-battle ship. Nelson, not wishing to miss a fleet action, interpreted this as an order to return to the fleet in the *Captain* himself and deployed other ships of his squadron to continue the blockade of Leghorn.

Determined to concentrate his fleet, Sir John had also ordered Rear Admiral Mann and his squadron to return from blockading Cadiz and to rejoin him. Having little confidence in Mann he wrote: 'Poor Admiral Mann has been afflicted with such a distempered mind during the last nine months that imaginary ills and difficulties have been continually brooding in it . . . When the Blue Devils prevail, there is an end of resource and energy.'

And to Lord Spencer:

> I beg I may have no more admirals unless they are firm men. Your Lordship will readily comprehend that persons holding high situations in a fleet who see everything with a jaundiced eye are a perfect nuisance; fortunately for me, Commodore Nelson and several of the captains of the line-of-battle ships and frigates under my command are of a temper that will work to anything.

A Spanish fleet of twenty-six sail of the line had entered the Mediterranean and had been seen off Cap Corse, the northern tip of Corsica. Jervis only had fifteen sail of the line under his immediate command but Mann's squadron would have increased it to twenty-two. Part of the Spanish fleet had earlier been sighted by Mann's squadron which was en route to Gibraltar to revictual and a brief action had ensued, in the course of which Mann lost a brig and a transport. After revictualling, he returned to cruising off Cape St Vincent, 160 miles west by north from Cadiz. On 16 October he received the order from the Commander-in-Chief, by frigate, to rejoin him off Toulon. Mann's astonishing reaction was to call a meeting of the captains of the ships in his squadron to discuss what to do. A vote was taken and a majority wanted to return to England, so after cruising for a few more days off Cadiz, and without informing Jervis, he simply returned to Spithead, arriving in time for Christmas. Surprisingly, Rear Admiral Mann was not court-martialled, but was ordered to strike his flag and was never employed again.

Meanwhile, the Corsicans were proving excitable and unreliable. Jervis described them as 'infernal miscreants' and had already told the Admiralty that 'strong nerves and manly sense' were superior to diplomacy in dealing with them. He was well aware that evacuation of Corsica would mean the virtual abandonment of the Mediterranean, leaving the French as masters of the Adriatic and rulers of Naples and Sicily, and would, as he put it, 'bouleverse the whole system of Italy'. He ordered Nelson to take instructions from Sir Gilbert Elliot and it was decided that Nelson should occupy the small island of Elba, between Corsica and the Italian coast, which had a good harbour on its northern coast.

Late in August the vacillating British government decided not only to withdraw its vice regency from Corsica, but the British fleet from the Mediterranean, retaining only Elba. Having first ordered Jervis to evacuate the Mediterranean, they later authorized the Admiralty to send him a secret letter telling him to remain there as long as possible under certain vague conditions – then, when it was too late, to hold Corsica and retain Elba. Lord Spencer, attempting to excuse himself for the vagueness and ambiguity of his recent orders, wrote: 'The orders we have sent have been purposely so framed as to leave a great deal to your discretion and judgement.'

Jervis then wrote to Nelson: 'The instructions I received yesterday have so many provisions founded on wrong principle, it is next to impossible to act upon them in the way you and I would wish.'

Nelson, bitterly disappointed, wrote to his wife:

They at home do not know what this fleet is capable of performing: anything and everything. Much as I shall rejoice to see England, I lament our present orders in sackclothes and ashes, so dishonourable to the dignity of England whose fleets are equal to meet the World in arms; and of all the fleets I ever saw, I never beheld one in point of officers and men equal to Sir John Jervis's who is a Commander-in-Chief able to lead them to glory.

On 2 October 1796, Jervis had written to Lord Spencer: 'Be assured I will omit no opportunity of chastising the Spaniards, and if I have the good fortune to fall in with them the stuff I have in this fleet will tell.'

Jervis ordered Captain Cockburn of the 12-gun frigate *Meleager* to take over the blockade of Leghorn and sent Commodore Nelson to undertake the highly responsible assignment of supervising the evacuation of Corsica. It was just in time. The Corsicans, fearing French retribution for their having hosted British sovereignty, had seized control from Sir Gilbert Elliot in Bastia and started to impound British property. Nelson arrived shortly afterwards and told the Corsican officials that unless they allowed the evacuation to proceed unimpeded, he would destroy the town with gunfire, which forced the Corsicans to permit the orderly evacuation of British nationals and property over the next five days. Late on 18 October, French troops landed in force on the northern tip of the island and began the 25-mile march towards the town. By evening on 19 October, the evacuation was complete and the British garrison marched out of the citadel. The French marched in an hour later and the last British boat, with Commodore Nelson and the army commander in it, shoved off and pulled out to the *Captain*. The convoy of transports and naval escorts then sailed for Elba, just 50 miles to the east. Meanwhile Jervis had brought his fleet to Fiorenzo Bay where Nelson later joined him, but before long the French made the anchorage untenable. When he heard, on 11 November, of Mann's shameful retreat to England, Jervis wrote to Spencer:

I cannot describe to Your Lordship the disappointment my ambition and zeal to serve my country have suffered by this diminution of my force, for had Admiral Mann sailed from Gibraltar on 10th October, the day he received my orders and fulfilled them, I have every reason to believe the Spanish fleet would have been cut to pieces; the extreme disorder and confusion they were seen to be in by the judicious officers who fell in with them leaving no doubt in my mind that a fleet so trained and generally commanded as this fleet is would have made its way through them in every direction.

When the news came that the Spanish squadron had entered Toulon, and running short of both food and basic stores, the Admiral set course for Gibraltar with his dozen line-of-battle ships, accompanied by frigates and transports. This was the prelude to an exit from the Mediterranean – an ignominious decision, damaging to morale, brought upon him by a weak government and defective Admiralty. Jervis had raised the fighting efficiency of his small fleet to an unprecedented level, with the support of Nelson and a handful of conscientious officers, but they had been obliged to abandon Corsica and Italy to the dictates of Napoleon.

The British fleet anchored in the bay west of the rock of Gibraltar – in theory sheltered from the east – on 1 December 1796. The men were put on full rations and extensive repairs of the wear and tear resulting from months of unbroken time at sea were put in hand. Jervis meanwhile was reprimanded by the Admiralty for sending one of the commissioners from Gibraltar to Naples to oversee the manufacture of some essential articles desperately needed as stores.

Five days later the Spanish admiral, de Langara, with twenty-six line-of-battle ships and a dozen frigates, sailed into Cartagena, while the French admiral, Villeneuve, proceeded west, bound eventually for Brest. Villeneuve was unaware of the British fleet in Gibraltar, but luck was on his side. The same easterly gale which swept Villeneuve's warships through the Strait drove the British ships towards the coast north of Algeciras and made it nearly impossible to weather the rocky points south-east of the Spanish town. The rotten-hulled 74-gun *Courageux* – captained by one of the outstanding officers in the fleet, Hallowell, a Canadian, who was ashore at the time on court-martial duty – tried to escape under the command of her first lieutenant. She succeeded in getting out of the bay, but was driven ashore on the Barbary coast where 464 out of her 593-man crew were drowned, a loss that was magnified by the shortage of crew in many of the British ships. Two other ships, the 80-gun *Gibraltar* and the 74-gun *Culloden*, were also driven ashore and seriously damaged while a few days later the 74-gun *Zealous* struck a rock in Tangier Bay. Jervis wrote:

> At any time the loss of such a ship to His Majesty, so manned and commanded, would have been very great, but in the present circumstances of my force, compared with that of the enemy in these seas, it is beyond all calculation. I shall endeavour by every means in my power to support and encourage Captain Hallowell who has lost all except his honour in this deplorable misfortune, and I beg leave to recommend his situation in the Lords Commissioners of the Admiralty as peculiarly worthy of their Lordships' attention and regard . . . The *Gibraltar* struck twice on Cabrita Point in getting out of the Bay after parting her cables: her foretopmast was carried away by the shock, but she does not make water . . . The *Zealous* struck twice on the reef off Cape Malabata and makes a little water . . . the *Andromache* is returned with a sprung bowsprit and *Niger* without any injury except the loss of two anchors.

As if these losses of men and ships were not enough to bear, Sir John now received orders to abandon Elba. Inevitably Commodore Nelson was sent to organize this final act: the evacuation of the naval and military garrisons together with their stores and equipment. He went, not in the *Captain* which could not be spared from a fleet reduced to eleven line-of-battle ships, some unseaworthy, but with his broad pennant hoisted in the frigate *Minerve*, with another frigate *Blanche* in attendance. Nelson sailed on 15 December and the following day Jervis departed with the rest of his small fleet for Lisbon, because Britain's ally Portugal was now under threat from the powerful Franco-Spanish alliance.

Entering the Tagus on 21 December, yet another misfortune occurred – the 74-gun *Bombay Castle* ran aground and stuck so hard and fast that she had to be abandoned. The lack of pilots had cost Jervis another ship. He made the most strenuous efforts to save her and asked the Minister to get aid from the Portuguese; but the

Minister was too slow. As for the Portuguese: 'the festivals happening at the moment, they were more intent on prayer and rejoicing than in preserving the officers and seamen of the *Bombay Castle*.' *Zealous* was by this time leaking so badly that she had to be laid up for repairs, the *St George* had lost her mainmast and the *Gibraltar* was sent limping back to England.

The Portuguese arsenals were empty, no stores of salted provisions were to be obtained, the naval hospital was in a deplorable state and medicines had not yet arrived. Jervis wrote:

> I find this Court more intent upon avoiding giving offence to Spain than desirous to coalesce with us . . . The expected reinforcement is whittled down very low . . . I will not lay here a moment longer than is necessary to put us to rights, for you well know that inaction in the Tagus must make us all cowards.

Despite all this, the fleet had a merry Christmas with welcome fresh food and wine, liberally provided by their Portuguese hosts. Jervis himself was in a grimly serious frame of mind, however, and issued orders that no boats were to be sent ashore unnecessarily for fear of drunken quarrels with the Portuguese, which he suggested 'always leads to assassination'. A captain, accompanied by a boatswain's mate, had to visit the hospital daily 'to see that the patients conduct themselves properly and orderly' and if not 'to punish them agreeably to the rules of the navy' – the word 'agreeably' here is used in an uncomfortably different sense to its modern meaning.

When *St George* collided with a Portuguese frigate and went aground, with exemplary patience and greater magnanimity Jervis wrote to the unfortunate captain:

> At the same time that I express the painful surprise I felt on observing His Majesty's ship under your command in the perilous state she appeared in on the 19th instant, I have great pleasure in assuring you that before I received your letter of yesterday I did justice to your character as an officer, of which I have had too great experience to doubt your having used

every means in your power to conduct the *St George* safe through the channel.

Ten days later the *Meleager* sprang her bowsprit and had to be sent back to Lisbon for repairs. The *St George* was refloated, but had to undergo major repairs so was out of action when the squadron put to sea in January, leaving Jervis to cruise with ten ships off Cape St Vincent, waiting on events.

Such was the close of 1796 – a year of defeat, disaster and disappointment – but the main objective was still clear: to prevent a junction between the combined French and Spanish fleets, currently split between the Mediterranean, Cadiz and Brest. The setbacks he had suffered only strengthened Sir John's resolve to achieve that objective.

Chapter Seven

Diplomat and Strategist

There is no better way of illustrating Admiral Sir John Jervis' great gifts as a strategist and diplomat, supported by a scrupulous attention to detail, than by quoting some of the letters he wrote and orders he issued over the last five months of 1796, while the government in London vacillated and evaded responsibility, and the French Republic swept all before it in Europe.

The British foothold in Corsica˙ and the anchor-hold in San Fiorenzo Bay were precarious, being dependent upon the co-operation of the Corsicans, who were at best self-interested and at worst treacherous. Opinions regarding the importance of retaining the island differed widely but by July 1796 the Admiral was already contemplating the removal of the naval establishment from Ajaccio to Porto Ferrajo in Elba. Meantime, he gave Commodore Nelson complete freedom to confer with and follow the advice of Sir Gilbert Elliot, the British Viceroy. The latter seemed to stand higher in his regard than any other diplomat representing the British government in the Mediterranean and Iberian peninsula, while Nelson wrote to Jervis:

> I experience the highest degree of pleasure which an officer is capable of feeling, the full approbation of his commander-in-chief, which must not be a little increased by knowing that his commander is such a character as Sir John Jervis, without disparagement or flattery, allowed to be one of the first in the service.

And he most probably meant it, as he already knew that he was due for promotion to Rear Admiral within a year. Jervis in return wrote to him while cruising off Toulon to maintain the blockade:

Dear Sir

There is a great wisdom and sound judgment in every line of the viceroy's letter; act up to it and you cannot err. We have no business with Vado or Port Especia, until the Austrians enter Piedmont. Do not Let any vessel come out of the Leghorn Mole, full or empty, unless the Viceroy advises . . . I wish you would send *Petrel* to Trieste, to reinforce Miller and recommend to Colonel Graham, if you have any means of communicating with him, that the Austrian flotilla shall be put under Captain Miller's orders. If you can write in cipher to Drake at Venice, to this effect, it perhaps may be more speedily carried into execution.

I have ordered two transports, wanting repair, to Genoa for that purpose; and they may be employed afterwards in bringing bullocks and lemons. Two, under the like circumstances, are ordered to Naples and, after repairing, to load with valuable articles from thence. When you write to Mr Jackson at Turin, make my excuses for not replying to his letter, on the score of ignorance how to convey it. T . . . is ordered to Ajaccio, to complete his sails, cordage and slops and then to follow your orders.

I have sent the proposals of Messrs. Coffarina to Heatly. I think the lemons high. I, the other day, purchased of a Dane, who loaded there, at nineteen livres the case. Go on and prosper.

Captain Ralph Willet Miller, by birth a New Englander, had been put in command in the Adriatic in the frigate *Unite*.

On 8 August, Jervis wrote to the British Consul in Leghorn, the Hon. F. Wyndham, who complained that he had not been informed of the move to occupy Elba:

Sir

I was unacquainted with the enterprise against Porto Ferrajo until it came into our possession. Having given orders to

Commodore Nelson to co-operate in all respects with the Viceroy. Had the concerting of this measure rested with me, I could not, consistently with the plan I have laid down, impart to you this or any other plan of operation previous to its execution, secrecy being the life and soul of every military undertaking; neither am I furnished with a cipher; and as my military correspondence is chiefly confined to the Viceroy, I refer your Excellency to him for general information. With respect to your Excellency's proposition for the departure of vessels belonging to Messrs Porter and Hudcert from Leghorn, it is out of my power to show partiality to any individuals, but particularly in the present instance, for reasons I will give you when I may have the honour of a personal interview. The plan suggested in your Excellency's letter of the 21st requires mature deliberation. I shall revolve it in my mind and write you fully on the subject by a future conveyance.

The island of Elba now offered the best, if not the only source of fresh food for the fleet, although Jervis did suggest to Sir Gilbert Elliot that, as current relations with Tripoli, Tunis and Algiers – all ruled by independent Beys – were good, they could be useful sources for supplying Gibraltar, or ships, in an emergency. He wrote to him on 22 August:

Dear Sir

Totally ignorant as I am of the intention of government respecting Corsica, or indeed, of the plan of operation in Italy, farther than being ordered to co-operate, my opinion upon the critical state of the island as it regards us is not worth sending. At the same time, that I may not appear shabby to withhold it, I am free to say, that if the Corsicans do not manfully resist the machinations of the enemy, it would be very bad policy indeed to continue in possession of the ports, longer than is absolutely necessary for our own convenience. Porto Ferrajo will be a very good transfer, equally à porté to Leghorn; and while the Austrians make any stand in Italy, I conclude it will be the policy of our cabinet to bolster them up; for should the fleet be withdrawn, the French will be masters of the Adriatic, give the law to Naples, take possession of Sicily and, in short, *bouleverse* the whole system in Italy.

Later the same day, having received letters from Sir Gilbert, Jervis wrote to him again, referring both to the French advance into Italy and, obliquely, to those in authority in Gibraltar as well as to Rear Admiral Mann and Commodore Nelson:

Dear Sir

Many thanks for your interesting letters of the 17th . . . You have drawn the exact type of Lord Bute and General O'Hara; nevertheless, they may by accounts prove true prophets; of course I must attend to their reveries until I have better evidence. Their constant communications with Rear-Admiral Mann have not contributed a little to his malady. He certainly should not have quitted his position before Cadiz until he saw the combined fleet under sail; and even then he should not have passed Gibraltar without filling his ships with provisions and water and gaining intelligence of the route of the enemy. But, if I were to tell him so, he would die instantly.

I agree with you in every part of your reasoning respecting Leghorn. The commodore is the best fellow in the world to conduct the naval part; but his zeal does now and then (not often) outrun his discretion. If Marshal Wurmser has fairly beaten the enemy in the field, poison and stiletto will do the rest, and the attempt at Leghorn ought to be made.

Eventually, Jervis received orders from the Admiralty, dated 17 August, to evacuate Corsica but to retain Elba, based on the mistaken assumption that his fleet had by then been reinforced by Rear Admiral Mann's squadron. Jervis had calculated the Spanish fleet in Cartagena at twenty-six sail of the line and the French in Toulon at twelve to fifteen, which made it essential to concentrate every available British line-of-battle ship.

When the King of Naples, whose dominions were scattered over southern Italy, heard that the British were vacating Corsica he appealed in alarm to the Admiral not to desert him. Elba was the last hope, but it meant putting the crews of the British ships onto short rations. The Neapolitans should have been eager to help but their officials – fearful of the French threat and greedy – were obstructive. Jervis' remonstrances to Sir William Hamilton were ineffectual and supplies from Genoa were exorbitantly expensive. He wrote angrily to Mr Joseph Braame, the British Vice-Consul in Genoa:

> Sir
> It having been represented to me by the officers who went to Genoa in the *Diadem* to purchase stock and refreshments for the fleet that you, in your own person, caused the price of every article to be raised upon them, for the sordid emolument of some creature of yours. I lose no time in communicating this foul charge, that you may have an opportunity of vindicating yourself; feeling, as I do, myself implicated for having recommended and obtained the consulship for you from his grace the Duke of Leeds.

To General O'Hara the Governor of Gibraltar, he wrote a prophetic letter:

> My dear Sir
> Richery [the admiral of the French squadron] has gone into the Bay of Biscay to see his crippled ships safe out of the track of the escorts of our trade, and then intends to proceed on his former mission, as the whole are gone to Brest, where they have seventeen more; and the invasion of Ireland is probably in contemplation, or threatened, to mask some other important design.
> The Portuguese will make no effort unless the British troops are sent to support them, which I expect to see; and my excellent friend Sir Charles Grey, if he will go, at the head of them. What do you think of the large importation at Brest from the Tagus, while we are looking for the defence of our own coast?

On 17 September, Jervis wrote to the British Minister in Venice, Francis Drake:

Sir

I am honoured with your Excellency's letter of the 30th August, with two very interesting papers of intelligence inclosed.

I had long foreseen the fate of Genoa and gave Commodore Nelson particular direction to keep his eye upon it; I also discouraged some merchants retired from Leghorn from sending a valuable cargo thither, but their spirit of adventure outran my discretion; two empty transports were also ordered to repair to Genoa, to receive the effects of our merchants.

I despatched orders to the commodore, by his Majesty's sloop *L'Eclair* to temporise with the Serene Republic, until he can retire the Factory and their property. Your absence is deplored by us all; Mr Braame being in a state of imbecility during his best days, was never fit to stand as your *locum tenens*.

Your commissionaire gives a very exact account of the number of French ships of the line, frigates and corvettes at Toulon, apparently ready for sea, with the exception of their sails not being all bent. We are frequently inferior to them in the number of our line-of-battle ships, and they have between twenty and thirty corvettes and frigates, while I have not one, the whole of mine being employed in the Archipelago, Adriatic, blockade of Leghorn, covering Corsica and convoying between Naples and Corsica. I believe Spain lays upon her oars, until she sees what effect the rash though feeble measure she has taken in the detention of our merchant ships, and those of the Portuguese, in her harbours, will produce. I have the satisfaction to assure you that there never was a squadron in higher health order or government, than the one I have the honour to command. I have caused every ship to be caulked at sea, and we are, for the most part, patched and painted; and when I reflect that we are in the close of our three-and-twentieth week at sea, I cannot be too thankful for the goodness of divine Providence.

The emperor must employ young and uncorrupt men in the command of his armies, or these devils will run over them every where. I fear French gold has been successfully distributed, both in his camps and councils.

That same day Jervis wrote to Nelson and then on the following day to Lieutenant General Trigg, commanding the troops in Bastia:

Dear Sir [to Nelson]

Persevere in your plans, both respecting Leghorn and Genoa, first withdrawing the merchants and their property from the latter. The lieutenant of the watch onboard the *Captain*, who suffered the boat to be run away with, deserves to be dismissed the service . . . The *Egmont* will be ten days or a fortnight at Ajaccio, getting her mainmast replaced by a repaired one. I therefore wish the *Captain* to follow close upon her heels, as I think it probable those devils will make some attempt on Ajaccio. It would be wise in the viceroy to take *Gentile* under his protection; the refugees are tired of wandering and I really believe would prefer our protection to that of France.

Dear Sir [to Lieutenant General Trigg]

I believe the transports with foreign troops for Trieste must touch at Bastia, for I have neither tonnage of transports, nor provisions, sufficient for the whole voyage. I begin to fear you will receive no direction about Corsica, but that ministers will leave the destiny of it entirely to you and the chapter of accidents. The person I conversed with about it never treated the subject seriously and the few observations I have lately received in a letter are of the same cast. If Commodore Nelson can contrive to get the British merchants and their property from Genoa, you will probably take possession of Capraja and destroy the batteries and remove the civil government.

On 2 October Jervis proposed to Sir Gilbert Elliot that he should send his wife in the *Gorgon* to take up temporary quarters in the *Britannia* off Toulon rather than sending her to Naples:

It is not in my power to exercise the smallest discretion, for they have sent me out no provisions and I very much doubt whether I shall not be compelled to touch at Lisbon for a supply. Thus circumstanced, there is not an hour to be lost. In the seventh month of our cruise, it is a hard measure to put the people to two-thirds allowance, but I cannot help it. If you do not withdraw the cannon and ordnance stores from Bonifaccio, Ajaccio, and Calvi, there will be very little to do. Captain Macnamara will carry into execution any orders you are pleased to give him on those heads; and I shall soon be able to furnish you with two fine copper-bottomed transports for the most valuable stores. Gibson is gone to Naples, with letters from Lord Grenville to Sir William Hamilton, announcing this event; and I have sent orders by him, for the frigates to retire from the Adriatic and to pick up Prince Augustus at Naples on their return. It will be, therefore, highly improper for Lady Elliot to go to Naples, unless she intends to fix there; for it will be to give the *Gorgon* to the enemy, to send her into the Adriatic after we are off. I trust, by the 20th or 25th instant, everything will be ready for us to proceed. The war with Spain is certain, for I have orders to attack ships of war of that nation, in fleets or singly, wherever I meet them. How unfortunate that Commodore Nelson could not have been put in possession of this in time! I only got it last night.

On 7 October Jervis wrote a furious letter to Joseph Braame, whom he now detested:

Sir

I have read with astonishment and indignation the paper sent to you by the secretary of state of the most Serene Republic of Genoa, wherein he charges Commodore Nelson with making use of a subterfuge to justify the boarding and carrying off a French tartan, that was disembarking cannon and ordnance stores at San Pietro d'Areno. I have no doubt you repelled this shameful attack on the bright honour of the commodore, which you was fully enabled to do, by the deserters being actually in your possession at Genoa, and the boat in a bay near it. In addition to this, the enemy having erected a battery to cover and protect their depot of military stores in the territory of the most Serene Republic, was justifiable ground for the commodore to have acted upon, exclusive of their shameful fire on a small open boat. I have always respected the flag, and shown friendly regard to the subjects, of the Genoese government; and I am very solicitous to continue this practice, conformably to the will and pleasure of the King, my royal master, who is renowned for his good faith; but I desire you will take the earliest opportunity to make known to the most Serene Republic that, if the representations lately made by the Viceroy of Corsica, Commodore Nelson and myself are not listened to and summary justice done thereon, I shall feel myself bound, by every principle which can govern an officer invested with the high command I have the honour to bear, to proceed to Genoa with the fleet, and exact it from the mouths of my cannon.

P.S. If you should find the government of Genoa disposed to accommodation, and to make amendment for the outrage offered to the British flag, you will govern yourself accordingly; for I shall feel the greatest repugnance to batter down the Mole-head and deface the beautiful city, which has been long the great object of my admiration; and I am anxious to avoid doing injury to the innocent inhabitants who, I believe, are as much dissatisfied with the conduct of their government as I am; but justice must be done. I desire you to write to Commodore Nelson and tell him that I have pledged my honour to the deserters from the *Captain* being pardoned.

A Most Secret letter was sent to Rear Admiral Mann on 8 October, proposing the best route to follow to join the fleet in San Fiorenzo Bay, avoiding areas where he might encounter a superior enemy force, keeping 'well to the south of the islands of Majorca and Minorca, so as not to be seen from either' and telling him that his 're-junction with me has become more essential than ever'. Of course Mann ignored the letter.

Towards the end of the month, having virtually given up hope of being reinforced, Jervis gave orders for the two principal forts commanding San Fiorenzo Bay to be dismantled, the heavy guns which had been carried up by British seamen re-embarked and the Martello tower blown up. His letter to Captain George Towry of the *Diadem* reads:

Sir

The experience I have had of your zeal and judgment, gives me the most perfect confidence that you will make the best possible disposition for retiring such artillery and ordnance stores as the viceroy may direct to be withdrawn from Ajaccio and Bonifaccio, with the troops, baggage, etc. Naval hospital and yard establishments. I wish as many of the Swiss corps of De Rolle's to be received on board the *Diadem* and sloops of war, as they can conveniently stow, it being my intention to embark the whole of them in ships of war, when they arrive at San Fiorenzo. The gun-boat will be very useful in embarking the cannon and heavy stores – the best use that can now be made of her. When all the transports, already at Ajaccio, are cleared of the spars, and other naval stores, on board them, and the victuallers of the provisions (with the stores I now send) there will be a considerable tonnage; should more be wanted, you must send to San Fiorenzo for them, but you are not to regard the men being a little crowded during the short passage to that bay. I shall be very glad to hear the *Tarleton* is got round safe to Ajaccio, her captain, officers and men, moved into the *Téméraire;* but if there is any risk, send the latter to Bonifaccio and direct the transhipping to be performed there, and the *Tarleton* sent to the bottom, without the harbour's mouth. You will receive on board the *Diadem* as much gunpowder from the garrison as the magazine will stow.

Sir John wrote again to the wretched Joseph Braame in Genoa on 1 November:

Sir

Not having heard from you since my letter of 7th October, by a Genoese boat which brought refreshments to the fleet off Toulon, I have only to observe that, although I have been prevented by the peculiar circumstances which have lately arisen, from appearing before Genoa with his Majesty's fleet under my command, I desire that you will seize the earliest moment to convey to the most Serene Republic that the event is not the less certain, unless the most ample reparation is made for the flagrant breach of neutrality and hospitality in prohibiting the exportation of the bullocks belonging to the crown and intended for the use of the fleet and for two violent and unjustifiable acts of hostility committed upon his Majesty's ship *Captain* bearing Commodore Nelson's distinguishing pennant and another afterwards upon his Majesty's sloop *Sardine*.

I am, Sir, etc J.J.

Sir Gilbert Elliot was still in Bastia, and Jervis wrote to him on 11 November:

Dear Sir

I have had no opportunity till this moment of acknowledging your letter of the 3rd instance. I agree with you that it is scarce within possibility that the Court of Naples should hesitate a moment to comply with every reasonable request we make. By the *Cygnet* cutter which joined last night, I have orders to support your sovereignty of Corsica; and in case of the evacuation having taken place, to establish ourselves at Porto Ferrajo. Thus far we sail before the wind; but alas! Poor Admiral Mann has, for the present, frustrated my plan of operations by a resolution (taken in concert with the captains under his orders) to cruise off Cape St Vincent until the latter end of October and then to proceed to Spithead with his whole force, in direct disobedience to the orders he acknowledges to have received from me. His reasons are those of a man who has lost all his powers and I conclude the queries he put to the captains were so formed as to point their answers, which happened on a former occasion. Thus circumstanced, it is my intention to proceed to Gibraltar with the convoy, in hopes of receiving a reinforcement. Should none appear in a reasonable

83

time, I will make the best of my way to Porto Ferrajo, where I hope to arrive before your return from the Continent. Although I have nothing to offer against your retiring from a scene where you cannot act with the dignity and authority necessary to justify to the public and your own character a longer continuance with us, I look forward with very great anxiety indeed to the situation I may be placed in by the loss of your able counsel and honest support.

I entertain the highest opinion of General de Burgh [officer commanding British troops on Elba]; but, inexperienced as he is in business of such a complicated nature – diffident and doubtful, where prompt decision is requisite – I dread the moment of your final departure. I will, however, hope for the best; and in truth I form great expectations from the plan of operations you have in contemplation to lodge with the General.

On 1 December, Jervis sent secret orders to Captain Thomas Trowbridge in *Culloden*:

Whereas I have received intelligence, that a Spanish ship of the line is cruising before Cadiz for the protection of the trade passing in and out of that port; you are hereby required and directed to proceed thither, with his Majesty's ship under your command; and the *Zealous*, Captain Hood being instructed to obey your orders, and endeavour to cut her off. In the performance of this service, you are not to hazard an action with a superior force, which may, possibly have joined that ship from Cadiz, since Captain Bowen of *Terpsichore* was off there; nor are you to cruise – the sole object of your mission being strictly confined to the making a stroke at the afore-mentioned Spanish ship and joining me in Rosier Bay with the utmost possible despatch.

For your guidance and that of Captain Hood; in case the easterly wind should bring down the combined fleets and place them between you and Rosier Bay, so as to defeat your junction with me during this short absence, you will receive therewith two sealed rendezvous addressed to each, of the most secret and important nature.

Given, etc, Gibraltar, 1st December 1796 J.J.

(Rendezvous)

In case your junction with me in Rosier Bay is defeated by the combined fleet being placed off Cape Spartel, or in such other position as may put that object to extreme hazard, you are to proceed to Lisbon, and use the utmost dispatch in filling your water and refitting his Majesty's ship under your command and then wait my arrival.

On board *Victory*, anchored in Rosier Bay on the west side of the Rock of Gibraltar, on 10 December, Admiral Sir John Jervis composed four very important communications, which must have taken him most of the day. There was no room for error or procrastination. Although some of the detail is not directly relevant to the main course of events, these letters are reproduced in full because they offer a vivid insight into the way his clear and incisive mind worked.

First, to Sir Gilbert Elliot, now removed to Elba and awaiting conveyance back to England. In due course, Nelson would bring him as far as Lisbon, where he and Jervis met.

Dear Sir

I return you many thanks for your interesting letter of the 5th and 6th November with the important enclosures.

There being two captains of frigates senior to Captain Fremantle in the eastern parts of the Mediterranean – Captain Tyler, who commands in the Adriatic and Captain Curzon, cruising between Sardinia and the coast of Barbary – I have given the command of the whole to Commodore Nelson, whose firmness and ability will very soon combine and fix all the parts of our force, naval and military, unless there is a greater disposition to doubt and fear – I only mean as far as relates to diffidence and want of experience – than I am aware of.

As the commodore intends to push for Naples in hopes of catching you before your departure to England, he will inform you of the extent of my new instructions, dated 7th November and the plan I am about to pursue to form a junction with the reinforcements which I am told will sail as soon as it can be collected. The westerly winds are so prevalent in the English channel, until the approach of Christmas, that I do not expect it to reach the Tagus before the beginning of January, about which time I shall probably be there, unless I am detained at Gibraltar longer than I look for, by the want of a Levanter to carry me through the Gut.

The evacuation of Porto Ferrajo, both in respect to period of time and manner, I have left entirely to the judgment of Commodore Nelson and it cannot be in better hands. The ratification or entire dissolution of the preliminary treaty between the directory and the Prince of Belmonte, must take place ere the Commodore can be in forwardness to carry this part of my instructions into execution.

Your observations on [probably referring to Joseph Braame] are confirmed by a variety of incidents which have come officially to me. It is some comfort that he will very soon be removed to a distance from this command. It is a matter of astonishment that with my impatient temper, we could have kept on any reasonable terms for so long.

You make me very happy by expressing a wish that our acquaintance may not end with the close of our public character in the Mediterranean; for I beg leave to assure you that in the course of my service I never acted with a man whose conduct in all respects inspired me with so much confidence and that claimed a higher degree of respect and esteem, than yourself and I will lose no occasion to testify the regard and affection with which I have the honour, etc.

To Commodore Nelson he sent an order to shift his broad pennant from *Captain* for a particular service:

You are hereby required and directed to hoist your distinguishing broad pendant on board his Majesty's ship *Minerve* to take her and the *Blanche* under your command, their respective captains being instructed to obey your orders and proceed forthwith to Porto Ferrajo. On your arrival (or falling in with them on your passage there) you will take under your command the ships and sloops named in the margin, numbering seventeen, whose captains are also instructed to obey you; and you are to carry into execution his Majesty's commands relative to the disposition of the troops and stores lately removed to that garrison from the island of Corsica, a transcript of which is enclosed. You will observe that the British artillery and the 1st regiment or Royal Scotch are to be disembarked at Gibraltar and the whole of the remaining troops, British and foreign, are to be landed at Lisbon and you will make your arrangements according. It will be advisable to put as many of the troops on board the frigates as they will conveniently stow, particularly the Royal and British artillery, as there may be more difficulty in landing them at Gibraltar, than in conveying the others to Lisbon. The *Tartar* and *William* and *Ann* transports are well adapted to carry baggage and valuable stores, being roomy and fast-sailing ships. With respect to the three frigates stationed in the Adriatic, under the orders of Captain Tyler, and *L'Unite,* you will take them under your command, in case of falling in with them, or not, as you will think fit. The accompanying orders for Captain Tyler, with duplicate and triplicate thereof (and copy for your information, enclosed) you will forward through Sir William Hamilton, his Majesty's minister at the court of Naples, Mr Graves, agent at the court of Rome, or any other of his Majesty's ministers in Italy, whom you may judge most likely to give them a speedy and safe conveyance.

Having experienced the most important effects from your enterprise and ability on various occasions since I have had the honour to command in the Mediterranean, I leave entirely to your judgment the time and manner of carrying this critical and arduous service into execution, for which this shall be your order.

Given on board the *Victory*, at Gibraltar, 19th December 1796.

To Lieutenant General de Burgh, in command of the troops now on Elba he wrote:

Sir

The events of this war are so fluctuating that it is very difficult to keep pace with them. In the present conjuncture, I have thought it necessary to send Commodore Nelson to co-operate with you and he will communicate my movements, with the plan for carrying into execution the last orders I have received, touching the troops etc under your command.

I have the honour, etc.

To Sir William Hamilton, British Ambassador in Naples:

Sir

I return your Excellency many thanks for your letter of the 31st October which I had the honour to receive on the 6th instant, and am very happy to learn that the resolution I came to met the approbation of his Sicilian majesty, to whom I beg you will express the high sense I am penetrated with by the gracious manner in which he has accepted my efforts to support the common cause.

I shall avail myself of the first spurt of easterly wind after the fleet is victualled, watered and refitted, which we are hard at work upon, to proceed to the coast of Portugal, where I am led to expect a powerful reinforcement. In the meanwhile, Commodore Nelson, than whom a more able or enterprising officer does not exist, will repair to Porto Ferrajo and take upon him the command of the naval force there. He has in contemplation to visit Naples, when he will confer with your Excellency on the measures necessary to be taken in the crisis the operations of the armies in Italy may be in at the time he arrives; for there is such continual fluctuations as to render it impossible to form a fixed plan to act upon. He will, at the same time, communicate to you the orders he is under, and the extension of my command, which calls for great exertions.

Sir Gilbert Elliot communicated the very interesting papers

alluded to in your letter and I consider myself under great obligation for the justice you did to my views and honest endeavours, which my friend General Acton, from a thorough knowledge of my character, arising out of an acquaintance of very many years standing ought not to have doubted.

Jervis would write one more letter to Sir Gilbert Elliot before they met again at sea off Cape St Vincent. He was sixteen years Jervis' junior, having been born in Edinburgh in 1751 and educated there, in France and at Oxford. He became a barrister in 1774. His political views were similar to those of Jervis and he entered Parliament as a Whig. He went on to become Governor-General of India from 1807 to 1813 as the first Earl of Minto. Like many successful Scots, he was adopted by the English in death and buried in Westminster Abbey. On 13 December Sir John Jervis wrote to him:

Dear Sir

It appears by my instructions, and other communications lately received from England, that the defence of Portugal and the prevention of the fleets of France and Spain combining in an attack on Lisbon or an invasion of England or Ireland, with the protection of Gibraltar, are expected from me. Of course all operations that depend on my support in Italy must be suspended until I am reinforced and see my way more clearly than I do at present.

The commodore will relate to you the dreadful weather we have experienced and the casualties produced by it. I am thankful we have not suffered more.

I rejoice we have obtained so much from Naples, before the arrival of the ratification.

Yours my dear Sir, most truly

The following day he wrote to one of his frigate captains:

Sir

Notwithstanding the instructions contained in my order of the 10th instant, advising you to proceed close along the coast of Africa until you reach the length of Cape Bona and

89

recommending a given route afterwards, it is more than probable that the enemy, under an impression of my intending to steer the same course with the fleet in my passage to Porto Ferrajo, may station cruisers off the different headlands and projecting points of Barbary. A good look-out is essentially necessary; and an endeavour to gain intelligence by speaking with central vessels, when this can be done without hazard of separation from the valuable ships you are charged with the protection of; and you will vary your course accordingly. The Bocca of Bonifaccio may become the safest, as it is certainly the shortest passage; and it frequently happens that running near the ports of an enemy is the least dangerous. But the whole will depend on the advices you may receive of the actual position of the combined fleet or the frigates belonging to it.

I am, etc

Sir John was no more averse to giving good advice to newly appointed British consuls than to castigating those who failed to meet his standards of conduct. To Richard Master, the newly arrived Consul in Algiers, he wrote on 15 December:

Sir

I am favoured with your letter by the *Meleagar*. The conversation I wished to have had with you before you entered upon the important and ticklish functions of your office comprised in two paragraphs – namely always to be the first (if possible) to communicate frankly any event which happens, wherein British concerns of any kind affect the interest of the Dey, or of his subjects; never to give way to him or appear to sink under his passions and menaces, at the same time showing the outward respect due to the presence. By these means I am persuaded you will be on better terms with him than any of your predecessors.

Having fully answered all the late complaints of the Dey, in the letter his Highness acknowledged to you he had received from me, of which a copy is enclosed, I do not trouble you with further detail on the subjects of it, because the answers are complete and we have only to maintain the ground

on which they rest. African princes always begin with griev-
ances which must be heard patiently, but pretended ones never
submitted to.

The history of passports, both at Algiers and at most of
the consulates on the African and European side of the
Mediterranean, is disgraceful to the British character . . .
Much caution and circumspection is therefore necessary in
complying with the Dey's demands on this head . . .

It will be very desirable on all accounts that you should
endeavour to live on terms of civil discourse and society with
consuls and merchants of other powers, even of our enemies.
The consuls being for the most part merchants are in perpetual
intrigue against each other; nevertheless, with your superior
manners and knowledge of the world, I trust you will be able
to command respect from them by your dignified conduct.

Commodore Nelson had not in his possession any property
belonging to the Dey. The following is an extract of his letter
to me dated the 10th August, relative to the transaction
alluded to:

*I have also granted permission at the request of Mr North,
that some goods and the American tribute to the Dey of
Algiers be shipped on board a Venetian vessel that is to come
here for them, and load under my guns. One of the Dey's
principal officers has been on board the Captain and appeared
much pleased with his entertainment.*

This was a favour refused during the blockade, to all powers
except those in strict alliance with us and great stress should
be laid on its being granted to the Dey.

I am, Sir, yours, etc.

Following the arrival of Admiral Jervis' small fleet in the Tagus, he
wrote to the Hon. Robert Walpole, the British minister in Lisbon:

Sir

I have the honour to acquaint your Excellency with the
arrival of part of his Majesty's fleet under my command and
to express an anxious hope that I shall soon be joined by the
rest, when I will not lose a moment in facing the combined

fleets of France and Spain, wherever they may be. I enclose a few propositions which I trust will not be found incompatible with the laws and customs of Portugal in like cases; persuaded that you will give us your influence to obtain a compliance with them.

I have the honour, etc.

It was from thc Tagus that Jervis would sail to the site of the battle which made his name.

Chapter Eight

The Battle of Cape St Vincent

The dispositions of the British fleet throughout the Mediterranean area on the eve of the battle from which Sir John Jervis would take his title were a remarkable combination of limited resources and concentration of strength. A comparison with a rugby team boasting a powerful pack of forwards but with backs lacking pace and stretched in defence, is not entirely inappropriate.

While the British squadron – hardly big enough to be called a fleet – lay in the Tagus over Christmas, the French made an attempt to invade Ireland as a stepping stone to England itself. Setting sail from Brest on 15 December 1796 with 14,000 men in forty-three ships, the great convoy ran into fierce winter gales. Once again, as in the defeat of the Spanish Armada more than two centuries earlier, the weather was the staunchest ally in helping to repel a foreign invasion of British soil.

While the French were storm-tossed off the south coast of Ireland, Commodore Nelson with two frigates, under Jervis' orders, was en route to evacuate the British garrison, and Sir Gilbert Elliot, from Elba. Off Cartagena the *Minerve* and *Blanche* fell in with and engaged two Spanish frigates and succeeded in taking one of them as a prize. When they reached Elba, neither Nelson nor Elliot was able to persuade the obstinate officer in command of the troops there, Lieutenant General de Burgh, to evacuate his garrison. Nelson knew that Jervis urgently awaited his return so on 29 January he sailed from the island, leaving the garrison behind, and headed for Gibraltar to store ship and leave his prize before seeking to rejoin the Admiral off Cape St Vincent.

On 11 January 1797, Jervis had left Lisbon and the River Tagus behind him and set sail west into the Atlantic, escorting a Portuguese convoy on the first stage of its voyage to Brazil. As they sailed down the Tagus, one of his most powerful ships, the three-deck, 98-gun *St George*, Captain Shuldham Peard, ran aground and could not be refloated, reducing the squadron to nine line-of-battle ships. Expecting to meet three times that number of Spanish ships of the line, they were nevertheless able to escort the Portuguese convoy well out into the Atlantic without sighting the enemy, and set it on its way before then altering course to the south-east and steering for Cape St Vincent. The wind had veered to the south-west and they made steady progress to the south on the starboard tack.

Two days after Commodore Nelson left Elba, the Spanish fleet – commanded by a lieutenant general with the courtesy rank of admiral, Don Jose de Cordova – comprising twenty-seven ships of the line and twelve frigates, had sailed out of Cartagena and headed for the Atlantic, running before a Levanter, a strong east-erly wind. They must have been some distance ahead of Nelson's two frigates. Their eventual plan after convoying merchantmen to Cadiz was to combine with the French fleet in Brest and then escort an invasion army from the Dutch coast to England. It is probable that they were as yet unaware of the failure of the attempted invasion of Ireland in December. News travelled slowly and the lines of communication between France and Spain were stretched and brittle.

The Spanish fleet ran before the gale-force Levanter, passing Gibraltar on 5 February and was blown much further out into the Atlantic than they had intended. Nelson, in *Minerve* and with *Blanche* in company, having delivered his prize and revictualled in Gibraltar, sailed right through them at night as they beat back towards Cadiz. Two of the Spanish warships pursued *Minerve* but she was able to elude them, despite having to alter course and 'bring to to pick up a man who had fallen overboard'. This manoeuvre

94

mystified the pursuing Spaniards, allowing Nelson to outstrip the enemy ships and rejoin Jervis off Cape St Vincent on 10 February, where he informed him of the position and approximate size of the storm-battered Spanish fleet. He then re-hoisted his broad pendant in the 74-gun *Captain*.

Four days earlier, the British force had been augmented by the arrival of five sail of the line, hurriedly sent out from England as a consequence of Rear Admiral Mann's unauthorized return. Jervis was delighted with the reinforcement brought out by Rear Admiral Parker and wrote to the First Lord of the Admiralty: 'I thank you very much for sending so good a batch. They are a valuable addition to my excellent stock.'

His fleet now comprised: the 100-gun flagship *Victory*, flag captain Captain Robert Calder; chief of staff Captain George Grey; and Captain Benjamin Hallowell as a supernumerary.

The 100-gun *Britannia*,	Vice Admiral Charles Thompson, Captain Thomas Foley.
The 98-gun *Barfleur*,	Vice Admiral William Waldergrave, Captain Richard Dacres.
The 98-gun *Blenheim*,	Captain Thomas Frederick.
The 74-gun *Captain*,	Commodore Horatio Nelson, Captain Ralph Miller.
The 74-gun *Goliath*,	Captain Sir Charles Knowles.
The 74-gun *Excellent*,	Captain Cuthbert Collingwood.
The 74-gun *Egmont*,	Captain John Sutton.
The 74-gun *Culloden*,	Captain Thomas Trowbridge.
The 74-gun *Diadem*,	Captain George Towry.
The 98-gun *Prince George*,	Rear Admiral William Parker, Captain Irwin.
The 98-gun *Namur*,	Captain James Whitshed.

The 74-gun *Irresistible*,	Captain George Martin.
The 74-gun *Orion*,	Captain Sir James Saumarez.
The 74-gun *Colossus*,	Captain George Murray.

In support of the line-of-battle ships the Admiral had seven smaller vessels: the 38-gun frigate *Minerve* (Captain George Cockburn); the 32-gun frigates *Lively* (Captain Lord Garlies), *Niger* (Captain Edward Foote) and *Southampton* (Captain James Macnamara); the 18-gun sloops *La Bonne Citoyenne* (Captain Charles Lindsay) and *Raven* (Captain William Prowse) and the 12-gun cutter *Fox* (Lieutenant Gibson).

Appendix A – Table of Rates, taken direct from John Masefield's *Sea Life in Nelson's Time,* published by Methuen & Co Ltd in 1905, gives information on ship categories.

Now, with fifteen sail of the line, Jervis continued to cruise off Cape St Vincent, scouring the horizon for a sight of the enemy to the south-west. The weather had been rough, but by keeping under the lee of the Cape he had protected his ships from the worst effects of the easterly gale which had moderated and veered to the south-west. Jervis wrote to Nepean, Secretary to the Admiralty: 'In case of the Spanish fleet being disabled I flatter myself we shall be able to deal with them.' He held to a southerly course to intercept them before they could reach Cadiz.

Numerous accounts of the Battle of Cape St Vincent have been written. Some of the detail in them is corroborative, some of it contradictory. In the description which follows, only details and incidents which have been reported in more than one of the previous accounts have been included and the aim has been to produce a narrative which is both credible and accurate.

It was by sound, not sight, that the approach of the Spanish fleet was first detected, their minute guns being first heard during the night of 12 February. These were customarily used as signals of distress or mourning, but on this occasion their purpose was to reassemble the ships which had been scattered by the storm. The Spanish fleet was in disorder. Jervis altered course a point or two to maintain the distance from the enemy during the hours of darkness.

The following night, as the faint thuds of the Spanish minute guns grew louder, Sir John gave a dinner party in his quarters for his subordinate admirals and Sir Gilbert Elliot, who had taken passage in *Minerve* from Elba, Commodore Nelson and the three captains with whom he was most closely associated, Calder, Grey and Hallowell. With a long-awaited battle against a Spanish fleet double their own size imminent, the atmosphere must have been electric. The Commander-in-Chief proposed a toast, 'To victory over the Dons in the battle from which they cannot escape tomorrow.' Then, because he was in the habit of retiring early, his guests departed by boat for their various ships. It may seem strange to the landsman, but officers frequently socialized at sea while ships were under sail, provided it was not too rough to lower and hoist boats.

Jervis did not, however, retire to his bunk. Being sixty-two years old, he made his will and then paced the quarterdeck, waiting for the dawn. At 2.30 am the Scottish captain of a Portuguese frigate, Captain Campbell, sent a boat to the *Victory* to report that the enemy fleet was only 15 miles away. Three hours later Captain Foote of the *Niger*, sent on a reconnaissance sweep to the south-west, reported that they were closer still. The fleets were eight leagues, or approximately 24 miles, west by south from Cape St Vincent.

The dawn was unspectacular – cold with a thick mist and nearly windless, with just a faint breeze from the west-south-west. The British fleet was deployed in two parallel columns, steering due south on the starboard tack. To his flag captain, Robert Calder, within hearing of others on the quarterdeck, Sir John announced with solemn emphasis, 'A victory to England is very essential at this moment.' He had already hoisted the signal 'Prepare for battle'. He then closed his fourteen line-of-battle ships into 'close order' and dispersed his frigates, which were not required to take station in a line of battle, but to be readily available for communication, reconnaissance and rescue duties. At 5.00 am the *Minerve* signalled that the main body of the Spanish fleet was in sight to windward. Such wind as there was remained steady from the south-west.

The *Culloden* was in the van of the leeward column – a tribute to her captain, Thomas Trowbridge, who had suffered damage in a collision with the *Colossus* two days previously but had contrived to bring his ship to battle readiness by effecting repairs at sea. *Culloden* now signalled that five enemy sail were bearing south-east, separated from the main body. When the morning mist began to lift, Jervis could see a gap of 2 or 3 miles between the two enemy bodies – in reality, the Spanish fleet was in some confusion. It consisted of seventeen to windward of the British line and another nine to leeward which had been escorting merchantmen loaded with a valuable cargo of mercury – essential for amalgamating the silver brought to Spain from the New World. Had Jervis known about this convoy, he might have acted differently, but in the event he reacted logically to the reports he had received, first altering course a few degrees towards the ships to leeward reported by *Culloden* – because they were closer to Cadiz – and then when it became clear that the main body were to windward, altering course again and steering for the 3-mile gap to split the enemy and isolate the leeward group. The *Minerve*, having first reported eight sail of the line to windward, continued to signal as more enemy ships hove in sight, the flag captain repeating the reports to the admiral.

The story is told that when Captain Calder reached a total of twenty-six, Admiral Jervis interrupted him saying, 'Enough, Sir, the die is cast and if there are fifty sail I will go through them.' With a lack of ceremony perhaps born of his Canadian origins, Captain Hallowell thumped the Admiral on the back and added enthusiastically, 'That's right, Sir John, that's right! And by God we'll give them a damn good licking.' Whether or not the story is apocryphal, Jervis was wise not to thump him back because Hallowell was much larger than the stocky little admiral.

Meanwhile, the Spanish fleet continued to run east before the wind. Their ships were described by the signal lieutenant of *Barfleur* as 'thumpers, looming like Beachy Head in a fog'. The merchantmen they had been escorting were already out of sight over the horizon, making for Cadiz, and to that extent the Spanish Admiral had successfully achieved his object.

Jervis signalled to his ships: 'Form single line of battle ahead and astern as convenient'.

His manoeuvre placed *Culloden* in the van, *Victory* exactly in the centre, with seven ahead and six astern, and Commodore

Nelson, in *Captain,* third from the rear of the line. The aim of the Commander-in-Chief was still to keep the two groups of Spanish ships apart, hoping to engage the larger group with approximate parity of numbers. He reasoned it would be difficult and take time for the smaller group to beat to windward and link up with the rear of the larger group, which had altered to a more northerly course, apparently with the intention of passing astern of the British line and taking the rear with their broadsides. However, they were in such disorder that this would have been impossible for the majority of them without firing through or over whichever of their own ships were nearest to the British line.

The larger Spanish group and the British line of battle were now approaching one another on approximately reciprocal courses, which presented Sir John with a problem requiring fine judgment. If he held on too long on the starboard tack, on a southerly course between the two Spanish groups, he risked making it easier for the larger group to pass astern of his line of battle and join up with the smaller group. Conversely, if his fleet went about in succession onto the port tack too soon, his van would engage the leading ships of the larger windward group and the smaller leeward group would be able to link up with their rear unimpeded.

Looking at a plan of the dispositions of both fleets before the action started, it is easy to suggest what Sir John should have done, but that is a very different matter from having to take a decision under pressure, at sea, with no plan of the enemy's deployment and no gull's-eye view of the relative dispositions of both fleets. What in fact Jervis did was to give the order to go about in succession onto the port tack so that his ships theoretically remained in line ahead. Thus the fleet came into action one after the other, giving the nearest Spanish ships the opportunity to concentrate their fire initially on *Culloden.* Had Jervis ordered his fleet to go about together at the crucial moment when his rear was nearly abeam of the leading Spaniard, his whole line would have come into action simultaneously, the rear becoming the van and the van the rear. Any junction between the two Spanish groups would have been prevented and about half of the larger Spanish group might have been neutralized, only able to fire through their compatriots. The victory could have been complete. Remarkably, Nelson was able

Battle of Cape St Vincent – 14 February 1797
Sketch plan of the fleets in early stages of the battle.

NORTH

DIADEM

CAPTAIN

EXCELLENT

CULLODEN

VICTORY

COLOSSUS

IRRESISTIBLE

MAIN
SPANISH
FLEET

WIND WSW

to visualize this from his station three from the rear and he then had the moral and physical courage to act on his assessment without waiting for an order from Jervis. He could have been court-martialled, had not his initiative saved the day for Jervis.

Nelson wore *Captain* to avoid interfering with his own squadron, passed between the two ships astern of him, *Excellent* and *Diadem,* and swung north-west on the port tack between the leading Spanish ship, the huge 130-gun *Santissima Trinidad,* and the Spanish group away to leeward. What might have become a long stern chase with only the British van engaged, and which the Spaniards with their greater spread of sail might have won, became a general action.

The Spanish Commander-in-Chief, Cordova, appreciating that Nelson's manoeuvre had foiled his attempt to join the leeward group under Vice Admiral Moreno, gave the signal for a general action. Rear Admiral Parker signalled his division to 'fill and stand on' in support of *Captain.* Trowbridge in the *Culloden* forced a huge Spanish three-decker to go about to avoid collision and sent two rapid double-shotted broadsides crashing into her, 'fired as if by a seconds-watch in the silence of a Port Admiral's inspection'. Jervis, in *Victory* seven astern of her, commented proudly, 'Look at Trowbridge, he takes his ship into battle as if the eyes of all England were upon him and would to God they were!'

Ship after ship of the British line now came into action, while Nelson kept the Spanish van occupied. Vice Admiral Moreno, seeing that Cordova's division could not join him from the west, altered course to the south, hoping to tack around the British line and join the rear of the main Spanish group. Four of them did contrive to engage the British rear and centre. Moreno in the 112-gun *Prince d'Asturias,* together with two smaller three-deckers and one 74-gun ship, held on to attack *Victory.* In imminent danger of colliding with her, the *Prince d'Asturias* swung away to port, giving *Victory* the chance to rake her with two massive broadsides. Moreno's flagship, shattered, retired downwind with her consorts, having only succeeded in delaying the moment when *Victory* could engage the main body of the Spanish fleet on her port side.

The battle reached its climax about one hour after noon. All the British ships passed through the gap between the two Spanish divisions with the exception of the unlucky *Colossus*. When her turn came to go about in succession she was hit by a single cannon ball which wrecked her steering; she then had her topmast shot away. She swung across the bows of the next astern, *Irresistible*, and fell out of the line, exposing her vulnerable stern to enemy broadsides. Captain James Saumarez in *Orion* went to her aid but *Colossus* could take no further part in the battle. Soon the British centre and rear were being engaged on both sides. A gunner on *Goliath* wrote later: 'We gave them their Valentines in style!'

On the quarterdeck of *Victory* Sir John was splashed with the blood of an unfortunate marine, struck by grapeshot. Captain Grey rushed to the Admiral but was reassured when he said, 'I am not at all hurt, but do you, George, see if you can get me an orange' – whether for himself or for the marine is not recorded.

Nelson now found himself in close combat with five of the largest Spanish ships, including the *Santissima Trinidad* which was the largest warship in the world. She was closely supported by two first-rates of 112 guns, *Salvador del Mundo* and *San José*, and by the 84-gun *San Nicolas* and 74-gun *San Isidro*. *Captain* opened fire on the *Santissima Trinidad* as soon as she came within range and for several minutes fought the massive Spanish ship alone, her foremast shot away and her wheelpost snapped. Then Trowbridge in *Culloden* came up in her support. The two ships were soon joined by Collingwood in *Excellent* and, still outgunned by at least 2:1, they continued the battle, their superior accuracy and skill more than compensating for the inferior weight of their broadsides. Robert Calder, fearful of the odds against the three 74s suggested to Jervis that they should be recalled but he replied, 'I put my faith in those ships . . . it is a disgrace that they are not supported.'

Before long they were. The Spanish van, prevented by Nelson's action from joining Moreno's group, swung north. Three more British ships from the rear half of the line – *Blenheim, Orion* and *Prince George* – entered the fray. After an hour of intense action the *Salvador del Mundo* struck her colours to the *Orion* and soon afterwards the *San Pedro* struck to the *Excellent*. Collingwood disdained the opportunity to take possession of the *San Pedro* and to quote Nelson, 'most gallantly pushed up with every sail set to

102

save his old friend and messmate'. With the *Captain* now closely engaged with the *San Nicolas*, Collingwood ran the *Excellent* between the two contestants, so close he afterwards said, 'you could not put a bodkin between us,' and emptied a lethal broadside into the 84-gun Spaniard. The *San Nicolas* thereupon swung to port, fouling the *San José*.

At this juncture Nelson told Captain Ralph Miller to lay the *Captain* aboard the starboard quarter of the *San Nicolas*. Her spritsail yard crossed the Spanish ship's poop and locked in her mizzen shrouds. Captain Berry, who had been a reluctant passenger on the *Captain*, awaiting a ship to command, was the first to board, followed by soldiers who were serving on board as marines. Captain Miller made to join the boarding party but was stopped by Nelson saying, 'No Miller, I must have that honour myself!' The boarding party fought its way to the quarterdeck, Nelson entering through a quarter-gallery window; on the poop Captain Berry was already hauling down the Spanish ensign. Nelson shouted to Miller to send more men across and immediately turned his attention to the huge three-decker *San José*, lying alongside with her yards and shrouds entangled with those of *San Nicolas* which was, by now, on fire.

Nelson, dramatically and somewhat obscurely (either with an eye on a seat in the House of Lords, or a tomb in Westminster Abbey) shouting 'Westminster or victory', led the boarding party over the side from one ship to the other. Minutes later *San José* also surrendered. The Spanish captain gave Nelson his sword and the news that his admiral was dying of wounds below. In the words of Nelson's subsequent account of the action:

and on the quarterdeck of a Spanish first-rate, extravagant as the story may seem, did I receive the swords of vanquished Spaniards; which, as I received, I gave to William Fearney, one of my bargemen, who put them with the greatest sangfroid under his arm. I was surrounded by Captain Berry, Lieutenant Pierson, 69th Regiment, John Sykes, John Thomson, Francis Cook, all old 'Agamemnons' and several other brave men, seamen and soldiers; thus fell these ships.

Meanwhile the centre and rear of the British line had been fiercely engaged. Following the example of *San Isidro,* the *Salvador del Mundo* now surrendered to the *Victory.* The battle was nearly over. The *Santissima Trinidad*, pride of the Spanish fleet, struck her flag to Captain Sir James Saumarez, a Channel Islander, but because all the serviceable boats from *Orion* were already away with a prize crew to man the *Salvador del Mundo*, he could not take possession of her, so she re-hoisted her colours and escaped in the fading light.

Although the Spanish fleet still outnumbered the British by at least eight ships, they were in no mood to renew the action. Jervis reformed his ships in a line between them and his four prizes while the twenty-three Spanish line-of-battle ships fled away into the darkness like a flock of sheep escaping from a pack of wolves.

It has been suggested that Jervis could profitably have renewed the action the following day, but he only had eleven ships still fit for further action and four battered prizes to attend to. He therefore deployed his ships in readiness to meet any attack at first light and, at the same time, to protect both his own ships and the four prizes. However, dawn found the Spanish fleet over the horizon, running for Cadiz before the south-westerly breeze.

After securing his two prizes, Nelson returned to *Captain*, thanked Miller for his unstinting support, and presented him with the sword of the captain of *San Nicolas* and a large topaz ring – legitimate booty. Then he shifted his broad pendant to *Minerve* because his quarters in his own ship were a shambles. The ship had lost twenty-four killed and fifty-six wounded, almost a third of the casualties suffered by the British fleet. When one of the officers unwisely remarked to Jervis that Nelson had disobeyed orders in breaking from the line to attack the Spanish van, he got a sharp rejoinder, 'Yes and if ever you commit such a breach of your orders I will forgive you also.'

Nelson went on board the flagship that evening with mixed feelings: trepidation, because he knew that he had broken the rules and was aware of Jervis' reputation as a severe disciplinarian; satisfaction because he knew that his initiative had turned what might have become an indecisive stern chase into victory; disappointment because he must have realized that if Jervis had shown greater tactical awareness the victory could have been overwhelming. In the event he reported, 'The admiral received me on the quarterdeck and, having embraced me, said he could not sufficiently thank me, and used every kind expression which could not fail to make me happy.'

The following day Jervis took his fleet and their prizes to Lagos Bay on the Algarve coast, just east of Cape St Vincent, to recuperate. The Admiral also took the opportunity to write his dispatches.

News of the battle did not reach London until 3 March. Jervis' dispatches, which he had entrusted to Captain Calder to take to England in the frigate *Lively*, were brief and to the point. He singled out Nelson, Collingwood, Trowbridge and Calder for particular mention. Hallowell was also complimented: 'His conduct on board the *Victory* during the action has made him more dear to me than before.' Saumarez was amongst those whose distinguished service was overlooked, and in those days, of course, it was rare indeed for anybody below the rank of lieutenant to get an official mention. Cannon fodder was simply for consumption!

Ten days after the action, the battered fleet returned to the Tagus. For the next two years Lisbon would be Jervis' principal base from which to prevent the Spanish and French fleets linking to threaten invasion of the British Isles. The Battle of Cape St Vincent had reopened the Mediterranean to the British fleet and given Great Britain a second chance to thwart Napoleon's plans to dominate Europe and control the road to India.

Formal acknowledgement and rewards came quickly. The House of Commons passed a Vote of Thanks immediately after the news came through – proposed by the Secretary of War, Dundas, and seconded by the Leader of the Opposition, Fox. The House of Lords followed with a similar vote on 8 March. Although the victory had not been decisive, it had done much to restore national confidence. Sir John Jervis was created Earl of St Vincent with a pension of £3,000 a year – a huge sum in today's terms – and was given the Freedom of the City of London with a key in a gold box. This was followed by similar gifts from most major cities in the United Kingdom. The two Vice Admirals, Parker and Thompson, were made baronets; Nelson was made a Knight of the Bath (better than the waters of Pisa!) and promoted to Rear Admiral; Robert

Calder was knighted, others were promoted and every admiral and captain received a gold medal. It is to be hoped that the ships' companies at least received their just share of the prize money from the four splendid prizes.

Chapter Nine

The Battle against Mutiny

In a year when the Royal Navy won significant victories over the Spaniards off Cape St Vincent and over the Dutch off Camperdown, the nation's shield was severely dented by a series of debilitating mutinies. Admiral Sir John Jervis' victory was won before the first concerted outbreak at Spithead on 12 April 1797. Admiral Adam Duncan's much harder-won victory over a highly trained and powerful Dutch fleet was achieved in the aftermath of the mutinies, and despite the recent inactivity and collapse of discipline which had undermined the efficiency of Britain's navy in the Western approaches, the Channel and the North Sea. Admiral Duncan had succeeded in blockading the Dutch fleet in the Texel only by a sustained but desperate ruse: showing his one or two loyal ships off the Dutch coast and sending signals to an imaginary fleet out of sight of the enemy over the horizon. By demonstrating exceptional powers of leadership, he had eventually been able to confront and defeat a skillfully commanded fleet of comparable strength.

From April to mid-June, the Navy was in open mutiny from Devon to East Anglia. The ingredients of the frustration which erupted into mutiny had been simmering for years: meagre and irregular pay; vile food; spartan living conditions often without shore leave for long periods; completely inadequate provision for the sick and wounded; all bolstered by discipline which varied from cruelly vindictive to barely tolerable, depending upon the policy and humanity of a particular ship's captain and officers.

The simmering discontent boiled over, inflamed by reports of the

107

recent revolution in France and fanned by discontent among Irishmen who comprised up to one fifth of the crew and were only there because the alternative was famine at home – or because, like many of their shipmates, they had been press-ganged from some port, merchant ship or fishing vessel. About half of the crew of an average British warship were Englishmen; the remainder were a mixture of Irish, Scots, Welsh and others pressed or voluntarily enlisted from almost anywhere in the world where British ships were to be found. In 1797 Britain faced Napoleon virtually alone. The dictator had made up his mind to invade the British Isles and was only prevented from doing so by Britain's command of the sea and by his own lack of suitable craft to take troops across the English Channel and North Sea. Echoes of mutiny in the Royal Navy were music to his ears.

Admiral Lord Howe, Commander-in-Chief of the Channel fleet, which was anchored at Spithead between Portsmouth and the Isle of Wight, had received petitions from the crews of four of his line-of-battle ships in March, asking very reasonably that an increase of pay recently granted to the Army and the Militia, together with provision made for their wives and families whilst serving abroad, should also be given to the seamen of the Royal Navy.

Unfortunately, because the separate petitions appeared identical in terms of both handwriting and content, Lord Howe attributed them to a single troublemaker and failed to appreciate their significance. Although he informed Lord Spencer, First Lord of the Admiralty, and the port admiral at Portsmouth, Sir Peter Parker, no action was taken. On 17 April Sir Peter learned of a concerted plan to seize the four ships. The Admiralty responded, using the mechanical telegraph which linked London with the Home Ports, by ordering the ships to sea. However, when the signal to weigh anchor was received, sixteen ships of the line refused to obey. Their crews climbed the shrouds and gave three cheers as the signal for mutiny. Unpopular officers were put ashore and two delegates from each ship met in the Admiral's cabin of the flagship *Queen Charlotte* to draw up terms to be presented to the Board of Admiralty.

It is noteworthy that Admiral Lord St Vincent wrote to Lord Spencer later that year: 'You may rest assured, the civil Branch of the Navy is rotten to the very core.'

Nevertheless, the Admiralty responded to the mutineers' terms by making a series of concessions. As the seamen began to realize the power they wielded by joint action, so their demands increased. Lord Howe found himself powerless, but fortunately the Spithead mutineers behaved with restraint and made it clear that if the French put to sea they would shelve their discontent, submit to discipline and go out to do battle with the enemy. By 15 May the Spithead mutiny had been resolved by conceding the more reasonable of the seamen's demands, but another more serious mutiny had broken out at The Nore, the anchorage of the North Sea fleet at the mouth of the Thames estuary. It lasted for nearly five weeks. The mutineers pirated merchant ships, went ashore and made trouble in local towns and virtually blockaded London. They were finally obliged to surrender when the navigational markers in the Thames estuary were removed at night, making it impossible for them to negotiate the difficult waters. This was followed by severe treatment of the ringleaders, the most determined of whom were hanged from the yardarms of their own ships, their shipmates forced to act as executioners.

There had been a marked difference between the two outbreaks. The Spithead mutiny was a genuine protest against hardship. At The Nore, the mutiny was led by Richard Parker, an ex-naval officer who had been dismissed for insubordination. He then became a schoolmaster, got heavily into debt and was imprisoned. From the debtors' prison he had been drafted into the North Sea fleet where his education, experience and bitterness combined to make him the focus of discontent. The Nore mutiny also had political undercurrents animated by the French Revolution and by the Irish republican movement which, organized as the 'United Irish', had developed a system of communication between ships.

An individual who has not been given the credit he deserved for the part he played in overcoming the mutinies was Admiral Lord Keith, who was soon to relieve St Vincent as Commander-in-Chief in the Mediterranean. He already had an excellent reputation for maintaining good relations with the men under his command. Within a fortnight of his appointment in May 1791 as Commander-in-Chief the Nore, based at Sheerness on the south side of the Thames estuary, he had persuaded the men of the ships which had mutinied, immobilized by the removal of the navigation markers, to surrender their ringleaders. Within days the mutiny was over. He performed the same role at Plymouth with regard to ships of the Channel fleet based there.

In the Mediterranean theatre, the ships under Admiral Lord St Vincent's command were tightly disciplined, more or less isolated from troubles at home and so highly trained that mutiny had much less opportunity to spread through the lower decks. The first signs of trouble had appeared in March, independently of the mutinies at Spithead and The Nore, and some contagion infected them by way of ships sent out from England to join the fleet, which was engaged in blockading the surviving ships of the Spanish fleet in Cadiz. St Vincent forbade any visiting between ships. Any overt act of insubordination resulted in an instant court martial, with the culprit being hung from the yardarm of his own ship. Two offenders found guilty on a Saturday were executed on the Sunday. Rear Admiral Nelson warmly approved, but when St Vincent's deputy, Vice Admiral Thompson, called it a 'profanation of the Sabbath', the Commander-in-Chief responded by insisting to the Admiralty that the Vice Admiral be 'removed from this fleet immediately or that I shall be called home'. He added, with irony: 'I hope I shall not be censured by the Bench of Bishops . . . I do entreat that no more admirals are sent hither!'

The situation off Cadiz deteriorated with the arrival of rein-forcements from the Channel fleet and Ireland in May 1798 under Rear Admiral Sir Roger Curtis. The ships were ninety-one short of complement. Captain Ellison of the ship of the line *Marlborough* reported that his crew would not permit a shipmate, who had been convicted of mutiny and sentenced to death, to be hanged on board his ship. St Vincent immediately sent for Captain Ellison and listened to his request to have the man hanged aboard another vessel. St Vincent's reply was, 'Do you mean to tell me that you cannot command His Majesty's ship *Marlborough*? If that is the case, Sir, I will immediately send on board an officer who can! That man shall be hanged at 8 o'clock tomorrow morning by his own ship's company, for not a hand from any other ship in the fleet shall touch the rope!'

Next morning boats from every available ship were ordered to surround *Marlborough* and to fire into her if there was any sign of revolt against the hanging sentence. The man was duly hanged and an incipient mutiny snuffed out.

St Vincent's fleet of fourteen line-of-battle ships blockading Cadiz was outnumbered by the twenty-three Spanish survivors within the harbour. News of the Spithead mutiny had not reached the fleet until it was joined by Sir Roger Curtis' squadron, but St Vincent's attitude to mutiny was uniformly ruthless and uncompromising. Asked to pardon a man of good character who had shown temporary insubordination in the face of provocation, he replied that he was glad to hang such a man because henceforward everybody would know that 'virtue and good character would not atone for mutiny'.

Such was St Vincent's faith in Nelson that he ordered the flag of the newly promoted Rear Admiral to be shifted to *Theseus* which was one of the ships worst infected with the virus of mutiny. It was a shrewd decision and confirmed his belief that a ship's officers were more often than not responsible for insubordination on the part of the seamen.

Following Nelson's transfer, St Vincent wrote to Nepean, Secretary to the Admiralty:

> I found it expedient to communicate to the officers and crews of the respective ships of the squadron the Order their Lordships gave to Admiral Lord Bridport, dated 1st April 1797, extracted from a newspaper, to prevent any ill impression being made of the excellent discipline of this fleet by an indirect communication of the events which have taken place at Spithead.

Admiralty instructions were addressed more to the officers than to the men: they were not to absent themselves without leave, they were to wear uniform on shore as well as on board, they were not to select the best food for themselves to the detriment of the men ... St Vincent passed the instructions to his flag officers. To Nelson he wrote: 'I dread not the men. It is the indiscreet, licentious, conversation of the officers which produces all our ills.'

111

Nelson commented: 'The overflow of Honourables and the disciples they have made among the plebeians has been the ruin of the service.'

While St Vincent believed that the threat of mutiny depended less upon the personalities of potential mutineers than upon the skill and humanity of their officers, he equally appreciated that there were limits to the extent he could pick, choose or reappoint officers. There was a shortage of properly qualified and reliable lieutenants. In one notorious case two men from the ship of the line *St George* had been tried and condemned for buggery. Their shipmates, disgusted, assembled on the upper deck to protest that if the guilty men were executed for this offence the reputation of the *St George* would be disgraced and they demanded their release. Without doubt the accused would have been dealt with by their own mess-mates. However, Captain Beard and his first lieutenant, Hatley, attempted to disperse the gathering. They were ignored, where-upon they rushed into the mob, each of them grabbing two of the ringleaders and handing them over to the custody of marines who customarily provided a safety barrier between the wardroom and the lower decks. The four prisoners were put in leg irons and taken to the flagship. Before they were court-martialled Admiral Lord St Vincent told them, 'My friends, I hope you are innocent, but if guilty I recommend you instantly set about making your peace with God, for if you are condemned, and there is daylight to hang you, you will die this day.'

The four were condemned but it was late on a Saturday. When the president of the court martial told them they would have until Monday morning to prepare themselves for execution, St Vincent overruled him, 'Sir, when you passed the sentence your duty was complete. You had no right to say the execution of it should be delayed.' He then ordered the sentence to be carried out on Sunday morning at 9.00 am. In the past, in similar circumstances, it had been the practice for the boats' crews of other ships in company to draw lots to decide which of them should go on board the ship where the condemned man was held, to man the yard rope and carry out the execution. On this occasion, to indicate his anger at the conduct of the crew of the *St George*, St Vincent ordered that the condemned men should be hanged from the yardarm of their own ship by the ship's company, that the execution should be witnessed by boats' crews from every ship in the fleet and that immediately thereafter every ship should proceed to the performance of divine service. As the fatal gun was fired at 9.00 am, the four guilty men were run up to the yardarm and the pendants signalling divine service were hoisted at the mizzen peak of every ship present. The Admiral wished to create an awesome and indelible impression of the horror and severity of the ultimate punishment for mutiny.

At the time of this shocking spectacle the fleet was anchored just outside the range of the shore batteries of Cadiz. The Spaniards, learning what was happening, decided it was an auspicious moment to attack the British inshore squadron, which comprised a number of small but well-armed sloops, cutters and launches. When boats from the main British fleet failed to retaliate, they thought that a minor victory was imminent, but St Vincent was only waiting until divine service was over. Immediately the pendants for prayers were hauled down, he ordered all ships' boats, manned and armed, to attack the Spaniards. Unpleasantly surprised and badly mauled, their swarm of little craft retired in disorder into the harbour and did not venture out again for as long as the British inshore squadron patrolled the exits.

St Vincent pursued his unremitting policy of appointing the best officers available to the command of ships showing signs of insubordination or latent mutiny, but was sometimes restricted by the availability of good officers. The captain of *Goliath,* Sir Charles Knowles, whom he described as 'an imbecile, totally incompetent' and whom Betsey Wynne considered a 'real bore', was replaced by Captain Thomas Foley. *Goliath* was soon restored to order, but St Vincent, presumably from lack of alternatives, then appointed Knowles to the command of *Britannia* where the impression he made was so feeble that 'the very first night . . . the ship's company took the command from him' and the ship deteriorated into a 'state of licentiousness'.

When the *Barfleur* arrived from England, her commanding officer, Captain Dacres, reported to the Commander-in-Chief that he knew there were letters on board from ships of the Channel fleet containing exhortations to mutiny. He suggested that they should

113

be withheld. 'Certainly not,' the Admiral replied. 'I dare say the Commander-in-Chief will know how to support his own authority.' It was his opinion, constantly repeated, that 'the present indiscipline of the navy originated with the licentious conduct of the officers.' Because Lord Harvey, captain of the *Jealous* had got his ship 'in a most undisciplined state, the people incessantly drunk', he was replaced by Captain Sam Hood who had the greatest difficulty in restoring order because of the shortcomings of the ship's officers. However, by the end of July the measures taken and the discipline imposed throughout the fleet appeared to have been effective. The Admiral was able to write a private letter to one of his frigate captains:

> We have had five executions for mutiny and a punishment of 300 lashes given alongside two disorderly line-of-battle ships and the frigate to which the mutineer belonged. He took it all at one time and exhorted the spectators to mind what they were about, for he had brought it upon himself. Two men have been executed for sodomy and the whole seven have been proved to be most atrocious villains, who long ago deserved the fate they met with for their crimes. At present, there is every appearance of content and proper subordination.

The Admiral was supremely aware that idleness and lack of diversion led to discontent and indiscipline. For this reason alone, he ordered the inshore squadron to bombard the city of Cadiz at night. It is to be hoped that the cannonade was directed at warships and military installations within the harbour area and that the residents of the city did not suffer for the mutinous tendencies of the British seamen. The first attack took place on 3 July when the bomb *Thunderer* went close to the city walls and started a heavy bombardment. She was attacked by Spanish launches which, in turn, were challenged by barges commanded by Nelson, Fremantle and Miller. There were casualties on both sides, but the Spaniards were forced to retire. Two further bombardments were organized but the second had to be cancelled because of the weather.

For some time the First Lord of the Admiralty had been pressing

St Vincent to send Nelson with a squadron to the Adriatic, but this had been resisted because the Admiral felt he could not spare ships from the blockade. Now Spencer pressed him to undertake an operation against Santa Cruz, capital of the Canary Island of Tenerife. There were two possible purposes: a diversion to allay discontent in the fleet; and the possibility of capturing Spanish treasure ships. There was little, if any, strategic justification. St Vincent's first reaction to the proposal was not enthusiastic: 'I am not competent to decide whether taking possession of the island of Tenerife would be of much importance at this stage of the war. With troops coming from Porto Ferrajo and what might be furnished from the squadron, the enterprise is practicable.' Apparently Lord Spencer encouraged him to go ahead. Nelson was chosen to lead the attack and suffered the one disastrous failure of his career. By this time the *Captain*, desperately in need of repairs, had been sent home and his flag transferred to *Seahorse*.

The attack was organized on the basis of inadequate intelligence – a fatal defect. The defences were underestimated, despite the fierce reception which had greeted the frigates *Lively* and *Minerve* under Captain Hallowell, when they had successfully cut out a French brig in the harbour of Santa Cruz in May.

By 14 July a squadron of three ships of the line, three frigates, a cutter and a mortar-boat, all hand-picked by Nelson, were assembled under his command. On board were extra marines from the fleet. St Vincent's parting words were, 'God bless and prosper you. I am sure you will deserve success. To mortals is not given the power of commanding it.'

It took the expedition five days to come within sight of the Canary Islands. The landing parties were transferred to the frigates while the line-of-battle ships stayed over the horizon. After dark the frigates stood into the bay of Santa Cruz, which is surrounded by high mountains from which unpredictable gusts of gale force sometimes sweep down. The plan was to attack the fort to the east of the town but to leave Santa Cruz itself initially unmolested; its surrender would be demanded once the fort had been captured.

The landing parties embarked in the dark, but were still 3 miles off shore when the dreaded wind swept down and the light of dawn exposed them to the enemy only a mile from the fort. Any element of surprise was lost. From that moment everything went wrong. With the boats forced to return to their parent ships, a half-baked plan was formulated and approved by Nelson: to land on a beach beside the fort and attack it from above. When the boats eventually got to the beach three hours after dawn, the sailors and marines scrambled up a mountainside to find Spanish troops facing them from a hilltop between them and the fort. Captain Trowbridge, who had been given command of the landing party, eventually decided to re-embark the men and return to the frigates, which then stood out to sea.

Typically, Rear Admiral Nelson would not admit failure, but reported to St Vincent and submitted another plan: to anchor the frigates near the beach short of the fort, and then to send the boats under the cover of darkness direct to the mole in the centre of the town harbour – and to lead the 1,000-man expedition in person. It was a foolhardy decision. The officers, and Nelson himself, were painfully aware of the possibility – even the likelihood – of failure. In a letter written to his family before the attack, Nelson had written: 'I think there is a chance of my never returning.'

At 5.00 pm the frigates anchored as planned. The landing parties were not embarked in the boats until 11.00 pm, but a gusting wind made it impossible for them to stay together in an orderly flotilla and they arrived off the mole in twos and threes at 1.30 in the morning. Alarm bells started pealing and a heavy fire from cannon and musketry tore into them. The *Fox* cutter was sunk with nearly one hundred men aboard. Nelson, in the act of leaping ashore, sword in hand, had his right arm shattered by grape and fell back into his boat. Two of his captains were also wounded but the landing party succeeded in capturing the mole and spiking the guns before advancing on the town itself. There they were met by devastating fire from the citadel and fortified houses on the water-front. Captain Bowen of the *Terpsichore* and half a dozen of his men were killed simultaneously. The rest of the party were held in a murderous crossfire, unable to advance. Captain Miller, the senior officer still on his feet, ordered the inevitable retreat back to the boats.

Stories are told of Nelson's selfless courage as he lay in the bottom of a boat, being rowed out to the frigates; how he refused to be taken aboard the *Seahorse* for fear the sight of him would frighten Betsey, Captain Thomas Fremantle's wife, who was on board. He knew Fremantle was wounded but did not know how badly. In fact he was safe. On reaching *Theseus*, Nelson climbed unaided up the side, using his good arm and immediately sent for the surgeon to amputate the shattered one. Meanwhile a second party under Trowbridge had landed south of the citadel, where they found themselves outnumbered by more than a hundred to one, covered by artillery in every direction and unable to advance. After threatening to burn down the town unless permitted to withdraw under a flag of truce, the Governor of Santa Cruz not only agreed but entertained him and Captain Hood to dinner before permitting their departure with colours flying – and provided them with boats. With astonishing chivalry he gave the eighty men in Trowbridge's party food and wine, treated the wounded and invited them to purchase whatever provisions they needed. Nelson, in acute pain, later ordered a cask of English ale and a cheese to be sent to the Governor and made an offer, which was accepted, to report his own defeat to the Court of Spain.

The casualties of Nelson's expedition were 280 men killed and wounded. His self-confidence, like his right arm, had been shattered. Three days after excruciating surgery he wrote to St Vincent with his left hand: 'I am become a burthen to my friends and useless to my country.' He asked to be sent home. His self-confidence would recover but his empty right sleeve would always be pinned to his coat. Following the failure, St Vincent wrote to Spencer: 'My mind labours under too much anguish to enter into details upon the subject. It has been my fate during this war to lose the officers most dear to me: by that of poor Bowen I am quite unmanned.' Bowen, captain of the *Terpsichore*, had fallen in the crossfire from the citadel of Santa Cruz and the fortifications on the waterfront. He was the midshipman who had served under Captain Jervis in *Foudroyant*.

The Commander-in-Chief continued to suffer from lack of reinforcements, ships desperately in need of refit and shortages of men, having to retain ships on the station when the crews were expecting to be sent home, which encouraged insubordination. Even those men who had gone to England as prize crews after the Battle of

Cape St Vincent had not been sent back to their ships. The masters of American vessels, who could offer better pay and conditions, took every opportunity to bribe men to desert to them. Meanwhile the French continued to do their utmost to deprive the British fleet of bases by both military and diplomatic means. St Vincent was under unmitigated stress and pressure. He was sixty-four and his health was failing.

1. Portrait of Admiral Lord St Vincent. (*After a painting from an engraving owned by Messrs T.H. Parker Bros, printsellers, 45 Whitcomb Street, London WC*)

2. Meaford Hall, Stone, Staffordshire – birthplace of John Jervis.   (*Author*)

3. Earl St Vincent Square, Stone, Staffordshire.   (*Author*)

4. The hulk of HMS *Foudroyant*, the ship in which John Jervis made his name.
(Picture courtesy of the Mary Evans Picture Library)

5. HMS *Victory* – flagship of both St Vincent and Nelson – the oldest warship still in commission. *(Author)*

6. Cadiz harbour – early nineteenth century.
(*Picture courtesy of the Mary Evans Picture Library*)

7. Port Mahon, the harbour at Minorca. (*Picture courtesy of the Mary Evans Picture Library*)

8. Action off Cape St Vincent – 14 February 1797: main fleet action. (*From an engraving owned by Messrs T.H. Parker Bros, printsellers, 45 Whitcomb Street, London WC*)

8a. HMS *Captain* (Horatio Nelson) engages the *San Nicolas*. (*From an engraving owned by Messrs T.H. Parker Bros, printsellers, 45 Whitcomb Street, London WC*)

9. Lisbon on the River Tagus.   (*Picture courtesy of the Mary Evans Picture Library*)

10. Flogging at the gangway. (*From* Sea Life in Nelson's Time *by John Masefield, published in 1905 by Methuen & Co Ltd, 36 Essex Street, London WC*)

11. Gibraltar, early nineteenth century. (*Picture courtesy of the Mary Evans Picture Library*)

12. Entrance to Brest harbour, early nineteenth century.
(*Picture courtesy of the Mary Evans Picture Library*)

13. The Rochetts, South Weald, Essex – Lord St Vincent's home from the time of his marriage. *(Photo by kind permission of Mr Alan Ford).*

14. The mausoleum in Stone churchyard, Staffordshire, where Admiral of the Fleet Lord St Vincent is interred. *(Author)*

Chapter Ten

Return to the Mediterranean

By the close of 1797 hopes of an early end to the war against France and her allies had evaporated – St Vincent had lost a bet with one of his captains, Sir James Saumarez, that it would be over by the autumn. After diplomatic negotiations in Lille broke down in September he paid Sir James the equivalent of £100 in Spanish currency. Napoleon's threat remained and the French put diplomatic pressure on the rulers of the North African states to make it as difficult as possible for British ships to replenish from that coast. In November 1797, following a show of hostility by the Dey of Algiers, St Vincent sent a letter of instructions from his flagship *Ville de Paris* to Captain Thomas Thompson of *Leander* who had joined the squadron from the Baltic in time to accompany Nelson on the final evacuation of Elba. Now he was sent with a small squadron to show the flag off Algiers. This letter is one of the best examples of the Admiral's incisive and uncompromising attitude in executing his duty as he perceived it:

> Whereas Mr Master, His Majesty's Consul-General at Algiers, has represented to me that his Highness the Dey has made the most extravagant, unjust and inadmissible demands upon the government of Great Britain, intermixed with unfriendly expressions, even to menaces of hostility, if he does not obtain the sums of money he has laid claim to early in the ensuing year.

You are hereby required and directed to appear before Algiers with the vessels under your order and endeavour to have an interview with Mr Consul Master, and concert such proper measures to be pursued as his situation may require; whether to have an audience of the Dey and explain with firmness the unreasonableness of his demands and the exposure of his trade and marine to annihilation, if he is rash enough to commit the most trifling act of hostility against the persons or property of his Majesty's subjects; to expose the acts and intrigues of the Spanish and French agents and Jewish merchants who conduct the trade of Algiers; or to embark Mr Consul Master, his suite and baggage, with any British subjects and their property who may wish to make their retreat.

In your conferences with the Dey, it will be absolutely necessary to preserve your temper although he should show the most violent and indecent passion, but not to give way to the absurd positions he may lay down, or to admit that his Majesty's ships have, on any occasion, committed a breach of neutrality; and finding all remonstrances ineffectual and that his Highness persists in his exorbitant demands, and carries the threats notified to the Consul-general into execution, by offering any insult to his Majesty's flag, or other flagrant violation of the treaties subsisting between the two governments you are to make known to his Highness that from the instant such an act of hostility should be committed by his orders, the war will be declared between Great Britain and Algiers and that you have my instructions to punish the injustice and temerity of his Highness by seizing, burning, sinking or otherwise destroying all ships bearing the Algerine flag; and to block up the ports of his Highness and to cut off all commerce and navigation between them and the ports of other nations; and having fulfilled the object of your mission, you are to lose no time in communicating to Lieutenant General O'Hara, Governor of Gibraltar, and to me, the event thereof, by despatching the sloop of war for that purpose.

Given on board the *Ville de Paris* in the Tagus, the 16th day of November, 1797.

The blockade of Cadiz continued without respite whilst the Royal Navy also kept a close watch on the continental North Sea ports and Channel ports from Calais to Brest. Throughout the autumn and winter, St Vincent never relaxed his iron discipline of the fleet or ceased his unbroken surveillance of Cadiz, whilst at the same time doing everything in his power to maintain the health and morale of the men he commanded. In his book, discipline, health and morale were inseparable. Complaints, if reasonable, were met with practical solutions but, if unreasonable, with contempt. When one captain objected to the removal from his ship by the Governor of Gibraltar, of soldiers who had been serving as marines, St Vincent told him: 'There are men enough to be got at Gibraltar and you and your officers would be better employed in picking them up than lying on your backs and roaring like bull calves.'

Although the Admiral preferred volunteers to conscripts he raised no objection to the use of the press gang. When he noticed that some of the lieutenants were getting a bit portly he forbade them to enter their ships by the usual entry port but made them climb the ship's side instead. Nevertheless, his underlying humanity was revealed by a few recorded acts of kindness, humour and generosity. One sailor who had his savings stolen while he was swimming, had them replaced from the Admiral's own pocket. To a frigate captain of very limited means, who had given outstanding service throughout the harsh demands of the blockade, he gave the opportunity – and some of his own money – to fit out his ship for a cruise which was likely to yield some prize money. To a lieutenant who had circulated a brilliant lampoon of his personal custom of attending morning divisions in his gold-braided admiral's full-dress uniform – regardless of the conditions – he responded by making the young man recite his composition before a table of captains from the fleet, whom he had invited to a dinner party, before sending him back to England on three months' leave. Finding a sailor from the flagship lying drunk in a Gibraltar street he asked the man why he had not returned on board. Amused by the answer that he feared 'old Jack' – the sailors' affectionate nick-name for the Admiral – would have him strung up to the yardarm, he arranged to have the man brought back to the ship and he went unpunished.

121

By the spring of 1798 it was estimated that the number of line-of-battle ships available to France and her allies – outside the Mediterranean – outnumbered the British by at least sixty-seven to fifty-eight. The Spaniards had thirty in Cadiz, the French a similar number at Brest while seven Dutch ships which had survived Camperdown were blockaded in the waters east of Texel. Britain had thirty-four ships of the line in home waters and twenty-four off Cadiz. It was basic strategy to prevent the French and Spanish fleets from joining one another. In the circumstances the government in London considered it too risky to detach any ships for service in the Mediterranean, which left the ports along the Riviera unobserved, and gave Napoleon freedom of movement between the Iberian peninsula and the Nile.

Britain's only real ally was Portugal, with Austria and Naples – the kingdom of the two Sicilies – amicably disposed but powerless at sea. Ireland was in a state of rebellion and in May 1798 the French were able to recapture Santo Domingo in the Caribbean. Yet on 2 May Lord Spencer, sitting in his office in the Admiralty in London, wrote to St Vincent:

> The appearance of a British squadron in the Mediterranean is a condition on which the fate of Europe may at this moment be said to depend. If you determine to send a detachment into the Mediterranean, I think it almost unnecessary to suggest to you the propriety of putting it under the command of Sir Horatio Nelson.

St Vincent responded by sending Nelson with three line-of-battle ships and five smaller vessels, which he could ill spare from the blockade of Cadiz, to cruise off Toulon and report on the disposition of the French fleet. These were to be reinforced by a squadron under Trowbridge as soon as they could be spared. He described them to Lord Spencer as 'in excellent order, and so well officered, manned and appointed I am confident they will perform everything to be expected from them.'

Off Cadiz he awaited a reinforcement of eight ships under Rear Admiral Sir Roger Curtis which had been cruising off the south coast of Ireland, and were described by Spencer as 'not fitted for foreign service' and 'not exactly such as I should have chosen to send out to you on a less pressing emergency'.

Writing to Nepean at the Admiralty from Gibraltar on 16 April St Vincent said: 'I heartily hope Sir Roger Curtis will not have a seditious squadron for he has no *fortiter in re* although he abounds in the *suaviter*. I never in my life saw a man who shrank from the audacity of united Irishmen like him, or who sacrificed discipline to the popularity of the moment.'

On 24 May, the eight ships made contact off Cadiz and Trowbridge's squadron sailed for the Mediterranean. St Vincent, ill and over-burdened, was left to face a formidable task. The anger of his subordinate flag officers at the appointment of an officer junior to themselves to command the Mediterranean squadron, and the dubious discipline of the new arrivals, riddled with dissension and incipient mutiny, added to his worries. He immediately received applications for courts martial from three of the eight newly arrived ships. In another, several Irishmen had already been found guilty of mutiny and summarily hanged – their plan to murder, capture or hang the officers, including St Vincent himself, and then to return with the ships to Ireland, having been found out.

While St Vincent dealt ruthlessly with mutiny and insubordination he never ceased to work to improve the ordinary sailors' living conditions within the realm of possibility, from food and clothing to the payment of prize money. Wherever possible he also removed officers whose behaviour provoked insubordination.

Information had been received of ominous concentrations of troops, transports and warships in Provencal and Italian ports – evidence of an impending operation on a huge scale. The *London Times* had reported in detail on the armada on 24 April, which was just twelve days after embarkation orders had been issued from Paris, but the destination of the expedition was not disclosed. Naples, the Neapolitan dominion of Sicily, Portugal, Ireland and England were all suggested. The true destination was hardly considered, despite the intelligence report to London that 400 French officers had been sent to Egypt. It seems that St Vincent alone considered Egypt as a possibility. With the reinforcement under Captain Trowbridge, Nelson would now command a fleet of some fourteen ships of the line. Their orders were to locate and engage the French force from the Riviera, replenishing with provisions wherever they could be found. Captain Hardy in the frigate *Mutine* had been sent to find Nelson and inform him of the coming reinforcement and by the same means a despatch went from St Vincent to the British Embassy in Naples, stating:

> I have a powerful squadron ready to fly to the assistance of Naples the moment I receive a reinforcement from the West of Ireland, which is on passage hither and I hourly look for its appearance with the utmost degree of anxiety and impatience. Rear-Admiral Sir Horatio Nelson will command this force, which is composed of the elite of the navy of England.

Reinforced, Nelson set off on a frustrating search for the French convoy. After just missing it twice, he wrote to St Vincent asking to be superseded if he was to blame. He was probably aware that his appointment to the command of the squadron, over the heads of two flag officers senior to him, had caused controversy and some dissension in the fleet. He was still suffering physically and mentally from the costly failure at Santa Cruz and some thought his judgement was impaired.

Only by the intervention of Sir William Hamilton in Naples was he able to get supplies for his ships. He wrote again to St Vincent: 'Your Lordship deprived yourself of frigates to make mine the first squadron in the world . . . but if [the French] are above water I will find them out and if possible bring them to battle. You have done your part in giving me so fine a fleet, and I hope to do mine in making use of them.'

Sailing east on 25 July the Rear Admiral deployed his ships in three widespread divisions, to cover the maximum area, linked by the invaluable frigates. As they sailed they carried out exercises and made detailed preparations for battle – Tenerife had taught the young flag officer a bitter lesson in forward planning. On 28 July they encountered Greek fishermen in the Gulf of Koron who informed them that a large French fleet had been sighted proceeding south-east. Considering all the circumstances, and aware of the Commander-in-Chief's strategic genius and assessment of Napoleon's probable destination, Nelson correctly deduced it. On 1 August he found a French fleet of seventeen ships, which outgunned his own fourteen line-of-battle ships, anchored in the shallow water of Aboukir Bay at the mouth of the Nile. The troops had already been disembarked and the ships were deployed in a defensive line with little water between them and the shoals which lay parallel to the line.

Nelson immediately attacked from the north, risking half his fleet between the French ships and the shoals. One of the best accounts of the Battle of the Nile is found in Ludovic Kennedy's *Nelson's Band of Brothers*. The unpredictability of Nelson's tactics took the French by surprise – with devastating effect. All but four of the French ships were either captured or sunk. In one stroke Napoleon's army had been isolated in North Africa, his communications with France severed and his occupation of Malta neutralized.

Rightly the main credit for this important naval victory belongs to Nelson, but too little is accorded to St Vincent for his strategic judgement and foresight and for his relentless vigilance, determination and insistence on training, which placed the best units in the Navy at his subordinate's disposal. Nelson knew this, even if the British public did not. The victory began, at last, to turn the tide in favour of Great Britain and against Napoleon Bonaparte and his ambitions.

After the battle, Nelson returned with his fleet to Naples where he was submerged in adulation. Suffering from a head wound received in action, his empty right sleeve pinned to his gold-embroidered jacket, he was the target for every kind of flattery. He wrote to St Vincent that he found himself in a country of 'fiddlers and puppets, whores and scoundrels . . . a dangerous place . . . We look up to you as we have always found you, as to our father, under whose fostering care we have been led to fame.'

Meanwhile the government in London, who had yet to learn of the naval victory in Aboukir Bay and were unwilling to accept responsibility for strategic decisions, were more than ready with their criticisms. Lord Spencer wrote to St Vincent on 16 September: 'I have seldom experienced a more severe disappointment than in the accounts which have lately reached us from the Mediterranean.' Adding that he had: 'Little hope that anything very decisive can take place . . . a very great degree of the effect and impression which the existence of a British squadron in the Mediterranean produces on the politics of Europe will be entirely lost if our fleet is tied down to a station as distant and so unproductive as a cruise off Alexandria.'

Nevertheless, the First Lord retained a modicum of confidence in Nelson. To Henry Dundas, Secretary for War, who would succeed him at the Admiralty before the Battle of Trafalgar, he replied to a criticism of Nelson: 'I hope he will have a pretty good story to tell at least. His missing the French fleet both going and returning was certainly very unfortunate, but we must not be too ready to censure him for leaving Alexandria . . . till we know the exact state of the intelligence which he received on his arrival there.'

A few days later the news of the resounding victory reached St Vincent – and then London, where it caused a nationwide surge of joyful relief. To St Vincent it was justification for all the difficult decisions he had taken, but his satisfaction was qualified by a sober assessment of the effect of the victory on the future course of the war. He hoped that it would 'Rouse the spirit of the Northern Powers and such of the Italians and Swiss who still retain any of their ancient character, and that we shall soon see a happy turn given to the war both on the Rhine and in Italy.' He was satisfied that for the time being Britannia ruled the Mediterranean waves.

The time taken for news to travel before the days of radio telegraphy is underlined by the action of the French in despatching an invasion force to Ireland just five days after the Battle of the Nile, unaware that an Irish rebellion had failed or that their navy in the Mediterranean had been practically annihilated, stranding Napoleon in Egypt. St Vincent appreciated that Nelson's victory gave him new responsibilities – and opportunities. Alexandria would still have to be blockaded as would Malta. He had been under pressure from Lord Spencer to take Minorca, the capture of which would be a mixed blessing – it would make a convenient strategic base but it would also put a strain on his limited resources. After careful consideration the Commander-in-Chief decided that the potential advantages outweighed the possible drawbacks.

He went to Gibraltar to plan the operation with General Sir Charles Stuart whom he respected, but found difficult to work with. The General had little sympathy for naval operations. St Vincent considered Commodore John Duckworth the most likely man to be able to co-operate with him and duly appointed him to convoy the troops to the island and to support the attack. It opened with a bombardment on 7 November by the six ships under Duckworth's command, and the island surrendered a week after the first landings. Once again the Admiral found himself subjected to the jealousies and umbrage of flag officers senior to Duckworth who resented both his appointment and the successful outcome. Duckworth sought a knighthood for the part he had played but St Vincent declined to recommend him. In any case, the main credit for the success rested with himself as Commander-in-Chief, and with the General who commanded the land forces.

The capital of Minorca, Port Mahon, would become an important British naval base, arsenal and ship repair yard for the next fifteen years. A month after its capture Russia joined the Anglo-Austrian alliance, which nominally included the Ottoman Empire as well as Portugal and the kingdom of Naples and Sicily.

Meanwhile the blockade of Malta continued. Its satellite island of Gozo was captured and presented, somewhat pointlessly, to the King of Naples although Malta itself, which had been taken by Napoleon's troops from the Knights of St John on their way to Egypt, would not fall to British forces until December 1800 – the beginning of a long and intimate relationship with Great Britain which would survive for more than a century and a half until the island became independent in 1961.

By 1799 St Vincent was becoming increasingly impressed with the potential of the undeveloped rock of Gibraltar. He wrote to Spencer: 'Much more may be made of this Arsenal than I was aware of until a three months' residence and unremitted attention to it shewed me the means.' He went on to describe its suitability for mooring ships of the line while refitting and also as a well-protected depot for stores and ammunition.

However, the ageing Admiral was still begging for replenishment of vital supplies. Early in the year he wrote to Nepean, Secretary of the Admiralty: 'Three-fourths of the ships under my command are so much out of repairs and shook that were they in England no one would go to sea in them.' Not only were they short of complement but: 'We are literally without a fathom of rope, yard of canvas, foot of oak or elm plank, board or log to saw them out of, have not a bit of iron except what we draw out of condemned masts and yards, not the smallest piece of plank.'

Some ships which were absolutely unseaworthy had to be sent home and the blockade of Cadiz was left to Rear Admiral Sir Roger Curtis with the discouraging directive that 'Intercepting the French squadron from Brest is of much greater importance than blocking the port of Cadiz against a few frigates, all the Spanish intend sending out at present.'

Following his success in Aboukir Bay, Nelson not only permitted himself to rest upon his laurels, but allowed his morals to rest upon the dubious if convenient assumption that King Ferdinand of Naples needed the presence of himself and the better half of the British fleet to bolster the defence of his kingdom. Rear Admiral Nelson had become infatuated with Emma, Lady Hamilton, the wife of the British Ambassador to the court of Naples and Sicily and used the pretext of supporting an ally to remain in Palermo. By neglecting the blockade of Alexandria he failed to prevent Napoleon in person from returning to France. At the same time he supported King Ferdinand's demands for yet more ships to protect his domains. St Vincent accepted the pleas of his favourite sub-ordinate and allocated ships that he could ill spare to Nelson's squadron. To Lord Spencer he wrote:

Their Sicilian Majesties and their Minister expect further naval support from hence, which it is morally impossible to furnish, for the blockade of Alexandria and Malta with the protection of the islands of Sicily and Minorca have swallowed up near half the force under my command and I will venture to assert that no officer in His Majesty's service but myself would have hazarded what I have done.

St Vincent's unenviable situation was aggravated by London government's clumsy decision (without informing him) to appoint Sir Sydney Smith, Captain of the *Tigre*, whom St Vincent described as 'this eccentric Knight of the Sword' with his 'romantic colouring', over Nelson's head to command naval forces off Alexandria and in the Levant. His main qualification for this appointment was his former residence in Constantinople and familiarity with Turkey – and his brother's being the British Minister at the Ottoman court. Sir Sydney had a variegated background, having served in the Swedish and Turkish navies and ably supported Lord Hood in the British evacuation of Toulon. Later, captured in the estuary of the Seine while attempting to cut out a French warship, he had been imprisoned in Paris and had not only succeeded in sending valuable intelligence reports back to England but had escaped and got back himself. However, both St Vincent and Nelson found him arrogant and presumptuous. While he famously and successfully bolstered the Turkish defence of Acre against a two-month siege by Napoleon's armies he also succeeded in antagonizing nearly everybody who had to work with him. He wrote to Sir William Hamilton that he was bound for Alexandria where he would meet Captain Hood – to whom Nelson had now delegated responsibility for blockading the port – 'who naturally falls under my orders as being my junior'. The letter was shown to Nelson. Because Smith had a dual appointment as Joint Plenipotentiary to the Ottoman Empire with his brother Spencer Smith, as well as his naval commission as Captain of *Tigre*, Nelson was put in an impossible position. His naval rank and the authority of the Commander-in-Chief had been undermined by an ignorant and thoughtless London decision. Furious, he wrote to St Vincent:

I do feel, for I am a man, that it is impossible for me to serve in these seas with the squadron under a junior officer – could I have thought it – and from Lord Spencer! Never, never, was I so astonished as your letter made me. As soon as I can get hold of Trowbridge I shall send him to Egypt to endeavour to destroy the ships in Alexandria. If it can be done, Trowbridge will do it. The Swedish Knight writes Sir William Hamilton that he shall go to Egypt and take Captain Hood and his squadron under his command. The Knight forgets the respect due to his superior officer; he has no order from you to take my ships away from my command; but it is all of a piece. Is it to be borne? Pray grant me your permission to retire and I hope the *Vanguard* will be allowed to convey me and my friends Sir William and Lady Hamilton to England.

Naturally St Vincent did not give permission to Nelson to retire. He, too, was furious with London and responded by formally placing Sir Sydney under Nelson's orders and protesting to the Admiralty. However, he was alert to Sir Sydney's influence with those in power and to the Spencer connection. In a letter to Nelson he commented: 'I foresee both you and I shall be drawn into a *fracasserie* about this gentleman, who having the ear of ministers and telling his story better than we can, will be more attended to.' In a further letter written from Gibraltar on 10 April he said:

I fancy ministers at home disapprove of Sir Sydney Smith's conduct at Constantinople: for in a confidential letter to me, a remark is made, that our new allies have not much reason to be satisfied with it. The man's head is completely turned with vanity and self-importance. Lady Hamilton has described him admirably in a letter to me. Lord Spencer is so wrapt up in him that he cannot avoid expressing displeasure at the statements I have made of his behaviour to us both, considering all my observations as arising from prejudice.

It was largely due to a hare-brained scheme of Sir Sydney's that Napoleon's return to France was facilitated, although others got the blame.

The 64-year-old admiral, suffering from a form of dropsy, no doubt exacerbated by the strain he was under, had asked in April to be replaced as Commander-in-Chief as soon as possible. He had told Lord Spencer that his successor would have to possess 'both temper and good nerves or he will be in continual hot water and [referring to the waters off Cadiz] terrified at this anchorage which appalls many a good fellow under my command.'

To him alone had been delegated the responsibility for judging the balance of necessity between blockading the Spanish fleet in Cadiz and watching Napoleon's preparations for expansion from his bases on the Riviera coast of the Mediterranean. He had waited with mixed impatience and trepidation for news of the success or failure of the squadron he had sent under Nelson to that vital area. Not only had his own reputation as a strategist depended upon it but he had fully appreciated that the containment of Napoleon's ambitions lay in his hands. Now it was time to shift the responsibility and burden of taking decisions to younger and less careworn shoulders.

Chapter Eleven

The Rift with Sir John Orde

Admiral Lord St Vincent, despite his great attributes, was not immune to making mistakes. They appear to have been due to two defects in his character: antipathy to having his authority questioned, and a lack of sensitivity or perception which sometimes blinded him to the compensating merits of those who had somehow earned his disapproval. However, when he fell out with Rear Admiral Sir John Orde, his third in command, the balance of blame fell heavily on Sir John's side. Had St Vincent mentioned that the appointment of Nelson to command the squadron detached to the Mediterranean had been made at the instance of the First Lord of the Admiralty, Sir John's resentment might have been diverted to London, but for St Vincent to have done so would have been to admit that he was not in command of his own station. As he famously said on a later occasion, 'Those who are responsible for measures have a right to choose their men.'

Sir John Orde was not the only officer to be offended by Nelson's preferment; Rear Admiral Sir William Parker, the second in command, was also affronted and several senior captains, who feared that the Commander-in-Chief's propensity for overlooking seniority might become habitual, were also unhappy. As third in line to St Vincent, Sir John Orde's pride was severely damaged and he was by far the most outspoken of his superior's critics. When St Vincent responded by summarily sending him home, the Admiralty, in the person of Lord Spencer, censured the C-in-C for his precipitate action. St Vincent wrote privately to Nelson: 'If he goes on goading I shall be off on a tangent and this fleet will go to the devil.'

The scene was set for a serious row which developed over a period covering St Vincent's final months in the Mediterranean and his first months back in England. The triangular correspondence between Sir John Orde, Lord St Vincent and the Admiralty, which took on another dimension when Sir John wrote to the press, and even the monarch became peripherally involved, tells the unedifying story with little need for further amplification.

Rear Admiral Sir Horatio Nelson had been despatched by St Vincent to the Mediterranean almost immediately on rejoining the fleet off Cadiz on 30 April 1798. He had been sent back to England in his decrepit flagship *Captain* to rehoist his flag in a more seaworthy ship of the line, the 74-gun *Vanguard*. On Nelson's return, St Vincent had written to Lord Spencer: 'The arrival of Admiral Nelson has given me new life. His presence in the Mediterranean is so very essential that I mean to put the *Orion* and *Alexander* under his command and to send them away to endeavour to ascertain the real objects of the preparation making by the French.'

On 2 May he had despatched the three ships of the line, accompanied by four frigates, to cruise off Toulon and the Riviera coast. It was at this point that Sir John Orde objected. On 16 June Sir John had written to Lord Spencer:

My Lord

Sir Horatio Nelson, a junior officer to me, just arrived from England, is detached from the fleet in which we serve, up the Mediterranean, with the command of twelve sail of the line, some frigates, etc; and Sir Roger Curtis has joined Lord St Vincent and taken the command in the second post, thereby lowering me to the fourth. I must not say I am surprised at this treatment, although very different from what I hoped to have experienced: but I cannot conceal from your lordship how much I feel hurt at the former, in particular. Indeed, were I insensible to it, I should be unworthy of the rank I hold and the distinction I have fought for and endeavoured to merit.

After having been employed the greatest part of last winter in the command of a strong squadron, a station honourable and confidential, in which I acquitted myself successfully and I have reason to believe entirely satisfactory to the Commander-in-Chief, I little expected to have been placed at this moment in the situation in which I now stand, so truly mortifying to an officer of any feeling or pretensions. I will not, however, on this occasion trouble your lordship with a recapitulation of the claims I conceive I have to a better lot than is now assigned to me; nor will I remind your lordship of the grounds on which I offered myself for service, and was accepted, on my return from a very troublesome service at Plymouth, when the mutiny broke out at the Nore; as both must be fresh in your lordship's recollection. I have felt from my earliest youth the debt I owe as an individual, to my country and have endeavoured faithfully to discharge it, but the sacrifice of my best days to the duties of my profession in any climate and country to which I was required to go. The same principles and the most disinterested motives, will lead me to persevere in a similar line of conduct, so long as my services continue to be called for my health will permit, and my character as an officer and a gentleman will suffer me to do.

A copy was sent to St Vincent, who replied on 18 June:

Dear Sir

The letter you have done me the honour to communicate, which I enclose, expresses precisely what I should have done under similar circumstances, for I never was blest with prudence and forbearance. At the same time, it must be acknowledged that those who are responsible for measures have an undoubted right to appoint the men they prefer to carry them into execution. You have a just claim to my entire approbation of your persevering services during the winter blockade of Cadiz.

An unfortunate incident, which aggravated the dispute, occurred very shortly after St Vincent had written his letter of the 18th. He had received a letter which displeased him from a colonel of marines. Unaccountably – even carelessly – he had assumed it was a reiterated complaint from Sir John Orde, to whom he sent a letter in reply which caused the Rear Admiral further offence. Sir John remonstrated that he was not the author of the letter referred to. St Vincent, realizing his mistake, sent for Sir John, and on the quarter-deck of *Ville de Paris* apologized to him and asked for his pardon. Sir John, instead of accepting the apology – which must have cost St Vincent a major instalment of pride – renewed his complaints. St Vincent reacted by interrupting him with the words 'Sir John Orde, I have begged your pardon. I can hear no more, no explanation or discussion.' He turned on his heel, leaving Sir John speechless.

A week or two later another incident further embittered the relationship between the two men. The Commander-in-Chief had been angered by the failure of an operation to cut out prizes from within the harbour of Cadiz, which had resulted in the loss of a launch from *St George*. St Vincent had consequently issued a general order to the fleet:

> It is very painful to the Commander-in-Chief to have to pass public censure on many of the officers who commanded boats of the fleet this morning, by whose misconduct a brilliant *coup* has been missed, and disgrace brought to his Majesty's arms. In future the lieutenants for this duty are to be selected and none but officers of approved firmness employed, who will be sure of their reward for any successful enterprise they exhibit.

Sir John Orde took immediate offence because two of his lieutenants from *Princess Royal* had been involved in the operation. He sent them on board the *Ville de Paris* with a request to know if these two young men 'had conducted themselves ill'. They were sent back with an answer that failed to satisfy Sir John who, thoroughly chagrined, demanded that the two men be court-martialled with the purpose of establishing their innocence. St Vincent refused. A lengthy correspondence ensued, politely acrimonious on Sir John's part, frustratingly laconic on the part of the Commander-in-Chief. Eventually, on 31 July, St Vincent wrote the following letter to Sir John, marked 'Private':

> Sir
>
> The moment you communicated to me the letter you sent to Lord Spencer, I considered it impossible you could remain an hour longer in this fleet than was necessary to make other arrangements, and I did not choose to leave it to Admiralty who should be sent to me. Sir William Parker, to whom I communicated the letter I received from Lord Spencer, touching the employment of Sir Horatio Nelson, knows that I had no share in the transaction. I certainly feel myself under no sort of engagement to you, under the quotation of which I admit to have passed in the presence of the persons you mentioned, at the same time that I shall be glad of any opportunity to bear testimony to your merits as an officer.

He followed this up with a further letter on 1 August, the very day that Nelson found and destroyed the French fleet in Aboukir Bay.

> Sir,
>
> Under the anxious desire I felt to give a prompt answer to your letter of yesterday, I omitted to mention that had you attended to the earnest wish I expressed, that you should not remonstrate against the measure of putting the detached squadron under the orders of Rear-Admiral Sir Horatio Nelson, you must eventually have succeeded to the command of this fleet, for my health will not admit of my continuing in the command of it many months longer.

Meanwhile, Lord Spencer had replied to Sir John Orde's letter of 16 June. It confirms another source of Sir John's discontent: that he would now be fourth in command – junior to both Parker and Curtis.

> Sir
>
> On the 5th instant I received your letter of 16th June and am sorry to find any event has happened to make you feel less

comfortable in the situation in which you are placed, than it is my wish every officer should feel, as far as circumstances allow of it. With regard to the first object of dissatisfaction to which your letter alludes, viz. the detachment of Sir Horatio Nelson, I cannot say that it strikes me in the same light it does you; nor can I conceive why it should not appear natural that a younger rear-admiral, in a two-decked ship, lately come out of dock, should be sent with two sail of the line on a service of that nature and, having been so sent, that it was not judged expedient when circumstances made it necessary to reinforce him, to send an officer senior to him especially as his seniors were all in ships less calculated for detached service. As to the arrival of Sir Roger Curtis, the very peculiar circumstances under which that squadron was detached from home sufficiently point out that it was a matter of necessity, and not of any arrangement calculated to displace you from a station in which your conduct had been approved by the Commander-in-Chief. Undoubtedly nothing but that kind of necessity would have occasioned such a measure. But I will dwell no longer on these points because, though I felt it due to you, and incumbent on me, to touch upon them, as you had thought fit to notice them in a letter to me, I have more satisfaction in acknowledging the handsome manner in which your sentiments, respecting the service of your country at this period, are expressed. Continuing to act on that principle, you cannot fail to deserve all the credit which is due to a zealous and active officer, and all the satisfaction that must infallibly attend a consciousness that you are performing your duty to the public.

I am, with great truth, Yours etc.

Having once made up his mind to be rid of Sir John Orde, St Vincent could never change it. To emphasize his letter of 31 July he followed it up by verbally informing the Rear Admiral's flag captain, Captain Draper, of his decision – an act of tactlessness by any standard! At the same time he asked Captain Draper to send two of his midshipmen, who were due for promotion, on board *Ville de Paris*. He then sent the Captain a note requesting details of the two young men so that their commissions could be made out. Sir John Orde, incensed, ordered his flag captain to decline. The two midshipmen may have suffered as a result of all this, but they were just pawns in the hands of two angry opponents.

The row intensified, stimulated by gossip amongst irresponsible officers, by disagreement over courts martial verdicts and by the exchange of inflammatory letters. Finally St Vincent ordered Orde to strike his flag on the 98-gun *Princess Royal*, to hoist it on board the 90-gun *Blenheim* which was in need of repairs, and return to England. On the day Sir John received this written order, 29 August 1798, he wrote to Sir Evan Nepean asking for a court martial on Lord St Vincent 'for conduct unbecoming the character of an officer by treating him in a manner unsuitable to his rank between 17th May and 29th August'. Sir John copied the letter to St Vincent who dutifully forwarded the original to the Admiralty. Sir John wrote two days later direct to St Vincent, strongly objecting both to the way he had been treated and to the order to transfer his flag. The reply he received dated 6 September guaranteed that the rupture would never be healed, forgotten or forgiven:

> Sir
>
> I have to acknowledge your letter, dated off Cadiz, 31st August, expressed in terms of insubordination, that even in these times I did not conceive could have come from an officer of your rank. I am, etc

The Rear Admiral sailed for England. On arrival he received an answer from the Admiralty refusing his request for a court martial. So angry was Sir John that he sat down to compile a pamphlet circulated privately, justifying his own conduct and condemning St Vincent's. Referring to himself in the third person he wrote:

> It has been conceived and generally credited, notwithstanding the pains taken to set the matter right in public opinion, through the medium of friends and private information, that the appointment of Sir Horatio Nelson to the command of a squadron, detached for particular service in the Mediterranean,

had alone created a difference and disagreement between Sir John Orde and the commander-in-chief of the station; which, after leading to the removal of the former by the latter (officer), occasioned his demand of a court-martial upon Lord St Vincent; and, on the refusal of the Admiralty to grant it his call upon the noble lord for personal satisfaction.

It has also been supposed and generally credited, that Sir John Orde, had, without reason, refused a very satisfactory proposal for *chief* command, made to him by the first lord of the Admiralty and, consequently, that his complaint of grievance and injurious treatment, was wholly ill-founded and unjustifiable.

In November Sir John heard formally from the Admiralty that although their lordships did not consider that adequate reasons had been given for sending him home, they had informed St Vincent accordingly and did not intend to take any further action. Meanwhile, in a communication of the same date the Admiralty commanded him 'to strike his flag on board the *Blenheim* and come on shore. Their lordships have, however, directed me to apprise you that they intend shortly to appoint some other ship for its reception.'

Soon afterwards, Lord Spencer sent for Sir John and not only told him that he was to be employed in the Channel Fleet, but also offered him the choice of two of the best ships available to hoist his flag – *Foudroyant* or *Neptune*. Sir John proved his intransigence – and perhaps his unsuitability for senior command – by refusing the offer, then applying for the command of a foreign station when it fell vacant. Lord Spencer's justifiable response was that 'As he had refused the service proposed to him, he did not choose to give him any other.'

On 9 October Sir Evan Nepean had written to St Vincent, with a copy to Orde:

My Lord
The Earl Spencer having acquainted my Lords Commissioners of the Admiralty that the King had received information that a challenge had been sent to your lordship

139

by Rear-Admiral Sir John Orde, on the occasion of some transactions that had taken place while he was employed under your lordship's orders, during your command of his Majesty's fleet in the Mediterranean; and having at the same time informed their lordships that his Majesty had been pleased to signify his express commands that your lordship should be restrained from accepting any challenge from Sir John Orde, on pain of his Majesty's displeasure; I have their lordships' commands to signify the same to your lordship; and to add that their lordships expect you will pay due obedience to their commands on this head.

I have the honour to be, Sir.

Between the date of that letter and 18 February St Vincent wrote on several occasions to Evan Nepean on the subject. Extracts from these letters are reproduced below. It should not be forgotten that while Sir John Orde was concerned primarily, if not exclusively, with his own wounded pride, St Vincent still carried the responsibility of a vital command on top of all his other worries, including ill health. Although Admiral Lord Keith arrived in Gibraltar to relieve him on 14 December, the Commander-in-Chief was so deeply involved, and so reluctant to delegate responsibility, that he unwisely hung on until June 1799.

Gibraltar, 5th December, 1798
I submit to the rebuke the Lords Commissioners of the admiralty have thought fit to convey to me, for sending Rear-Admiral Sir John Orde to England without their lordships' authority so to do; but my pride of character is very much wounded by the censure contained in the latter part of your letter of 13th October, denying positively, as I do, having ever treated him, or any other officer under my command, improperly, even when there were meetings and resolutions to resist the regulations I found it absolutely necessary to make, to preserve his Majesty's fleet under my command from the disgrace which it has suffered in other regions; and I am bold to affirm, that nothing short of the measures I have taken could have succeeded. I therefore desire you will state to their

140

lordships the extreme injury my reputation suffers by a sentence passed on me without being heard in my defence.

Gibraltar, 6th December 1798
My dear Nepean
I thank you kindly for putting Mr Pitt in possession of the facts relative to certain transactions, which have been most basely misrepresented. Sir William Parker and Sir John Orde will not deny that I used every argument in my power to prevent their writing to Lord Spencer. When I found the former had been wrought upon in a manner that I could make no impression on, I endeavoured to persuade him to delay his letter, which I was equally unsuccessful in; and I then told him, he was at full liberty to lay on upon me, as hard as he chose. Soon after this he sent me the letter to read, which bore no mark of the character of an officer or a gentleman. I returned it without remark; and, when sealed, it was forwarded in my packet. In respect to Sir John Orde, I did not know he had written until some time after his letter went, when he showed me a copy, which I told him was what I should not have been ashamed to have written myself, had I felt as he did, or words to that effect. I dare say he took them down, for I have discovered, since he left the fleet, that he is fraught with the most malignant policy.

Formed as your Board is, I am not surprised at the letter you were ordered to write. Which I would not endure for one moment, but for the critical state of naval operations in these seas which would suffer in the extreme, were I to avail myself of the permission I have obtained to return to England for the re-establishment of my health. But I confess myself not Christian enough either to forget or forgive those who have most unjustly condemned me, unheard. Much fitter would it have been to put me on my trial.

Yours, most truly

To Earl Spencer:
Gibraltar, 6th December 1798
The recollections of what passed at Cadiz made me very

141

circumspect in the choice of a colleague in General Stuart. I knew Commodore Duckworth to possess a large share of forbearance, which he acquired under the high hand of Captain Fielding, and the enclosed will justify my appointing him to the command. The general has many great and good points about him, but he is a niggard in his praise to the navy, and there are very few seamen who could act with him. I am about to send the regiment De Rolle to Minorca, at his earnest request.

I have the honour to be, my Lord, etc.

To Evan Nepean:
Gibraltar, 28th December 1798

I observe that in the close of your letter of the 2nd ultimo, wherein you communicate the permission given me by the Lords Commissioners of the admiralty, to return to England leaving the command of the fleet in the Mediterranean, etc to the next flag-officer in succession, and that I am not to avail myself of this indulgence, unless my health absolutely requires it; which not being the case at present, I shall conform myself to the pleasure of their lordships, until a return of the complaint I am subject to compels me to relinquish the command, when, I conclude, I am at liberty to go to Spithead in the *Ville de Paris*.

To Evan Nepean:
28th December 1798

Under the restriction at the close of your letter of leave, I dare not go to England. In truth, I am at this moment able to undergo more fatigue than any officer on this Rock or, I believe, in the fleet yet. As I approach the completion of my sixty-fourth year, and have never spared myself, I cannot long expect to be equal to the exertion, the great scene now before me requires.

I hear Sir John Orde is endeavouring to write me down and has not been over-scrupulous and accurate in his assertions, which I shall take no public notice of, unless you tell me it is necessary; nor will I mention his name to you, or any one, after this date. Neither you nor any of his nautical acquaintance, can be ignorant that he is not a practical seaman; neither has he the reach of sea understanding, ever to become a tactician.

To Evan Nepean:
Gibraltar, 23rd January, 1799
Sir John Orde has sent out a copy of his printed case to General O'Hara and artfully endeavoured to draw an opinion from him, in which he has failed. I am told (for I shall not deign to read his brochure) that he has printed private letters which passed between him and me and I think it more than probable he is practising upon the sea-officers under my command. As far as the matter relates to myself I am totally indifferent about the consequences; but if your Board suffers such proceedings to pass, without the most marked repro-bation, you will give a coup mortel to subordination, of which there is very little left.

To Evan Nepean:
Gibraltar, 17th February 1799
Many thanks for your letters enclosing Sir John Orde's Narrative, which I probably should never otherwise have seen. The conversations related in it consist of misrepresen-tations, partial statements and gross falsehoods; more especially the two between Sir William Parker and me and those between Captain Draper and me, on the subject of the supposed defection of the Irish militia, an account of which I received by two expresses in the course of the same day; and I did not lose a moment in making the signal for all captains and, having assembled them in my cabin, communicated under a seal of secrecy, to all except their flag-offices, the intelligence I had received and the measures I judged most advisable to be taken thereon. Every other conversation is most abominably twisted and distorted for the express purpose of stabbing my character; and he has concealed his own acts of disobedience to my orders, and arrogant presumption in counteracting them, during his sejour at Gibraltar, where he was sent for recreation, the public service

143

not allowing a trip to Lisbon as he wished. He has by this pamphlet proved himself so litigious a character.

There is an insinuation at the close of the pamphlet, that I withheld the original letter which contained his charges against me, forwarded by the *Blenheim*; and I request you will contrive some means to convey to me that it was received at the office. If I were disposed to rip him up, I could do it with great ease; but I feel so thorough a contempt for all he has said and done, that unless I discover that I am injured in the opinion of the King and his ministers, I shall certainly leave him to his own reflections – the greatest punishment which can possibly be inflicted on him.

To Evan Nepean:
Gibraltar, 18th February 1799
I have written to General Stuart assuring him that should he continue in the island of Minorca, I will endeavour to remove every obstacle to his ease and comfort; and I referred him to the major for the rest, having fully explained to him the difficulty I should have in finding an officer of sufficient rank to command the squadron, free from prejudices and qualified to be entrusted with the naval defence of the island. Between you and I, there is no such person here except Lord Keith, and the squadron is not of size for a vice-admiral without putting Lord Nelson under his command; which would revolt his feelings, and the squadron before Cadiz be deprived of the only man capable of commanding it. For I must continue to reside on this Rock, or the operations of the detached squadrons will be cramped and they in danger of starving, if I am not in the way to supply their wants and to decide with promptitude upon the various exigencies which must daily arise . . . I am not a judge of his [General Stuart, the army C-in-C in Minorca] military talents and fitness for so critical and important a trust. Where you will find a better I know not; for, if a money-making man is sent, the island will not long remain in our possession . . . Brigadier Stuart, Colonel Graham and Colonel Paget are very great characters. There are some good field-officers; and a very martial spirit

has been happily infused into the whole line; at which no man, since the days of Wolfe has such a knack as General Stuart.

Did you observe in Sir John Orde's Narrative, an avowal of his having convened some of the senior captains to sit in judgment upon my conduct towards him? You have no conception how far these meetings went; and with the exception of Sir Roger Curtis, and perhaps Collingwood, I do not believe there was an officer of any standing who did not, in some sort, enter into cabals to pull down my authority and level all distinctions . . . I saw this clearly and had no other card to play but to get rid of Sir John . . . in the most summary way; and, if your Board has half an eye, the necessity of the measure must have met it and, instead of a rebuke, my conduct merited silent *approbation*, at least, if public could not, with propriety, have been conveyed. In short, my dear Nepean, unless the promulgation of that narrative is stamped with some mark of high displeasure no commander-in-chief or minister is safe, and you will see your humble servant much sooner than you are aware of.

When St Vincent eventually returned to England in the summer of 1799, having been succeeded as Commander-in-Chief Mediterranean by Vice Admiral Lord Keith, Sir John Orde was waiting to attack him like a bull terrier at a garden gate. Sir John demanded 'private satisfaction for private ill-treatment'. He waited only until the elderly Admiral had begun to recover his health; then he set off for St Vincent's Essex home to make his despicable challenge. He sent a certain Captain Walrond to Rochetts to demand a meeting. Lord St Vincent declined by letter, reasoning that he was not personally responsible for his public measures, and that he was still indisposed. Sir John, frustrated, returned to London where he apparently intended to await developments before issuing another challenge. There he was visited by the civil magistrate and asked to give security to keep the peace. St Vincent was similarly bound to keep the peace – both men for very large sums of money. Obviously the intervention of the King had had its effect. While this brought the affair to a close at the personal and professional level, it had not enhanced the reputations of either party and the row would rumble on in gossip and argument between officers for decades to come. It was an unjust reward to Lord St Vincent for sustained and courageous devotion to duty, however tyrannical his conduct might have seemed to those under his command.

Chapter Twelve

Back to England

Sir John Orde was by no means the only prominent officer to fall out with Lord St Vincent. The renowned Cuthbert Collingwood who served under him with distinction as captain of the *Excellent* at the Battle of Cape St Vincent, having previously distinguished himself under Admiral Lord Howe in 1794 – when the French were defeated off Ushant at the Battle of the Glorious First of June – and who was later Lord Nelson's second in command at Trafalgar, found him overbearing on occasion; but Collingwood himself was inclined to be touchy. He had refused to accept a gold medal for his prominent part in the Battle of Cape St Vincent because he had been omitted from the medal list for the Glorious First of June. Yet St Vincent had a high regard for him, more than once entrusting him with the command of detached squadrons and special missions, and making him a Commodore when short of competent junior flag officers. He also made use of Collingwood's disciplinary success by drafting 'the most ungovernable spirits' into *Excellent*, with the maxim 'Send them to Collingwood and he will bring them to order'. Collingwood was one of the minority of captains who was able to maintain order with the minimum use of corporal punishment, although he was unflatteringly described in later years by George Elliot, the second son of the former Viceroy of Corsica, who had served under him as a young officer: 'I was many years in company with him and always considered him a selfish old bear. That he was a brave, stubborn, persevering and determined officer everyone acknowledged, but he had few if any friends and no admirers. In body and mind he was iron, and very cold iron.'

When *Excellent* was part of the blockading squadron off Cadiz a confrontation between St Vincent and Collingwood occurred which, although in itself insignificant, engendered lasting bad feeling between them. The *Excellent* was ordered by the C-in-C to weigh anchor and close the flagship. As she approached she was unaccountably signalled five or six times to alter course, then ordered to send a lieutenant to report on board the flagship. With increasing annoyance Collingwood watched from his own quarter-deck. Eventually he ordered his boat to be lowered so that he could accompany his lieutenant to *Ville de Paris*. Repairing on board with the lieutenant, he obtained a copy of the signal which explained why *Excellent* had been ordered to close the flagship, and then read it aloud to St Vincent and his flag captain, Sir Robert Calder, while the three of them walked the Admiral's quarterdeck. It was notifi-cation of the issue of two bags of onions to the *Excellent* for the benefit of the sick. Collingwood protested indignantly, 'Bless me! Is this the service, my lord? Is this the service, Sir Robert? Has the *Excellent*'s signal been made five or six times for two bags of onions?'

Turning to the officer of the watch, Collingwood ordered his boat to be manned so that he could return to his own ship. Determined to mollify him, St Vincent repeatedly invited him to stay for dinner but he refused and left the flagship. In rejecting the C-in-C's invitation in these circumstances, knowing the Admiral's uncompromising attitude to insubordination and his insistence that officers set an example, Collingwood was taking a real risk. He got away with it – at the price of a permanent scar on his relationship with St Vincent, who once said in a letter to the wife of the First Lord of the Admiralty: 'I pride myself in maintaining strict disci-pline when surrounded by factious spirits in the lower orders and discontent among the higher classes.'

According to his biographer the following words were written by Collingwood at the time:

This appointment of Admiral Nelson to a service where so much honour was to be acquired, has given great offence to the senior admirals of the fleet. Sir William Parker, who is a very excellent officer and as gallant as any in the navy, and Sir John Orde, who on all occasions of service has acquitted himself with great honour, are both feeling much hurt at a junior officer of the same fleet having so marked a preference over them, and have written to Lord Spencer, complaining of this neglect of them. The fleet is, in consequence, in a most unpleasant state; and now all that intercourse of friendship, which was the only thing like *comfort* which was left to us, is forbidden; for the admirals and captains are desired not to entertain, even at dinner, any who do not belong to their ships. They all complain that they are appointed to many unworthy services and I have my share with the rest. But I place myself beyond the reach of such matters; for I do them with all the exactness in my power, as if they were things of the utmost importance; though I do not conceal what I think of them. In short, I do what every body else does – wish myself at home very much.

Collingwood's objections to the methods used by St Vincent to maintain discipline were repeated after the latter became Commander-in-Chief of the Channel fleet and sought to raise the standard to that previously obtaining in the Mediterranean. To a friend, Mr Blackett, he wrote:

I do assure you, when I reflect on my long absence from all that can make me happy it is very painful to me; and what day is there that I do not lament the continuance of the war. We are wandering before this port with no prospect of change for the better. Nothing good can happen to us short of peace. Every officer and man in the fleet is impatient for release from a situation which daily becomes more irksome to all. *I see disgust growing round me* very fast. Instead of softening the rigours of a service which must from its nature, be attended with many anxieties, painful watchings, and deprivations of any thing like *comfort a contrary system is pursued* which has not extended to me, but I see its effects on others and deplore them. What I feel as a great misfortune is, that there is no exercise of the military part of our duty – no practice of those movements by a

149

facility in which one fleet is made superior to another. Whoever comes here ignorant in these points must remain so, for he will find other employment about blankets and pigsties, and tumbling provisions out of one ship into another.

The final sentence referred to the C-in-C's insistence that hammocks and bedding must be aired, his banning of the practice of keeping pigs and other livestock on board ship to the benefit of officers and the detriment of general health and his fair distribution of available stores. The obvious conclusion to be drawn from the views expressed by Collingwood is that the greater the responsibility shouldered by anybody, the greater their vulnerability to damaging criticism. Fortunately history has the retrospective capacity to condemn the critics and justify the actions of the criticized. Trafalgar would be the justification for all the harsh discipline imposed by Lord St Vincent, whilst the readiness for action of each ship remained the responsibility of her captain.

Vice Admiral Lord Keith arrived in Gibraltar to relieve Admiral Lord St Vincent on 14 December 1798, but the latter, despite his age and ill health, was reluctant to relinquish the command which he had exercised with such assiduous attention to duty and detail, strategic skill and inflexible discipline for over four years. He did not finally resign the command until August 1799, the Admiralty being content to leave the actual date of his departure to his own discretion – which was convenient for him but unsatisfactory and unfair to his successor.

Although Lord Keith arrived with an impeccable record of service and vast experience as a seaman, his appointment was not popular with Nelson's 'band of brothers'. He was senior to Nelson as a Vice Admiral, thoroughly professional and in no way encumbered by personal considerations. Even the most ardent male admirers of the victor of the Nile must have realized that, at the time, the combination of poor health and infatuation with Lady Hamilton impaired his judgement in regard to Mediterranean strategy. A supremely courageous tactician, Nelson never proved himself a strategist of the genius of St Vincent, and in early 1799 he appeared to put the safety and welfare of the royal family of Naples and Sicily – and of Lady Hamilton – above the demands of strategic control of the Mediterranean. On 16 January St Vincent wrote both to Evan Nepean and Lord Spencer:

My dear Nepean

The royal family of Naples have had a narrow escape. Tuscany is gone and Spain and Portugal will follow, whenever it so pleases the directory; for the governments of both increase in weakness and oppression in proportion to the dangers by which they are threatened from without.

My Lord,

An arrogant letter, written by Sir Sydney Smith to Sir Wm Hamilton, when he joined the squadron forming the blockade of Malta, has wounded Rear-Admiral Lord Nelson to the quick who, besides, feels himself affronted by his embassy *and separate command,* which compels me to put this strange man immediately under his lordship's orders or the king may be deprived of his [Lord Nelson's] important services, and those of many valuable officers as superior to Sir Sydney Smith in all points, as he is to the most ordinary of men. I experienced a trait of the presumptuous character of this young man, during his short stay at Gibraltar, which I passed over, that it might not appear to your Lordship I was governed by prejudice in my conduct towards him.

I enclose a copy of Lord Nelson's detailed account of the transaction at Naples, previous to the departure of the royal family, and of the passage to Palermo. These events make the island of Minorca of incalculable importance. I therefore trust the representations I had the honour to make to Mr Dundas two months ago have been attended to and we shall soon be supplied with the means of reinforcing the garrison; which becomes the more necessary because General Stuart (who is a host in himself) finds his health so much impaired by the air of the island, which I have known to disagree with many, that he cannot continue there; and where an officer like him can be found I know not. But it is of the most material consequence that an able and disinterested man should succeed him, or our tenure will be very precarious indeed.

St Vincent, exercising command from his hulk in Gibraltar harbour, ordered Keith to take over the blockade of the Spanish fleet in Cadiz. Initially Keith hoisted his flag in *Foudroyant*, later transferring it to the *Barfleur*. From December 1798 until the late spring of 1799, with a squadron varying from 11 to 16 ships, he continued to blockade the Spanish fleet of 11 line-of-battle ships within Cadiz harbour. He detached ships singly or in pairs to Gibraltar for stores, but the Rock was dangerously short of water. In the last week of March St Vincent authorized the squadron to sail to Tetuan on the Moroccan coast, 40 miles south of Gibraltar, to replenish with water and fresh provisions, leaving two frigates to watch Cadiz. On 13 February he wrote again to Lord Spencer:

My Lord,
Your lordship will learn, from the communications made by General Acton to Lord Nelson, and by his Excellency's letters to me, copies of which are enclosed, that their Sicilian majesties and their minister expect further naval support from hence, which it is morally impossible to furnish; for the blockade of Alexandria and Malta, with the protection of the islands of Sicily and Minorca, have swallowed up nearly half the force under my command, and I will venture to assert that no officer in his Majesty's service, but myself, would have hazarded what I have done. Lord Keith has seventeen ships of the line and three sloops under his command, some of the former in so crazy a state that they are obliged to come occasionally into the mole to be patched up. The *Princess Royal*, for instance, just gone out and the *Prince George* now lightening to come at her leaks, which are several streaks under water; we have also had to shift the mainmasts of *Edgar*, *Powerful* and *Marlborough* and are driven to our wit's end for resources. In truth, the mast last prepared could not have been effected without extracting the iron from those disabled in the action of the Nile; and we are without sails, canvass, cordage, oak, elm or fir planks and, what is still more alarming, our provisions run very short. Unfortunately Lord Keith has been forced, by blowing weather, to take shelter in

Tetuan Bay and only one ship *Hector,* off Cadiz, for the few remaining victuallers expected from Lisbon.

The want of frigates to communicate with Lord Nelson and Commodore Duckworth, is very distressing; and I cannot call the *Flora* and *Caroline* from the north-west coast of Spain, as they, with the *Speedy* and *Mondovi* sloops, compose all the force I can give for the protection of the outward and home-ward-bound Portugal trade; which has suffered much from the depredations of small French privateers and a great deal of clamour has ensued. Ten additional efficient frigates and sloops are absolutely necessary for carrying on the extensive service of this command, and there really should be something like a relief to the ships which form the blockade of Cadiz, some of them having been ten and eleven months out of port and the health of their crews put to great risk, although it has been hitherto miraculously preserved.

In this statement, however incredible it may appear, I do assure your lordship I have nothing exaggerated. Yet I am much more affected by the discontents of Lord Nelson and Captain Trowbridge; the former continuing seemingly deter-mined upon relinquishing his command and returning to England, and the latter in such a state of despondency, from the slight he has received, which he terms an indelible disgrace, that I really am at a loss how to act. The arrival of the *San Leon* (with a commission for his first lieutenant to command her) may operate to pacify him, although he left Palermo in a mood that has given me inexpressible pain.

Within days, St Vincent felt it necessary to write again to Lord Spencer about the condition of *Prince George* and *Princess Royal,* describing the 'tinkering' the latter had received in Portsmouth harbour as so superficial that they were obliged to lighten her to reach one considerable leak. They found that all her bolts were so loose that they could be removed by a blow from a hammer. The oakum in the seams on the *Prince George* was rotten.

On 21 February the Admiral wrote enthusiastically about the recently acquired facilities in Port Mahon:

My dear Lord [Spencer]

I have the honour to send you a plan of the arsenal of Port Mahon, which has received many improvements since I was acquainted with it. Commodore Duckworth says there is a new storehouse building upon the site of one pulled down which, if the island should become a permanent possession, might be turned into proper houses for the commissioners and officers of the yard; who certainly ought never to reside in the town (an opinion I join with him in most cordially) – for I well remember much delay, inconvenience, and peculation arising from the distant residence of the officers. Commissioner Coffin writes in raptures of the capability of his department; and Dr Weir reports, in the most favourable manner, of the naval hospital which is purified from the filthy state the Spaniards left it in, and is altogether the completest thing of the kind in Europe.

Happily there are few sick in either department; and as there is always a plentiful supply of vegetables and a prospect of getting cattle from Algiers, I am in great hopes the troops and seamen will continue healthy.

At this time, Lord St Vincent had disposed of his fleet so as to watch all the most important points of the enemy's coast. Lord Keith was off Cadiz, Nelson at Naples, Duckworth at Minorca. Sir Sydney Smith was at Acre, Hood and Hallowell at Alexandria and Sir Alexander Ball commanding the blockade of Malta, assisted by the Marquis de Nisa with the Portuguese squadron. However, early in March, he had to contend with the withdrawal of the Portuguese squadron leaving Nelson with insufficient ships to ensure the defence of Naples and Sicily. On 10 March St Vincent wrote a secret letter to Lord Spencer which, in the light of later developments in the Iberian Peninsula, is of particular interest. Strangely, he had been asked by a representative of the King of Spain if a British frigate could bring desperately needed 'specie' – coinage or bullion – from the Spanish colonies to Gibraltar for onward conveyance to Madrid. St Vincent, seeing this as a possible way of driving a wedge between Spain and her dominant French ally, had replied that he did not have the authority but would secretly convey the request to the British government. In his secret letter to Lord Spencer he said:

> It is evident that the court of Spain is trembling under the menaces of France; and the Spanish army is so ill paid, and the people so dissatisfied with the oppression they suffer, a revolution will be brought about whenever the French are able to march an army into the country; in which event Portugal must fall too; for the French opinions have gained great ground there, among all ranks of people; and as (without pretending to be a politician) I cannot conceive a greater evil to Great Britain than these two countries falling under the subjugation of France, I shall keep this proposition open, until I receive instructions upon a subject much too weighty for me to advance a step in without them.

While St Vincent controlled events from *Le Souverein* in Gibraltar harbour, Nelson was stuck in Palermo – immobilized by the head wound he had received in Aboukir Bay, by his obsession with the Neapolitan court, and by his infatuation with Lady Hamilton. His wound caused him fits of depression and affected his sight. He wrote to St Vincent that there was 'no true happiness in this life and in my present state I could quit it with a smile'. He was jealous of Keith's appointment but could not complain officially because Keith was his senior in the list of vice admirals. He was more upset by the unorthodox employment of Sir Sydney Smith in the Levant, which undermined his authority. Elsewhere, his close friend Trowbridge was dejected over his exclusion from the honours awarded for the Battle of the Nile – excluded because his ship *Culloden* had run aground before the main action. Meantime Captain Hood, on detached duty blockading the Italian coast, had lost his brother in action and sought permission to go home to settle his estate, while Captain Louis, lying off Leghorn for the protection of the family of the Grand Duke of Tuscany, was beset by the total lack of dependability on the part of those he was protecting.

All these diverse and splintered responsibilities weighed heavily on St Vincent, himself tired and in poor health. In a letter written on 16 April, he told Nepean that he had no information about what was happening at the eastern end of the Mediterranean, but expressed the hope that Messina could have been saved by the arrival of General Stuart and commented that 'two good regiments of British infantry would have taken Malta long ago'. He also touched on the question of his return to England, wondering whether he should travel in *Ville de Paris* or 'go like a convict as I came out'.

Meanwhile, the French had decided to attempt to relieve their army in Egypt and their garrison in Malta. This would require a naval force capable of competing with St Vincent's fleet, which, although widely scattered, consisted of thirty-five line-of-battle ships and a few frigates. The French admiral Bruix was determined to escape from Brest to enable the 25 ships of the line and 10 frigates blockaded there to join the 22 Spanish ships in Cadiz, combining to outnumber St Vincent. By the middle of April his fleet was ready to leave Brest. British intelligence was aware of this but wrongly concluded that its destination was southern Ireland. Lord Spencer instructed the Commander-in-Chief Channel, Lord Bridport (formerly Alexander Hood), who was then blockading Brest with sixteen ships of the line, to fall back to Cape Clear, the southernmost promontory of Ireland, in the event of the French escaping from Brest. On 25 April, Bruix put to sea in foggy conditions, with twenty-five sail of the line. Despite the fog, his ships were sighted by the British frigate *Nymphe* which reported their escape to Lord Bridport. He followed Lord Spencer's instructions and retired towards the coast of southern Ireland, thus allowing Bruix and his fleet to set course south across the Bay of Biscay for Cape Finisterre, where they planned to rendezvous with the Spanish fleet. The capture of a French cutter carrying dispatches enabled Bridport to send a warning by express packet to Keith off Cadiz and also to St Vincent at Gibraltar. By the beginning of May the Admiralty had decided it needed to send reinforcements to the Mediterranean.

On 6 May seven line-of-battle ships under the command of Rear Admiral Whitshed in the 110-gun *Queen Charlotte* stood down the English Channel in pursuit of the French fleet, but by then Bruix was already off Oporto.

St Vincent had to make his dispositions and give his orders on the basis of small pieces of information, often arriving long after the event, as evidenced in two letters he wrote to Lord Spencer four days after Rear Admiral Whitshed left England:

My Lord,

I may say, with my old friend General Wolfe, that I have had a choice of difficulties, very much increased by the want of frigates to obtain intelligence of the movements of the enemy; inasmuch that I am under the necessity of diverting the *Success* from the service she was ordered on; having literally no other resource; nor do I know when I may be able to part with her. Unless another ship is sent from England to convoy the homeward-bound Oporto trade, much clamour will ensue.

Your lordship will be aware that the moment I quit this bay, which I hope to do early in the morning, the coast from the Tagus to Gibraltar will have no protection and this garrison will be exposed to great distress for want of refreshments, until a powerful reinforcement is sent out to recover the dominion of this district under my command, which I must abandon in order to effect a junction with the ships of the line stationed about Minorca, before any hostile operation takes place against that island – the more to be apprehended because the Brest squadron is six nights and five days before us. All I can say is that every means shall be used to preserve it and to counteract the enterprises of the enemy wherever they may point. Having no information to guide my steps, nor means to trace the course of the Brest squadron, I must grope my way in the best manner I can.

Your lordship will perceive the difficulty of bringing the two regiments from Lisbon to Gibraltar, which General Cuyler informs me is now their destination. I nevertheless have orders for the *Haarlem, Europa* and *Pallas* to perform this service when they come down the Mediterranean – hourly expected. The *Calcutta* and *Ulysses* being so necessary as store ships, I cannot do without them; for, although I hope to be able to withdraw all the stores and provisions necessary for the defence and sustenance of the garrison from Port Mahon, it is a contingency not safely to be relied upon.

Lord Keith has shown great manhood and ability before Cadiz; his position having been very critical, exposed to a hard gale of wind, blowing directly on the shore, with an enemy of superior force to windward of him and twenty-two ships of the line in the Bay of Cadiz, ready to profit by any disaster which might have befallen him.

My Lord,

His Majesty's ship *Childers* arrived at daylight on the 4th instant with the enclosed and I did not lose a moment in sending off advices of the contents to Rear Admirals Lord Nelson and Duckworth and to Captain McDougal, of the *Edgar* in Tetuan Bay, with directions to him to apprise Captain Moore, of the *Vesuvius*, lying in Tangier Bay, of the approach of the enemy's fleet, by express from Tetuan; and I sent directions to Vice Admiral Lord Keith, in the event of his having an action, or a junction being formed with the Cadiz fleet without one to make the best of his way hither; but, the wind having continued to blow strong from the south-west, nothing could get through the Gut [Straits of Gibraltar].

The *Cameleon* arrived on the 5th, having passed through the French squadron, eight or nine leagues to the west of Cape Spartel; and at five o'clock the same evening twenty-six ships were observed passing through the Straits into the Mediterranean, nineteen of which, at least, appeared to be of the line. The weather was so hazy, with heavy rain, their force could not be ascertained with precision.

I enclose an extract from the journal of Captain Stiles, by which their lordships will perceive that the French squadron eluded the vigilance of Lord Keith by the darkness of the atmosphere; for the enemy was very near the position his lord-ship had, on receiving intelligence of his approach, determined to take, when Captain Stiles found himself in such jeopardy that he was forced to escape, through a channel pointed out by Mr Matra, the Consul general at Morocco, who happened to be at Gibraltar. An express was sent to Tangier, via Tetuan and a duplicate by Mr Jackson, master of the *Ville de Paris*, from hence, in an open boat, with orders to Lord Keith to make the best of his way hither. In the meantime all the stores, wine and provisions, which could be spared were directed to be shipped on board the *Calcutta* and *Ulysses*, armed transports. On the 6th, the *Cameleon* was despatched to Captain Ball, commanding the blockade of Malta and to Sir Sydney Smith at Alexandria, and the *Andentrine*, Portuguese Corvette, to Lord Nelson, at Palermo, with advices of the enemy having entered the Mediterranean; and the *Vesuvius* having arrived in the evening from Tangier, to give an account of what Captain Moore had observed touching the French fleet, she was detached to Minorca with the same advices and instructions to Rear Admiral Duckworth, to hold the ships of the line, under his orders, in constant readiness to join the squadron the moment he received intelligence of its approach and with directions to keep the Victuallers and the *Serapis* store ship ready to proceed to such port as should be pointed out; replacing the stores in the *Serapis*, that in case of a siege the stores and provisions should not fall into the hands of the enemy, which must be the case if Fort St Philip should be invested, the arsenal not being within its protection. In the evening of the 7th, the *Transfix* arrived with the enclosed reports from Lord Keith, which reflect great honour on his lordship's manner of conducting the squadron; and soon after the *Success*, Captain Peard, having found it impracticable to work out of the straits, after landing an officer at Tangier, would have been driven into the Mediterranean, had he not taken shelter in the Bay; for the weather was very tempestuous and has continued more or less so ever since, which put the life of Mr Jackson and his boat's crew to great hazard, and compelled him to return, as it did two Gibraltar fishing boats, which had been engaged for the same purpose, and very much retarded the embarkation of provisions and stores on board the *Ulysses*. It being therefore impossible to have any communication with Lord Keith through the Gut and having been informed that Commissioner Coffin (who had returned to this place from Minorca) was appointed commissioner of

Halifax yard, I desired him to proceed through Spain to Lisbon, and from thence to England in a packet, (which I requested him to apply to Mr Walpole for) with instructions to despatch a vessel to Lord Keith from Faro; which he most zealously undertook to perform, and accordingly set off on the morning of the 9th, by means of a passport obtained by General O'Hara from the Governor of St Roche. The squadron arrived from before Cadiz this morning at nine o'clock; and the moment the most pressing wants of the ships composing it are supplied, which I trust will be by the dawn of tomorrow, it is my intention to proceed with the utmost despatch, consistently with the preservation of the order of sailing, off Cape Mola and endeavour to collect the ships of the line under the orders of Rear-Admiral Duckworth, take a position before the island of Minorca and act afterwards as events may require.

Whatever ships of war their lordships may judge it necessary to despatch hither in consequence of the whole naval force of France and Spain being in these seas should have all the stores, of any description, that can be collected at the moment put on board them and be victualled for six months, and an additional supply sent afterwards in victualles, etc, powerfully escorted to prevent their being intercepted; for the Spaniards will naturally keep a squadron cruising at the entrance of the straits for this purpose, being very favourable for such an operation, and the coast of Andalusia provided with abundance of vessels adapted to it. Their lordships may rest assured that every nerve will be exerted to counteract the designs of the enemy; in which I rely with the utmost degree of confidence on all the officers, seamen, and marines of the fleet I have the honour to command, the present disposition of which I enclose.

I am, Sir

P.S. Lord Keith saw twenty-two sail of the line at anchor in Cadiz Bay last evening at sunset. Not having any frigate with me, I am constrained to keep the *Success*. The homeward-bound Oporto trade will consequently be without convoy.

As Keith's squadron was returning from Tetuan, they were met by two British frigates from whom they learned that five Spanish sail of the line had emerged from Ferrol, 650 miles by sea from Cadiz and that the French fleet had been sighted off Oporto. Keith immediately despatched the first frigate to Gibraltar to report the situation. In response to this news, St Vincent sent three additional ships of the line and one more frigate to reinforce Keith's squadron. Keith formed his fleet of sixteen ships in line of battle off Cadiz to await the French. The enemy fleet, which appeared on the western horizon at about 8.00 am on 6 May, consisted of thirty-three sail of the line. With the twenty-two Spanish vessels within Cadiz harbour, Keith's squadron found itself between enemy forces which outnumbered him by more than three to one. Nevertheless, he formed his ships on the same tack as the French and waited to receive them, whereupon, to his surprise, the French ships wore to the opposite tack and stood away to the south-west.

Keith's squadron had been deployed to prevent the Spanish ships from escaping from Cadiz and at the same time to prevent the French and Spanish from joining forces. At daylight on 7 May, when four French ships were seen to windward, Keith's squadron gave chase but the Frenchmen had more than a head start and the British ships had to return to their blockade, expecting orders from St Vincent to join him in pursuit of the main French fleet – now thought to be heading for Toulon. Receiving no orders, Keith decided to sail for Gibraltar, which lay only 50 miles to the east, leaving some of his ships off Cadiz. When they reached Gibraltar they found, to their astonishment, that instead of acting upon the intelligence conveyed by the frigates, St Vincent had ordered his ships to anchor and take on water and provisions, which took three days. When at last St Vincent hoisted his flag in the *Ville de Paris* and shaped course east, in company with Keith's squadron and other available ships, instead of pursuing the French on their presumed route to Toulon, he parted company and sailed for Minorca. There is no record of St Vincent's reasons for his actions. He was apparently under the misapprehension that the French were making for Port Mahon. He left Keith to pursue the enemy, who by now had had time to embark stores at Toulon and continue east before Keith could catch up with them. The British ships crowded all sail in pursuit and at length came in sight of their enemy's lookout frigates between Corsica and Genoa. Before the British squadron could contact the main French fleet, a fast-sailing transport hove in sight and fired guns, signalling Keith to bring to. Very reluctantly he did so and received an uncompromising order from St Vincent to return to Minorca. Lieutenant Thomas Cochrane was an eyewitness to Keith's chagrin on receipt of this order. In his autobiography he says:

> On Lord Keith receiving this order, I never saw a man more irritated. When annoyed, his lordship had a habit of talking aloud to himself. On this occasion, as officer of the watch, I happened to be in close proximity, and thereby became an involuntary listener to some very strong expressions, imputing jealousy on the part of Lord St Vincent as constituting the motive for recalling him. The above facts are stated as coming within my own personal knowledge, and are here introduced in consequence of blame being cast on Lord Keith to this day by naval historians who could only derive their authority from data which are certainly untrue, even if official. Had the command been surrendered to Lord Keith on his arrival in the Mediterranean, or had his lordship been permitted promptly to pursue the enemy, they could not have escaped.

There is no valid reason to suppose that, had the enemy been brought to action, the outcome would have been any less successful than the battles of the Nile and Trafalgar. No new tactics were employed in either of those two victories. Both were the outcome of boldness and initiative in attack, and superior gunnery. Lord Keith, who had entered the Navy at the age of fifteen, had proved himself over nearly forty years of varied action and experience in the Seven Years' War, the American War of Independence, the Mediterranean, the South Atlantic and – during a period on half pay after the Treaty of Versailles – in ships of the East India Company on voyages to the Far East. However, he never had the opportunity to command a fleet in action.

St Vincent had certainly experienced a choice of difficulties – and in this case he had clearly taken the wrong option.

By 15 June, St Vincent was writing to Mr Nepean:

Sir,

At a moment so eventful, it is with inexpressible regret I acquaint you, for the information of the Lords Commissioners of the admiralty, that the rapid decline of my health compels me to avail myself of their lordships conditional permission to return to England; for to continue at this place, without a prospect of being soon able to conduct the fleet at sea, would cramp the operations and prove very injurious to his majesty's service. I have, therefore, transferred the command to Vice Admiral Lord Keith, with their lordships' secret instructions, and other unexecuted orders relative thereto; and on the arrival of the detachment from Lord Bridport's fleet and the necessary orders being given for its conduct in the defence of the island, during the absence of Lord Keith, it is my intention to proceed to Gibraltar, in his Majesty's ship the *Argo* and to wait there the arrival of the *Ville de Paris* or *Princess Royal* to convey me to England.

The following day he referred to 'a rapid decline of health, as to bereave me of all power both of body and mind', but it was not until August that he embarked for England in the *Princess Royal*.

Chapter Thirteen

Commander-in-Chief, Channel Fleet

Lord St Vincent retired to Rochetts to recover his health and await events. This time was overshadowed by the actions of Sir John Orde, but by October 1799, both the symptoms of dropsy and the row with Sir John had begun to subside. The Lords of the Admiralty were already considering how they could exploit their most experienced and professionally reliable flag officer.

In March 1800 he accepted command of the Channel fleet, over the head of a resentful Sir Alan Gardner, who became his second in command. Among his junior flag officers were Collingwood and Whitshed. St Vincent hoisted his flag in the *Ville de Paris*, at the head of a fleet consisting of forty sail of the line.

The position of Commander-in-Chief, Channel fleet, was a crucial one for Napoleon was still threatening to invade the British Isles. St Vincent declared of his appointment: 'The King and government require it, and the discipline of the British navy demands it. It is of no consequence to me whether I die afloat or ashore. The die is cast.'

In an attempt to rescue Nelson from his entanglement with Lady Hamilton, St Vincent contrived to have him appointed to the Channel fleet. Nelson had already asked to be released from his duties in the Mediterranean, unwilling to play second fiddle to Lord Keith. He arranged to travel to England overland in the company of the Hamiltons, ostensibly to look after them on the journey. By now St Vincent had reluctantly admitted to himself that Nelson's capacity for taking balanced decisions was seriously flawed and a disagreement arose between the two which threatened to disrupt a relationship which had been more like that between a father and favourite son than between two admirals serving in the same navy.

Despite St Vincent's disapproval, it was not Nelson's affair with Lady Hamilton which caused a rift between them, but money – prize money. In October 1799 valuable prizes had been taken in the trade routes off Cape Finisterre. Although not strictly within the area of St Vincent's command, the prizes had been taken by ships acting under his orders. Under the prevailing rules for prize money, once the Admiralty prize court had 'condemned' the prizes and established their value, the money was due for distribution in legally recognized shares between the officers and men of the ships which had made the captures and the flag officer under whose orders they were operating.

A large sum of money was at stake. In this case the flag officer's share depended upon whether or not St Vincent had handed over the command to Keith. Although St Vincent had handed over operational command to Keith in August, the Admiralty did not formally terminate his command until 25 November – after the captures were made. Keith had left the Mediterranean in pursuit of the French fleet, sailing as far north as Brest, temporarily delegating command in the Mediterranean to Nelson.

Directly the news of the captures reached the Mediterranean, Nelson put in a claim for the flag officer's share. It is questionable whether he had any rights at all. The overall command lay between St Vincent and Keith, while Nelson only exercised temporary operational command within the Mediterranean from a base 1,200 miles from the area where the prizes were taken; nor were the ships which took the prizes operating under his orders. Keith made no claim and remained strictly outside the argument.

St Vincent held back, initially. He was doubtful of his own rights and in any case did not wish to contend with his favoured protégé. The Admiralty authorities were unhelpful, considering it a borderline case – presumably between St Vincent and Keith. On the face of it, Nelson's claim was very weak and the naval authorities eventually persuaded St Vincent to put in a claim. He could not legally transfer his rights, but he made it clear that, if successful, he wished to give away his share – to whom is not clear. He told his secretary to contact the agents acting for Nelson and to give them every assistance.

Nelson, caught up in the extravagant social whirl of Palermo, badly needed money to supplement his pay, blind to the advice of friends and the criticisms of the unsympathetic. Illogically, he resented St Vincent's claim although it had only been lodged under Admiralty pressure. The old Admiral had only asked for an amicable arbitration to settle a point of law and had declared that he would not be retaining any money awarded to him.

Emma Hamilton was now carrying Nelson's child and once back in London society, his need for money was greater than ever. Nelson visited St Vincent but lacked the moral courage to discuss the dispute openly with him. St Vincent, uncomplicated, straight-forward and, perhaps, lacking intuition, did not understand the emotional tangle behind the problem. He wrote to a friend:

> I am persuaded there is a serpent lurking somewhere deter-mined to create a rupture between Lord Nelson and me. Entre nous, I suspect Lord Hood who has been an adviser throughout. I could discover by the manner of Lord Nelson when he was here that he felt he had injured me, but we parted good friends, and he owes all the fame, titles, badges and distinctions he wears to my patronage and protection, and I still continue kind to him in the extreme. I hardly think it possible he can break with me. He is vain and weak, therefore open to flattery and all its concomitants.

Nelson wrote to his agent just a few days later: 'I have frequent letters from the Earl but not a word of the lawsuit. So best. But we will not lessen our exertions to get justice and I am sure his agents are not less active in trying to deprive me of my right.'

A week or so later, he wrote again to his agent:

> The Earl is nothing to either of us in his private character; therefore if you choose to come here, do so. When I went to

the Earl yesterday you would have thought he would have overwhelmed me with civilities, nothing equal to me as an officer. I hope he says true, but I will not spare him an inch in the point of law, and I only hope he will never open the subject. If he does I am prepared with a broadside as strong (and backed with justice) as any he can send.

When, in due course, St Vincent became First Lord of the Admiralty, Nelson commented that the appointment 'will, I hope, give a new spur to our just cause'.

After his triumph in Copenhagen in 1801 he declared: 'Justice is all I want. My Commander-in-Chiefs run away with all the money I fight for; so let them. I am content with the honour: there they cannot get a scrap. But damn me if I suffer any man to swindle me out of my property whilst he is at his ease in England.' He was speaking of a man who had served through fifty-three years of active service, physical hardship, mortal risk, crushing responsibility and bodily infirmity. Nelson was forty-three.

Surprisingly, Nelson won the lawsuit. Far from being magnanimous, he complained about the prize money and medals awarded after Copenhagen and at being kept with the Channel fleet until the peace of 1802 , declaring: 'I am used and abused and so far from making money I am spending the little I have.'

If Lord St Vincent was concerned at the deterioration of his relationship with Nelson, he had much else to occupy him. He was appalled by the state of discipline in many ships of the Channel fleet, and told Nepean: 'I could relate such atrocious proceedings in some of the ships that would make your hair stand on end.'

To Lord Spencer he wrote: 'You cannot conceive how few men are qualified to command ships of the line as they ought to be.'

He particularly objected to ships' captains bypassing him and communicating direct with the Admiralty. To Spencer he wrote: 'If your Lordship does not put an extinguisher upon the gossiping correspondence carried on between your Neptunes on the Board and the officers of every description in the squadron, neither I nor any other person who may be thought fitter for the purpose can command it.'

St Vincent was now under greater pressure of interference from London, and shortages of material than he had been in the Mediterranean. He was only separated from authority by the time it took for the mechanical telegraph to pass a signal, or a relay of horsemen to cover the 200 miles from London to Tor Abbey. He based himself there in January 1801, exercising command over-looking Tor Bay, when dropsy forced him to give his own health priority over his perceived need to be at sea with the fleet.

One of St Vincent's very first acts on assuming command was to issue the same strict disciplinary orders that he had enforced in the Mediterranean. Significantly, a toast had been proposed at Lord Bridport's table before St Vincent's appointment: 'May the discipline of the Mediterranean never be introduced into the Channel fleet.' Lord Bridport sat silent.

The behaviour of Sir Alan Gardner – the previous C-in-C, now second in command – had been outrageous. At first he had refused to hand over orders, signal books or 'official means of any kind'. It took the Admiralty five months to remove him.

Among new orders particularly resented by officers were these: the captain of the ship which had the guard must be present on shore night and day while the fleet was watering, to prevent desertions or disruptive behaviour; no boat should be away from its parent ship after sunset; no officer ashore on day leave was to go more than 3 miles from the landing place; and, causing particular indignation, no officer was to sleep ashore. The Admiral was aware of the disruptive effect of allowing officers to remain ashore overnight while the seamen and marines were not. He had received a moderately framed petition from the marines to this effect and he held them in high regard for their loyalty and discipline. He was adamant that officers should not enjoy fundamental privileges which were denied to those they commanded and equally he insisted that officers must totally fulfil the obligations of their rank: for example, captains were expected to be on deck when their ships were manoeuvring and not to delegate the responsibility to a junior. St Vincent was accustomed to appear on deck to satisfy himself that they did so.

The Commander-in-Chief gathered round him as many as he could of his Mediterranean captains and colleagues, in preference to 'the old women, some of them in the shape of young men, I am burthened with'. To a friend he wrote: 'There was a kind of tacit engagement that any interference of mine with the interior economy of the respective ships of the squadron should be resisted.'

He told Lord Spencer 'I will not be deterred from doing my duty by the ill-humour of individuals. I will be obeyed.' Fortunately he had some subordinates on whom he could utterly rely, such as Thompson, Saumarez and Foley, although some of his junior flag officers had threatened to haul down their flags if any of his nominees were appointed.

Although St Vincent condoned punishments of extreme severity when naval regulations authorized them, he made prodigious and sustained efforts to make good food, suitable clothing and proper medical care available to the least of the ordinary seamen. He awarded silver and bronze medals, which he paid for himself, for 'Uncommon merit . . . in resisting the wiles of mutinous spirits in the Channel Fleet and the blandishments and revilings of the courtesans at Plymouth and Portsmouth.'

He appointed his own physician, Dr Baird, as surgeon to the flagship and medical adviser to the whole fleet. This was an unpopular move both with surgeons in the fleet and officials of the Admiralty's Medical Board, but the combination of his persistence and Dr Baird's competence won over the Admiralty, who bypassed the Medical Board and offered to pay Dr Baird as Physician to the Fleet. Dr Baird wisely declined the offer, though St Vincent described him as 'the most valuable man in the Navy'.

St Vincent had found the sick quarters at Brixham and Dartmouth completely unsatisfactory and wrote to Spencer: 'I conclude neither my great predecessor, Lord Howe, nor the more immediate one, Lord Bridport, considered an inquiry into the state of these sick quarters, and shameful mode of transporting the patients to them, any part of their duty, or the evil could not have existed for such a length of time.'

He set up an inspectorate, telling Lord Spencer: 'I may be considered as travelling out of the pale of my duty. Humanity has dictated it and I am sure I shall stand excused with your Lordship, however much I may be condemned by others.'

Lord St Vincent appreciated that health and good medical care were fundamental to morale and discipline. He was a passionate exponent of good ventilation, avoidance of damp and dirt – and of curtailing the seamen's activities ashore. He urged officers to set a good example and to 'prevent, by whatever possible means, the profligate and abandoned life the crews of the Channel fleet have been and still are, in the habit of leading when in port, their only gratification being in getting beastly drunk with ardent spirits in the lowest brothels. From whence they return to their ships with their blood in a state to receive every disorder arising out of such practices.'

The success of St Vincent's strict measures could soon be observed in an improvement in conduct, health and efficiency. Within a few weeks of taking up his post he was able to report: 'This fleet, which when I came to it was at the lowest ebb of wretched and miserable discipline, is now above mediocrity.'

It was with this fleet that St Vincent had to counteract Napoleon's unquenchable fountain of ambition by preventing the escape of the French fleet from Brest. He tightened the blockade to make it impenetrable. The blockading fleet was increased from fifteen sail of the line to thirty, with five of them anchored between the Black Rocks at Porquette shore, just 10 miles from the harbour entrance, while frigates and cutters patrolled the Goulet. The main fleet was deployed off Ushant, where from two to four ships of the line cruised off the southern entrance to the Passage du Raz and others cruised the Bay of Biscay to intercept communications between the port and the outside world. They kept station off Brest for 121 days without a break through the summer of 1800. The strain on men and ships was immense and mutterings against St Vincent continual. Despite this, when the fleet returned to Torbay in November, there were only sixteen cases for the hospital. St Vincent wrote to Lord Spencer: 'I am at my wit's end to meet every shift, evasion and neglect of duty. Seven-eighths of the captains who comprise this fleet are practising every subterfuge to get into harbour for the winter.'

The threat of lower-deck mutiny lingered on. On 17 March 1800, the crew of *Danae* had taken her into Brest and handed her over to the French.

Although the British fleet had little to show for it, except wear and tear, the blockade was having its effect. As the forty-eight French and Spanish ships of the line ran short of stores and ammunition, their crews' morale deteriorated and their standards of seamanship and fighting efficiency declined through lack of exercise and practice. The primitive French road network was incapable of keeping the fleet supplied from landward, while coastal trade had been strangled by the blockade. It was not until after St Vincent had based himself on shore that a French squadron did make its escape. Sir Robert Calder followed with seven ships of the line, but lost them and they were able to reach Toulon.

Orders from Napoleon to the combined fleets to put to sea were simply ignored, but he contrived to form an alliance with the Baltic powers, Denmark among them, which between them had a potential fleet of 123 line-of-battle ships and twenty-five frigates. By this alliance he hoped to outflank the British. He was later to admit that it was the strict blockade of Brest which forced him to come to terms with the government in London. By November, following the expiry of the Austrian armistice and the defeat of the Austrian Army at Hohenlinden, Britain faced France virtually alone.

St Vincent was wearied with the continual strain and pressure of command. Stalemate had been reached: France seemed invincible on land while Britain ruled the seas. He wrote a surprising letter to his sister in which he advocated 'Dropping the farce of preparation for carrying on the war with vigour . . . negotiating a peace . . . and the more colonies we give up, both in the East and West Indies, with the single exception of Ceylon . . . the better.'

On 3 February 1801, William Pitt resigned as Prime Minister and was succeeded by Henry Addington, later Lord Sidmouth. Many of Pitt's colleagues resigned with him, including Lord Spencer. The threat facing the country was formidable. The Northern League of Armed Neutrals was formed to prevent their ships being boarded by the British Navy in their attempts to prevent trade with France. When Addington invited St Vincent to succeed Spencer as First Lord of the Admiralty, he reluctantly accepted the invitation and took office on 20 February 1801. The opportunity to tackle the ineptitude of the victualling and supply functions of the Admiralty, to have a leading role in maritime strategy and in the appointment of senior officers, and to combat the appalling corruption in the bureaucratic machine and the royal dockyards – that was a challenge he simply could not refuse. It was as well for Great Britain that he did accept the challenge. If he had not done so, the Navy would have been ill prepared to face the combined fleets of France and Spain in 1805 and Napoleon's chances of successfully invading the British Isles would have been dangerously enhanced.

Chapter Fourteen

First Lord of the Admiralty

The first year of St Vincent's tenure as First Lord of the Admiralty was one of onerous responsibility, frustration and ill health, brightened only by three victories in which he played an important strategic role, and the appointment of Nelson as second-in-command to the Channel fleet. In March 1802, the Treaty of Amiens was signed after nine years of war between Great Britain and France, but the British Navy still had to be kept ready for action.

St Vincent began the campaign which would become his greatest contribution to the nation at large and to the Royal Navy in particular: an unfaltering, sustained campaign to eradicate nepotism and corruption from the Admiralty, the royal dockyards and the Navy as a whole. In doing so he may have proved unfair to a few individuals, and sometimes to have put economy before efficiency, but nobody and nothing from royalty to bodily weakness could deter him from the assault on the evils which he perceived to be threatening his country and weakening his service.

There was no element of personal greed or ambition in the campaign. He was already wealthy, well-established at the top of his profession and in government. He could simply have sat back, enjoyed the fruits of his labours and concentrated on recovering his health, but his conscience would not allow it. What he held dearest was threatened by Napoleon's ambition from without and by corruption from within.

William Pitt had resigned after eighteen continuous years as Prime Minister, mainly because of opposition to his plans for Catholic emancipation. His successor, Henry Addington, proved to be neither a competent nor popular Prime Minister.

At the time of St Vincent's appointment the Admiralty's structure was very different from today. The First Lord did not have absolute control over the Navy. He controlled the Board of Admiralty, but it had to compete with the Navy Board and its Comptroller who was appointed by royal patent and with the Board of Ordnance headed by the Master-General. The two latter boards controlled supply of the Navy's stores, material, guns and ammunition. The First Lord's position might be compared to the trainer in a large racing stables with no control over fodder, bedding, harness, saddlery – or even when to call the vet. St Vincent was convinced that the power of the Navy Board had to be broken, that the Admiralty must have control over ships' armaments and supplies, and that 'nothing short of a radical sweep in the dockyards could cure the evils and corruptions within them; and this cannot be attempted until we have peace.' That is possibly the main reason why, when negotiations for peace were finally opened later in 1801, he was willing to support terms less advantageous to Britain than might have been expected.

The Admiral received many letters of congratulation on his elevation to the supreme position in his profession but he was restrained in his reactions. For example he wrote to Lord Keith, still Commander-in-Chief in the Mediterranean: 'Your friends will have told you how I came here. What sort of figure I shall make will be seen. I have known many a good admiral make a wretched First Lord of the admiralty. I will, however, support Commanders-in-Chief upon all occasions, and prohibit any intrigue against them in this Office.'

He noted in a letter to the Duke of Northumberland: 'A thousand thanks to your Grace for the interest you take in my appointment to this Board, where I hope to be some use in stopping, if not radically reforming, the flagrant abuses which pervade the naval service, both civil and military.'

St Vincent's Board of Admiralty comprised seven men: two other naval officers, Captain Sir Thomas Trowbridge and Captain John

Markham, and four civilians: Sir Philip Stephens, the Hon. William Elliot, James Adams and William Garthshore, all government appointed. They were served by Evan Nepean as First Secretary and by William Marsden as Second Secretary.

When he arrived at the Admiralty in February, St Vincent was faced with the paramount need to assemble an effective Channel fleet to counter not only Napoleon's threat, but a new threat from the Baltic where the League of Armed Neutrality had been revived. There was a chronic shortage of seamen and many of the ships of the line desperately needed refit and repair, but it was the bottleneck in the dockyards, due to inefficiency and corruption, which caused most of the delays. Shipwrights, the key men, were taking advantage of the threat from France to demand higher pay and to organize strikes. Delegates from the royal dockyards, expecting to meet the gentlemanly Lord Spencer, were met instead by the uncompromising Lord St Vincent. When the delegates turned down the Admiral's offer of increased rations for their families because the price of bread was unwarrantably high, he dismissed them, sacked the leaders from their jobs and threatened instant dismissal of anybody who sought to extort concessions by intimidation.

Vice Admiral Nelson was appointed as second in command of the Channel fleet on 17 January – a month before St Vincent took office at the Admiralty. Strangely it was St Vincent who had previously recommended Admiral Sir Hyde Parker as 'the only man to face them' – referring presumably to the League of Armed Neutrality comprising Denmark, Sweden, Russia and Prussia. St Vincent's failure to nominate Lord Nelson for the overall command can only have been due to one of two reasons – or perhaps both: that Nelson's emotional state was unsuitable or that the appointment of a newly promoted vice admiral over the heads of his seniors would have caused an outcry. Perhaps St Vincent was aware that Nelson, in the heat of battle, would unhesitatingly attack the enemy and this, of course is what eventually happened at Copenhagen. The story of Nelson turning his blind eye to Parker's signal to withdraw is well known to every British school child.

Denmark had the strongest fleet in the Baltic League and it was believed that defeat of her navy would neutralize the involvement of the other three members and disrupt the League. To attack the Danish fleet in the harbour of Copenhagen was a government decision in which St Vincent was a prime mover. He ordered the Channel fleet to assemble at Yarmouth and to prepare to sail at the first opportunity.

Sir Hyde Parker's flagship arrived in Yarmouth on 10 March. A ball was being arranged by his young wife and Sir Hyde was in no hurry to leave. Nelson wrote to his friend Trowbridge, complaining at the delay. When St Vincent heard of this, he wrote to Sir Hyde Parker on 11 March saying: 'Any delay in your sailing would do you an irreparable injury.' Sir Hyde immediately issued orders to prepare his fleet of fifteen line-of-battle ships, four frigates and a brig to put to sea the following day.

The Battle of Copenhagen has been described many times, one of the best descriptions being contained in *Nelson's Band of Brothers* by Ludovic Kennedy. Of the eighteen Danish ships anchored in the King's Channel, only three escaped entirely. The rest were either sunk, blown up, taken and burned, or captured. The outcome was the disintegration of the League of Baltic States. It took several days for news of how the victory had been achieved to reach the Admiralty but when it did, St Vincent decided to recall Hyde Parker and leave Nelson in command. He wrote to Nelson: 'Your Lordship's whole conduct from your first appointment to this hour is the subject of our constant admiration. It does not become me to make comparisons: all agree there is but one Nelson.' Sir Hyde Parker had been hoping for a peerage but did not receive one. He was, however, spared a public inquiry or court martial.

Before the Battle of Copenhagen, the First Lord had written letters which encapsulated the policy he intended to adhere to through thick and thin in regard to promotions. He had announced on his appointment that he would fill vacancies with the most suitable and efficient men he could find and would 'pay no regard to the recommendations of any person whatever'.

To Sir Charles Grey at the Admiralty he wrote:

Lieutenant K has been playing a game to get to Ireland, which has lowered him very much in my opinion. He is brave and enterprising, but, like the rest of the Aristocracy, thinks he has from that circumstance a right to promotion in prejudice to men of better services and superior merit, which I never will submit to. Having refused the Prince of Wales, Duke of Clarence, Duke of Kent and Duke of Cumberland, you will not be surprised that I repeat the impossibility of departing from any principle which would let in such inundation upon me as would tend to complete the ruin of the Navy.

To Rear Admiral Duckworth he suggested:

Allow me as an old friend to caution you against giving an order to act in a vacancy, to any person who has not duly served his time and regularly passed the examination for a lieutenant, in all forms. The Board has come to a strong resolution on this subject and such a proceeding will be a bar to promotion afterwards. The inroads and abuses which have crept into every department of the Navy require a strong hand to crush: regardless as I am of the unpopularity which attaches upon all attempts to correct abuses, I am determined to support the Board, *coute que coute* in every strong measure which it is judged fit to take, whenever these evils present (which God knows happen frequently) and by that means lay a foundation for my successor to restore the Navy to its pristine vigour.

Very soon after the Battle of Copenhagen, Lord Nelson asked to be recalled from the Baltic for reasons of health. St Vincent replied: 'To find a proper successor is no easy task; for I never saw the man in our profession, excepting yourself and Trowbridge, who possessed the magic art of infusing the same spirit in others.'

The successor finally appointed was the reliable Admiral Pole and on 19 June Nelson sailed for England as a passenger in the brig *Kite*. Almost simultaneously St Vincent despatched Rear Admiral Sir James Saumarez from England with five ships of the line on a secret mission, with orders that were not to be opened until they reached the latitude of Cadiz.

The eye of the First Lord of the Admiralty was not only on the Baltic and the latitude of Cadiz, but also on the eastern

Mediterranean where, early in March, Admiral Lord Keith anchored his fleet and the transports carrying General Abercromby's troops in Aboukir Bay. In a model combined operation all the troops were landed in a single day. The French Army was decisively defeated and pursued to Alexandria, although Abercromby himself was severely wounded and brought back to Keith's flagship *Foudroyant* where he died of his wounds. On 2 September, the French would capitulate and Alexandria surrender. St Vincent was able to note the second victory with naval involvement since he became First Lord of the Admiralty. At last there was some light on the horizon, although a blot appeared when the *Swiftsure*, Captain Hallowell, was captured in the Mediterranean after a gallant action against four French line-of-battle ships.

Meanwhile Napoleon Bonaparte, desperately hoping to win back Egypt, was endeavouring to assemble a combined French and Spanish fleet in Cadiz. Three French ships of the line left Toulon and headed for the straits of Gibraltar – called The Gut in naval slang because it was so difficult to sail through from the Atlantic. St Vincent had received intelligence of this move: the reason for sending Sir James Saumarez south under secret orders.

En route from Toulon to The Gut, the three French ships captured the brig *Speedy*, commanded by Captain Lord Cochrane, after a gallant rearguard action. When Cochrane finally hauled down his colours and went on board the *Dessaix* to present his sword to Captain Palliere, the Frenchman refused, saying he would not take the sword of an officer 'who had for so many hours struggled against impossibility'. Cochrane became an involuntary witness in the subsequent battle in the Bay of Algeciras to the west of Gibraltar. St Vincent had previously written to the Governor of Gibraltar: 'Sir James Saumarez will, I trust, be able to counter whatever plan of operations may be in contemplation at Cadiz.'

The three French warships were anchored under the guns of Algeciras, on the west side of the bay, when Saumarez's squadron approached from the Atlantic, handicapped by light winds. In the fierce ensuing action the three French ships, badly mauled, had to cut their cables and drift inshore. Lord Cochrane, who was later exchanged for a French officer of similar rank, was in Captain Palliere's cabin when a British cannon ball whistled through it, breaking glass and china. Of the British ships, one had to be towed out of action, one grounded and struck her colours, and the remainder of the squadron had to break off the action before retiring to Gibraltar harbour because, in the absence of any wind, they could hardly manoeuvre. Although French casualties were double the British, and the junction of the French and Spanish squadrons had been foiled, it could not yet be termed a victory.

The French Admiral sent a message overland to Cadiz for a reinforcement of six ships of the line. They sailed from Cadiz on 9 July and anchored in Algeciras Bay while the British ships were busy repairing their damaged hulls and rigging and preparing to renew the battle against a squadron double their number and three times their firepower. Action was renewed that night. Two of the Spanish ships were blown up and a third captured before Saumarez decided he could do no more and, assembling his scattered squadron, returned to Gibraltar.

St Vincent reacted with delight – a third victory to celebrate, if only a small one. 'I knew it, I knew it. I knew the man. I knew what he could do. It is the most daring thing that has been done this war. It is the first thing. I knew it would be so!'

To Saumarez himself he wrote: 'The astonishing efforts made to refit the crippled ships at Gibraltar Mole surpasses everything of the kind within my experience and the final success in making so great an impression on the very superior force of the enemy crowns the whole.'

French and Spanish casualties had been more than 3,000 – many of them passengers: women and children. Not only had the action scuppered Napoleon's plan to return to Egypt, but it also caused a significant rift between Spain and France.

Lord St Vincent had taken his seat in the House of Lords for the first time on 16 April when he moved a vote of thanks, in extravagant terms, to Lord Nelson and the officers and men of the ships under his command for the destruction of the Danish fleet at Copenhagen. He appeared again on 30 October to move a vote of thanks to Sir James Saumarez for his 'noble and gallant exploits on 12 July'.

St Vincent spoke in favour of the terms agreed for peace with France, claiming the terms were honourable and advantageous to

Great Britain, obtaining 'two of the most valuable islands in the whole world, whether considered in a political or commercial point of view – Ceylon and Trinidad'. His strategic thinking was that France should be confined to the European continent by a combination of enforced neutrality in the Baltic and British command of the seas from the North Sea to the Mediterranean, and from Gibraltar, by way of Malta, to Alexandria.

St Vincent understood that Napoleon only wanted peace to give himself breathing space to build up his army, his navy and his diplomatic network, but the First Lord of the Admiralty also desperately wanted peace to tackle corruption in the dockyards and to repair the ravages suffered by Britain's Navy in nine long years of storm-blast, blockade and battle. For the sake of national morale – and for his own peace of mind – he wanted Nelson in command of the fleet protecting the most vulnerable coasts of the British Isles, and he wanted the Navy to comprise sound and seaworthy ships of the line and frigates, well manned, well armed and well exercised – not William Pitt's idea of swarms of little gunboats to attack Napoleon's landing craft as they conveyed his troops to the British shores. Few questioned the French dictator's ambitions and intentions, but there was a chasm between the views of the fighting admirals who believed that any attempt at invasion could be defeated out at sea by a well-handled fleet of ships of the line, and the adherents of William Pitt's untried strategic theory that the way to defeat an invading force was by attacking it with gunboats and repelling it with shore-based artillery and infantry drawn up along the shoreline.

It was fortunate for Great Britain that Pitt had resigned as Prime Minister, that St Vincent had been appointed First Lord of the Admiralty and that Nelson had survived to command the fleet at sea. The government unwisely used the peace which followed the Treaty of Amiens to run down the country's militia, to build static coastal defences such as Martello towers and to pursue a pointless argument: line-of-battle ships versus flotillas of little gunboats.

Chapter Fifteen

The Battle against Corruption

Vice Admiral Lord Nelson, though a brilliant tactician, did not grasp the importance of the command allocated to him by the First Lord in 1801. He accepted it with reluctance, contemptuously referring to it as 'this boat business'. St Vincent wrote to Lord Keith:

> It is unfortunately the fashion of this day for many of our brethren to look to the right and left instead of that straightforward conduct which used to form the characteristic of the profession. When we meet I shall astonish your Lordship with the miserable attempts which have been made to give an unfavourable impression of the arrangements for the defences of the coast.

He tried to persuade Nelson that his presence was essential for reasons of morale: 'the country at large derive so much confidence from your Lordship being at the head of our home defence, that apprehension seems to be dispelled from the public mind . . . I differ with your Lordship *in toto* as to the importance of the command you fill.'

He urged him in no circumstances to relinquish it, but Nelson was not convinced and wrote to his agent: 'I am trying to get rid of my command, but I am forced to hold it, to keep the merchants easy till hostilities cease in the Channel. I must submit for I do not wish to quarrel with the very great folks at the Admiralty.'

181

After making two less than successful attacks on gunboats at Boulogne, he reported: 'The craft which I have seen I do not think it possible to row to England, and sail they cannot.'

Nelson had been given the added responsibility of organizing the Sea Fencibles, composed of fishermen and others with sea experience who had volunteered to serve in an emergency, but who naturally put their own livelihoods first and were unreliable.

It is true that the fleet Nelson commanded consisted mostly of frigates and gunboats, because the line-of-battle ships were employed in blockading Brest and the continental North Sea and Channel ports. He never accepted that the threat of invasion by Napoleon was a serious one.

The cessation of hostilities with France was proclaimed on 12 October 1801, although the Treaty of Amiens was not actually signed for another five months. As negotiations continued St Vincent was among the guests at a dinner party given by the Prime Minister, the principal guest being the French negotiator General Lauriston. St Vincent assured him that he had 'immediately ordered packet boats to be despatched to all quarters of the globe to cause hostilities to cease; that the least delay might occasion the death of multitudes of men: and that civilized Europe had suffered too much during this long war'.

He wrote to the Earl of Uxbridge that he considered the peace to be the very best the country had ever made, and regarded it as the 'happiest event of my life to have contributed to so great a blessing'. There had been considerable anxiety that if Thomas Jefferson was re-elected as President of the United States, that country would have entered the war on the side of France. The peace came before the election, but the newly elected President complained to Congress about 'the great depredations on the commerce of the United States by British cruisers'. St Vincent's view was set out in a letter to the American Minister in Lisbon: 'It is no less my duty than disposition, to cultivate the good understanding so necessary to the happiness and prosperity of both our countries.'

Despite this, he was still concerned at the continuing efforts by both American consuls and the captains of American ships to persuade or bribe British sailors and soldiers to desert to the American flag. It was therefore an embarrassment to him to have to apologize humbly to the Minister when a press-gang from the British frigate *Diana* boarded American ships in the Tagus and forcibly pressed British members of their crews.

Peace may have brought relief to a nervous government and cabinet, but to St Vincent it brought very little respite. He still had to fight his corner against the 'small boat' defence faction; to cope with a disgruntled Nelson, to parry requests for preferential treatment for individuals and, above all, he had to grapple with the poisonous dragon of corruption which tyrannized both the Admiralty bureaucracy and the dockyards. The shining armour of the old knight was creaking and rusting a bit, but his sword was burnished and as sharp as ever, and his shield a bond of consistency and integrity.

Amongst his problems was that of oversupply of middle-rank officers. The circumstances of the war had resulted in a huge list of post-captains and commanders, exceeding by far the availability of posts for them.

He wrote to Lord Keith on 4 September 1801:

> The list of Post-Captains and Commanders so far exceeds that of ships and sloops, I cannot consistently with what is due to the public and to the incredible number of meritorious persons of those classes upon half-pay, promote except upon very extraordinary occasions, such as that of Lord Cochrane and Captain Dundas, who have the rank of Post-Captain; nor can I confirm any of the appointments made by Commanders-in-Chief upon foreign stations, except the vacancies are occasioned by death or the sentences of Courts Martial; and as your squadron must be considerably reduced in strength of men by the very hard services in Egypt, it will be advisable not to commission any captured ship or vessel that is not very eligible.

St Vincent continued his fight for the welfare of his men and their families. He petitioned the government with a scheme to pension 'the widows and children of sea officers slain in fight with the enemy, and the widows of those who die a natural death'.

To overcome the crippling shortage of suitable timber in the royal dockyards, he started negotiations with the East India

Company, involving the Secretary for War, Henry Dundas, to have ships for the Navy built in Bombay. The idea was to freight them to England with cotton, then fit them out as warships – unfortunately the ships ordered as a result were found to be unsatisfactory on delivery.

In July 1801, the trial took place of two officials responsible for naval stores. In summing up, the Attorney-General stated, 'the depredations upon the King's naval stores did not annually amount to less than £500,000' (many millions in today's terms). He referred to direct theft but went on to say that losses from waste, carelessness, extravagance and misuse were much greater. The Board of Admiralty was the source of that information.

Throughout his time in office, the First Lord continued with almost unbroken consistency to refuse to accept unsolicited recommendations for appointments or promotion. He stated:

> It is my fixed determination to fill all vacant offices with the most efficient men I can find, and to pay no regard to the recommendations of any person whatever, where the qualification of the candidate will not bear me out in the appointment . . . As the Father of the Service I cannot travel out of this record except in very extraordinary cases.

His firmness extended to resisting the blandishments of the aristocracy. He wrote to HRH The Duke of Clarence on 7 May 1801:

> It is therefore very painful to have to state to Your Royal Highness that, although all the persons in the Transport Board agree with me that a more amiable or virtuous man does not exist, yet no one who is, or has been, a member of that Board, will say that Mr W. is by any means capable of fulfilling the duties of his present employment. This being unfortunately the case, I fear it will not be in my power to appoint him a Clerk of the Cheque of a Dock Yard, as under the new regulation a person filling that office ought to possess a degree of precision and energy not to be found in Mr W., and without these endowments the corruption and abuses, which are very much attributed to that department, never can be rooted out.

On being approached by HRH the Duke of Kent about a Mr R. he said:

> If Mr R. had any claim on the naval service I should perhaps have felt the propriety of giving way in the gratification of any private views to favour the wishes of his Royal Highness, but Mr R. is not a person under such circumstances; and, besides, it is not a seemly thing to place a gentleman who has contrived to get rid of a handsome fortune and who, it may reasonably be supposed, is not a man of business, to execute the duties of the office, with advantage to the public.

St Vincent was no less rigorous in his approach to workers at the royal naval dockyards. He emphasized to a dockyard commissioner the importance of appointing the most capable men as master shipwrights without reference to seniority or influence of any kind, and warned against taking the word of the person's teacher or advocate.

Throughout his time at the Admiralty, St Vincent continued to correspond with his old friend, Sir Charles Grey, with whom he had served on the Commission on Dockyard Fortifications in 1785–6 and as joint Commanders-in-Chief in the West Indies operation. Their letters ranged over a wide variety of subjects, including matters of health, the career of Sir Charles's son, cabinet appointments, the joint operations of Lord Keith and General Abercromby in Egypt, and the invention of a lifeboat by a Mr Greathead.

Although St Vincent had supported the terms of the Treaty of Amiens, it appeared to opponents of the government that Addington had been politically outmanoeuvred by Napoleon and had ceded most of his best bargaining counters: former French possessions in India, Africa, the East and West Indies and the Mediterranean, won by British arms, were won back by French diplomacy. Minorca, Corsica and Elba had been evacuated and even Malta had been ceded back to the Knights of St John, and the Cape of Good Hope to the Dutch. In return Britain had obtained the restoration of Egypt to Turkish rule, a guarantee of Portuguese territorial integrity and a promise to withdraw

French garrisons from south Italian ports. Although both St Vincent and Nelson had given public support to the government, privately Nelson wrote: 'There is no person rejoiced more in the Peace than I do but I would sooner burst than let a damned Frenchman know it.'

The French would later renege on almost all their promises and undertakings – to Napoleon the peace was a device to allow him to renew preparations for war.

The First Lord of the Admiralty cared nothing for popularity. He forced through a Parliamentary Commission of enquiry into corruption in the royal dockyards and, in anticipation, ordered all the dockyard books to be 'secured' against tampering before embarking on a thorough inspection of all the yards – something which had been contemplated but postponed for a decade. Meanwhile he imposed a regime of ruthless economy. Unreliable dockyard workers were dismissed, doubtful contracts withdrawn and surplus or defective stores sold off – some to French agents. The French meantime were replenishing their arsenals and planning to build twenty-five ships of the line per annum. Napoleon considered the British to be indolent, luxury-loving and effete. He knew that British sea power was the only barrier between himself and the world power he sought.

One of Lord St Vincent's first steps in his campaign to remove that colossal obstruction to improvement of Britain's defences represented by the royal dockyards, was to arrange for the transfer of key contracts to merchants' yards. On 20 August 1802, the Board of Admiralty approved the following Minute:

> The Lords taking into their consideration the extraordinary Expences incurred in the several Dock and Rope Yards, beyond what was known in any former period of war, in proportion to the number of ships employed; and having received Reports from various quarters of flagrant abuses and mismanagement existing in the several Departments, which there is reason to believe are but too well founded: and being determined as far as in them lies to discover and remedy the same, do judge it expedient forthwith to visit all His Majesty's Dock and Rope Yards, to examine into the conduct and

186

ability of the Officers, the sufficiency of the Workmen, the condition of the Ships and Magazines, together with the Works carrying on, in order that such Reforms and Improvements may be made as shall be found advisable to prevent an unnecessary expenditure of the Public Money; to see that the several rules and orders for the government of the Yards are duly enforced, that the ships and vessels of the Royal Navy are kept in constant readiness for service, and that the money granted by Parliament for keeping up the same is wisely and frugally expended; and they think proper to direct that the Comptroller and 3 other Members of the Navy Board do attend them in their visitation.

The Board left London the very same day and arrived in Weymouth on 22 August. Over the following eight weeks a comprehensive and conscientious inspection was made of all the naval installations between Plymouth and the Thames estuary, including Woolwich and Deptford, taking in ships, dockyards, anchorages, victualling offices, storehouses, timber stocks, rope yards, barracks and naval hospitals.

On 16 October the Board, having considered the Minutes of their tour of inspection and all the relevant correspondence, 'unanimously decided to transmit a complete Minute to the Navy Board together with a letter signifying their disapproval and reprimanding them for the same; as, by their failure in the execution of their duty, the Public has been suffered to be defrauded to a very considerable amount, and delinquencies passed unpublished.' It was signed individually by every member of the Board. A lengthy, but unsatisfactory, answer was sent by the Navy Board on 15 November, but the Secretary of the Admiralty replied on 26 November stating that Their Lordships 'did not form the resolution upon the neglects and abuses referred to in their said Minutes, without full and mature consideration of all the circumstances which related to them; and that they do not perceive any reasons set forth in your justification which should induce them to alter the sentiments expressed upon that occasion.'

William Pitt, in 1804, accused the Board of Admiralty under St Vincent of weakening the Royal Navy. This is belied by the fact that in November 1802, the King's Speech had enumerated the improvements in the force: 207 warships (compared with 115 in 1786), including 35 sail of the line in commission (compared with 23 in 1792) and 50,000 seamen (compared with 18,000 in 1792). During the debate on the Navy Estimates that October, Captain Markham had defended the Board of Admiralty against criticisms that it had dismissed large numbers of workers from the royal dockyards:

> Many men certainly had been discharged; but not one who was not either disabled by age from useful service, or from habitual inattention to duty, seemed unworthy of employment; or, from some acts of criminal misconduct, rendered much fitter objects for the severity of the law than for the lenient punishment of mere dismissal. But he could assure the Hon. Member, so far from the artificers and deserving men having been dismissed or maltreated, the good men were particularly sought out and rewarded; and more Artificers had received permanent provision than had ever before been usual. The full effect of those arrangements had not yet time to be matured; but he was convinced, when it was felt in the extent, it would be highly satisfactory. It was true that many of the Caulkers were dismissed, but it was for a conspiracy to raise their wages in time of Peace to the full war allowance, and for abetting another conspiracy of a similar kind in the service of the Merchants and Shipowners which must have been felt with extreme injury to the Commerce of the Country ... He felt it his duty to say this in vindication of the Noble admiral who had exercised the authority vested in him with respect to the dockyards, from charges that were either totally unfounded or misrepresented.

A common excuse for failing to execute a necessary transaction had been that the key individual had not been 'hampered', meaning that he had not been given a hamper of wine or some other such bribe. Eight months before Trafalgar, in February 1805, St Vincent would write a private and confidential letter to his friend Benjamin Travers:

I have, by means of the Commission of Inquiry, exposed the profligate waste and plunder of the public treasure, in the civil department of the navy. I hope there is sufficient virtue in the two Houses of Parliament to punish great delinquents and to enact laws to put a stop to their crimes. Unless there is, the country will not stagger long under the iniquitous weight of these blood-sucking leeches. All the sluices of corruption have been opened since I retired from the Admiralty.

Chapter Sixteen

Reconstruction – or Destruction

It is difficult to assess the balance between the positive and negative aspects of St Vincent's reign as First Lord. In the short term he may have weakened the fighting strength of the Royal Navy, but in the longer term his reforms were salutary and essential. After the signing of the Treaty of Amiens he was responsible for disbanding the Sea Fencibles, for paying off 40,000 seamen, for reducing the number of line-of-battle ships by half and dismissing thousands of dockyard workers. It is fair to suggest that if somebody had not tackled the dockyard corruption, the profligate and uncontrolled naval expenditure and the poor quality of ship construction, the war against Napoleon, which continued for nine years after the Battle of Trafalgar, would never have been won. It is equally fair to suggest that if the appalling problems in the dockyards had been tackled less precipitately and more gradually and methodically the same results might have been achieved at less cost – but that was not St Vincent's way. Nobody, from today's historical perspective, would doubt his complete integrity, moral courage and single-minded determination to put things right. His objectives were unexceptionable, his method and timing perhaps questionable.

The inspection of dockyards had uncovered a cesspit of inefficiency and corruption: no proper accounts kept of income and expenditure; repeated payments for the same piece of work; payment of 'extras' (overtime) for work not performed; irregular mustering of employees and stocktaking; and appropriation of stores for personal use. St Vincent wrote to Nepean: 'I am sorry to tell you that Chatham dockyard appears by what we have seen today a viler sink of corruption than my imagination ever formed. Portsmouth was bad enough but this beggars all description.'

The Admiral considered the only appropriate action was to form a Parliamentary Commission to investigate the dockyards and report to the House of Commons. He wrote to the Prime Minister in August 1802: 'We find abuses to such an extent as would require many months to go thoroughly into and the absolute necessity of a Commission of Enquiry to expose them appears to the Admiralty Board here in a much stronger light than ever.' When the Cabinet rejected his proposal, St Vincent threatened to resign as First Lord and to cease to sit in the House of Lords. The Commission was duly appointed.

In due course the Commission made twelve reports which resulted in termination of the system of piecework and contracting. The dockyards were finally brought under direct Admiralty control, which unromantic conclusion was perhaps the First Lord's most important contribution to the Royal Navy in the years preceding Trafalgar. He had been given the close and loyal support of Trowbridge and Markham throughout the difficult months.

It is not surprising that these reforms engendered unpopularity proportionate to the depth of corruption. The system was so deeply entrenched that it had become a way of life and its interruption deprived many of their accustomed sources of income: officials, contractors and suppliers. The rule had been: the highest rate for the minimum of work; the highest price for the lowest quality acceptable to the purchaser; acceptance of supplies regardless of their suitability for the purpose purchased; and jobs for all – whether or not able, fit or competent. Those in charge were paid twice: once by the government and a second time in the form of bribes from the contractor or supplier. The Navy Board, as distinct from the Admiralty, did not care because it was public money being spent. Everybody was happy except those with a conscience – and the seamen who had to make do with the end product: ships with rotten hulls, rigging and cables – even with defective compasses where iron bolts had been used to affix them instead of copper ones.

191

It took time for the Board of Admiralty to appreciate that government officials were every bit as corrupt as the contractors and suppliers. There were, however, a high proportion of good shipwrights working in the royal dockyards, doing their best within the corrupt system. That it took years for St Vincent's reforms to take effect was demonstrated by Captain Lord Cochrane's experience a year after Trafalgar. As a Member of Parliament, he had continually drawn attention to Admiralty and dockyard abuses in Parliament. To get their awkward critic out of the way the Admiralty appointed him to the command of the frigate *Imperieuse* fitting out in the royal dockyard at Plymouth. The ship was ordered to sea before she was anywhere near ready – she had lighters alongside, the guns were not secured, the ballast had not been put below and the rigging was not set up. She had to heave to in mid-Channel to finish basic preparations.

The Royal Commission of Inquiry's work continued for two years, making a series of devastating reports. St Vincent's unpopularity increased proportionately. Admiral Collingwood commented: 'It was part of Lord St Vincent's economy to employ convicts to fit out the ships instead of the men and officers who were to sail in them.'

Lord Nelson observed: 'There is scarcely a thing he has done since he has been at the Admiralty that I have not heard him reprobate before he came to the Board.' It was certainly the view of many that the First Lord's economies crippled the Navy.

St Vincent had long taken an interest in and had a special regard for the marines. He regarded them as supremely loyal and dependable. As a result of his approach to King George III, in April 1802, they became the Royal Marines, comprising 43 companies at Chatham, 51 at Portsmouth and 51 at Plymouth. The peace establishment was fixed at 100 companies in 1802: 36 at Chatham, and 32 each at Portsmouth and Plymouth, each company comprising 100 men. By January 1804, however, the First Lord was urging the Commandant at Portsmouth to 'exert himself to correct the abuses which have crept into the Staff Department of the Royal Marines whereby the embarkation lists have been loaded with heavy debts and in other instances the Public has sustained heavy loss'. This plea was repeated in similar terms to the other two divisions.

Despite his criticisms, the officers of the Corps asked him to sit for a portrait by Sir William Beeches because of the 'sense they entertain of His Lordship's kind and unmerited attentions to the honour and service of that Corps'.

This 'unremitting attention' extended to an objection to sending Royal Marines to relieve New South Wales Rangers in that colony, although he was willing to provide ships to convey convicts there. He commented, with considerable lack of foresight: 'The Colony of New South Wales has long appeared to me in a hopeless way and the expense of it is very heavy, but as I cannot suggest a better way of disposing of the increasing number of convicts, I shall say no more on that Head.'

Corruption in the dockyards was by no means the only problem confronting the First Lord and his Board of Admiralty. There was no feeling of urgency in the various sectors of the shore defence, probably due to a false sense of security. The English coast had not been invaded for nearly 800 years and the Navy had always won its vital battles. Only a small minority of the population read newspapers and before radio waves were discovered, news travelled slowly. The danger of invasion by Napoleon's armies was simply not a reality to most of the population of the British Isles. Gunbrigs deployed in creeks and inlets along the south and east coasts of England as the front line of coastal defence were, in many cases, used as houseboats with the lieutenant in charge working an agricultural smallholding alongside. The chances of such a gun-brig putting to sea in an emergency to repel an invader was less than slight. In ships of the line there was still a latent threat of mutiny, stimulated by some officers who were only too keen to go onto half pay when peace terms were agreed.

Not long after the Treaty of Amiens was signed, a squadron was detached from the Channel fleet to counter the threat of a French and Dutch concentration in the West Indies. A squadron of twelve ships of the line was victualled for six months' service and ordered to Bantry Bay, to be held in readiness to cross the Atlantic to the Caribbean. The ships' companies were taken by surprise. The fleet had been lying in Plymouth harbour with topmasts struck when the orders were received. Within four hours they were under sail in a severe gale and it took them eight days to reach the south-west extremity of Ireland. When the crews learned that their destination was the West Indies they determined to refuse to weigh anchor except for England, led by the men of the flagship *Téméraire*. The ship's officers suppressed the mutiny and had the ringleaders secured. Sadly, they were among the best of seamen and were objecting, not just to being sent abroad for an unspecified period when peace was imminent, but to inadequate pay and absence of any reward following long years of demanding war service. The men were tried and hanged. Even Captain Brenton, a relative and consistent champion of Lord St Vincent, was highly critical of him for sanctioning their execution.

The harshness of punishments makes the loyalty of the ships' companies at Trafalgar and in subsequent naval actions all the more remarkable, and emphasizes the supreme importance of maintaining morale and a good relationship between officers and men. In the interim, the Navy was forced to rely more than ever on the press-gangs to man its ships. St Vincent, obsessed with corruption in the dockyards and making economies in naval administration, was possibly guilty of turning a blind eye to maintaining morale.

He continued his campaign against nepotism, although a letter written to a young officer who was related by marriage to both his wife and himself, but of no proven merit, raises doubts as to whether the Admiral was as immune to the virus as he wished everyone to believe. He refused to give Francis Fane the two steps of commander and post-captain at once, but arranged to appoint him to the command of a sloop to hasten his progress.

It is fair to compare his attitude to this young man with his treatment of Lord Cochrane, whose exploit in boarding and taking the Spanish frigate *El Gamo* (32 guns, 190lb broadside, crew of 319) with the brig *Speedy* (14 guns, 28lb broadside, crew of 54) on 5 May 1801 put him at the very pinnacle of ship-to-ship action in the David and Goliath category. Unfortunately both Cochrane's father and uncle were unwise enough to write to the First Lord canvassing his promotion. St Vincent replied that while he had no difficulty in acknowledging Cochrane's feat, he noted:

The first account of that brilliant action reached the Admiralty very early in the month of August, previously to which intelligence had been received of the capture of the *Speedy* by which Lord Cochrane was made prisoner. Until his exchange could be effected and the necessary inquiry into the cause and circumstances of the loss . . . had taken place, it was impossible for the Board . . . to mark its approbation of his lordship's conduct.

When Lord Cochrane subsequently made repeated applications to the First Lord for a ship, he was still turned down. Eventually he outfaced St Vincent, who said to him, 'Well, you shall have a ship. Go down to Plymouth and there await the orders of the Admiralty.' He was then insulted by being appointed to a rotten-hulled converted collier which, he said, 'sailed like a haystack' and was incapable of carrying out her assigned duties.

In assessment of professional qualities this was probably the worst mistake St Vincent ever made. Cochrane was just the sort of officer he sought: every bit as courageous and resourceful as Nelson and with the same magical ability to inspire those serving under him. By failing to appreciate his qualities, St Vincent deprived the British Navy of the most brilliant officer of the post-Nelson generation. The victory he planned in Aix Roads in 1809 would have been as decisive as Trafalgar if Gambier, the Admiral in command, had not acted like a dowager with arthritis. Cochrane's command of the navies of Chile, Brazil and Greece, in their successful wars of independence from Spain, Portugal and Turkey respectively, are proof of the enormity of St Vincent's mistake.

When the First Lord wrote to a Rear Admiral Dacres offering him the choice of appointment as second flag officer at either Plymouth or Chatham, Dacres declined. St Vincent wrote to him:

Your letter reminds me of my old constituents at Yarmouth who, the moment I did them an act of great kindness, applied for another; and I cannot forbear telling you frankly that I am not a little disgusted with the repeated assumptions I have received from your house. The merits of other flag officers cannot possibly be laid aside for your sole aggrandisement.

St Vincent tried always to stay true to his ideas of what an officer should be, as expressed in a letter to Francis Fane dated 18 May 1802:

Dear Francis

I had not an opportunity to give you a few hints touching your conduct as a Commander before you left town which induces me to address them to you in a short letter.

Complacency to your Officers is the best principle you can act upon, respecting them, taking especial care neither to be too familiar with them nor allowing familiarity on their parts towards you; the best means of avoiding these evils is to observe a certain degree of ceremony upon all occasions, which may be done without imposing restraint upon them. To the inferior officers and men, your humanity and good sense will naturally incline you to show all manner of kindness consistently with the preservation of good order and due execution of the service. Upon complaint being made of any irregularity, investigate it with temper and never delegate these examinations to a lieutenant, much less the infliction of punishment; which never ought to take place but when absolutely necessary, and the strictest decorum observed in the conduct of it and whatever your feelings are, nothing like passion ought to appear.

An expensive way of living having crept into the service during the late war, I cannot avoid stating my decided opinion that it has done more injury to the Navy than can be described in a letter. I therefore recommend strongly to you to limit your Table to what is decent and proper, equally avoiding profusion and variety, and never to sit long after dinner.

At the end of December 1802 St Vincent wrote to Sir Andrew Hammond who, as Comptroller of the Navy, was Head of the Navy Board, responsible for the Navy's stores and supplies, including the contracts for building ships, although orders were initiated by the Admiralty.

It must be fresh in your recollection that I have seldom conversed with you upon any subject without introducing the urgent necessity of entering into Contracts for building as many 74-gun ships as you could find fit persons to undertake in every part of the Kingdom. I cannot therefore refrain from expressing a considerable degree of surprise at the tenor of your letter of yesterday which requires that I should repeat, in the strongest terms, the opinion I have so frequently given.

St Vincent's correspondence with Sir Andrew continued in January 1803, the Admiral expressing strong dissatisfaction with the Navy Board and with the Comptroller in particular for failing to make progress with the construction of ships, particularly 74-gun line-of-battle ships, using merchant yards in addition to the royal dockyards as necessary. This correspondence was significant and would be central to the controversy when William Pitt later accused St Vincent of failing to maintain the essential numbers of ships the Navy needed.

Chapter Seventeen

Prelude to Trafalgar

By the middle of May 1803, when war was declared, St Vincent had deployed his most reliable flag officers and their ships with strategic skill from the North Sea to the Mediterranean. He had appointed Lord Keith as C-in-C North Sea with 6 sail of the line in the Downs, 6 blockships at The Nore, a fast-sailing squadron of frigates and smaller ships in the Dover Straits, and 5 sail of the line off St Helens. Thornbrough cruised off Texel with five sail of the line and some frigates while Sir Sidney Smith in a frigate watched Flushing; Sir James Saumarez with a squadron of frigates was cruising off the Channel Islands; Cornwallis with fifteen sail of the line was blockading Brest, while another ship of the line supported by frigates watched L'Orient; Lord Gardner was off the south-west coast of Ireland with five sail of the line; Sir Edward Pellew with five sail of the line cruised off Ferrol; a frigate was watching Bordeaux; and Sir Richard Strachan with a ship of the line was off Cadiz. Vice Admiral Lord Nelson was in the Mediterranean blockading Toulon and keeping watch on the movements of the French and Spanish fleets. St Vincent wrote to him on 19 May:

> I very much lament your detention at Portsmouth, equally unpleasant to you and injurious to the public service. I was in hopes your Orders and Instructions would have followed you much quicker than they did; the delays of office are inscrutable and increase every hour . . .
>
> It is of the utmost importance that the junction of the

Victory with Admiral Cornwallis may be demonstrated as soon as possible to our Enemies in Brest and should the Admiral not find it necessary to detain her, you will part company in the night, otherwise proceed in the *Amphion*.

Your Lordship has given so many proofs of transcendent Zeal in the service of your King and Country that we have only to pray for the preservation of your invaluable life to insure everything that can be achieved by mortal man.

Pray take care of your health and spare your eyes as much as possible and with my fervent wishes for a prosperous voyage believe me to be, my dear Lord, Your very faithful and obedient servant

In a letter to Lord Hobart, a member of the court of King George III, written on 23 June 1803, St Vincent gave a comprehensive summary of his naval defence preparations in reply to various queries from the King. He was able to state with truth that he had already taken account of every point raised: signal stations had been established and manned up and down the coast and additional ones were planned where necessary; the corps of Sea Fencibles had been re-established for coastal defence, comprising men with maritime experience, presumably unsuitable for the press-gang, but an 'Impress-service' was operating to secure as many seamen and 'seafaring men' as possible for service in the fleet. He enclosed a list of all the ship dispositions, already summarized, and assured His Majesty that if ships had to leave their stations others would replace them.

From August 1803 to March 1804 he continued to correspond with Nelson on a variety of matters affecting the Mediterranean squadron. It should not be forgotten that these letters, meticulously polite, were written by the most senior officer in the Royal Navy to a vice admiral who was not only his junior in rank and age, but who was no longer on the best of terms with him:

21st August 1803
Your Lordship is so thoroughly acquainted with the court of Naples that it is unnecessary for me to urge the taking every precaution to prevent the French from getting a footing in

Sicily by lulling that Court into security or operating upon it by intimidation.

I am assured by Mr Marsh, Chairman of the Victualling Board that a large supply of casks is sent out for your Squadron; but without due economy nothing we can furnish will suffice. I well know Your Lordship will enforce it to the utmost of your power. The store-ships are loading with cordage, sails, etc. and will sail the moment they can be got ready. Men you can never be in want of while we are in possession of Malta, which will supply the squadron abundantly and I have no idea under the vigour of your character that there will be an imaginary difficulty; real ones cannot exist. In short, cordage may be manufactured at sea; caulking and every other refitment which in England requires Dock Yard inspection, Your Lordship knows is much better performed by the Artificers of the squadron; and barring accidents by shot, there is nothing that cannot be provided for.

The blockade of Genoa and Spezzia is published in the Gazette and all the steps you have advised taken, excepting warfare against the Kingdom of Etruria which for wise political reasons is suspended.

Your nephew Bolton in the *Childers* will join you soon: the *Victory* was close upon the heels of the *Amphion* and Rear-Admiral Campbell is with you before this. Admiral Campbell will second you. He is a proved man and will, I am persuaded, act most cordially with you. Have the goodness to remember me to him and to Murray, for I have not time to write to either and with my most ardent wishes for your health and aggrandizement, be assured I am, etc.

24th September 1803

I have to acknowledge your Lordship's letters of the 12th, 13th and 21st July and Sir Evan Nepean has communicated letters from you of a later date to him from which I have the satisfaction of learning that you have changed the cruising position of the squadron. Experience having taught me that any attempt to preserve a situation to the westward of Cape Sicie must tear away the best fitted squadron to pieces in a very short time, while a station between Cape Sicie and the islands of Hiers may be maintained with the utmost precision, running under the lee of the Levant Island when the N.W. winds blow so strong as to hazard being driven off the coast . . . It is intended that a ship of the line shall accompany every convoy which sails for the Mediterranean which will enable you to send the ships purchased from the East India Company, so much complained of, to England in return, as by the accounts we have received of them they are most applicable to convoy service.

20th November 1803

The *Leviathan* and *Terrible* will be soon added to your Lordship's squadron which we are anxious to reinforce, but the great demands made upon us for the defence of the coast of Great Britain and Ireland swallow up such a number of men, we have not been able to equip so many ships of the line as we otherwise should have done.

7th March 1804

The *Leviathan* with three Bombs and their tenders will proceed to join Your Lordship on the 14th of this month, having under their convoy the trade for the Mediterranean. The *Royal Sovereign* has, I trust, arrived long before this, as the wind was favourable for many days after the 12th February, when Admiral Cornwallis detached her. A convoy sailed from Plymouth on the same day, under the protection of a Troopship, with a reinforcement of Artillery for the garrison of Gibraltar and the *Hindostan* with a large supply of naval stores, which I trust will arrive safe.

The Board has adopted Your Lordship's proposition of arming the *Niger* with 28 guns . . . in quoting my dissatisfaction of Lord Spencer having loaded me with so many officers to provide for, perhaps your Lordship does not know that I carried to the Mediterranean a much longer list than I have troubled you with, and the moment that was fulfilled I received another, and never uttered a murmur until it was so often repeated as to wound my feelings in the extreme. No promotion being made at home, unless on occasion of distinguished service against the enemy, there is much stronger ground for the measure than during the last War.

Despite his ill-health at this time, St Vincent continued to correspond with flag officers from the West Indies to the North Sea as well as carrying out his duties in respect to the royal dockyards and the Admiralty itself. While Napoleon prepared to invade the British Isles, the First Lord declared, 'I do not say the French cannot come. I only say they cannot come by water.'

Napoleon involved himself in the minutest details of his plans for cross-Channel invasion: boat-building, construction of barges, and adaptation of ports. However, with oars and without keels, his barges were helpless in wind and tide. St Vincent was contemptuous of them and insisted that continued preparation of the battle fleet was the best answer, although his former economies led to difficulties. Some ships in a poor state of seaworthiness had to run for shelter in stormy weather, but the same storms played havoc with Napoleon's barges in Boulogne, Rochefort and elsewhere. The City of London passed a Vote of Thanks to the Navy for 'Their great zeal and uncommon exertions by which our enemies have been kept in a constant state of alarm nor dared for a moment to show themselves upon that element which has so often been the scene of their defeat and disgrace.'

Nelson's attempts to destroy the landing craft and facilities in Boulogne harbour had been of doubtful benefit, but St Vincent was still keen to put the port out of action. He responded to a plan by English smugglers from the east coast to neutralize the French port by sinking blockships in the entrance. They were familiar with the port and offered to carry out the operation for financial reward. Three old three-masted merchant ships were filled with masonry, bonded with iron and cement, and were to be towed into the harbour entrance and sunk. The plan received the approval of the Prime Minister, but had eventually to be abandoned after several attempts to position the ships for scuttling were defeated by adverse weather.

St Vincent still found time amongst all his myriad responsibilities to take an interest in the naval education of a friend's son. On 10 June he wrote to him:

In my judgement he is too young to embark and I advise his being instructed in Arithmetic, Geometry and trigonometry; for without these foundations of the Theory of Navigation, he will have a very uphill game to fight, and there are so few Schoolmasters in the Navy that there is little chance of obtaining this essential part of his education at sea: thirteen years of age is certainly early enough for any youth to engage in such a Profession as ours . . . I would with the greatest degree of satisfaction assist you in making choice of a proper Seminary to prepare our young Sailor for the Navy if I was able, but I really have no information whatever upon the subject. He is too young to be admitted into Portsmouth academy, twelve being the age prescribed by the Regulations or he should be entered on the first vacancy.

St Vincent also had to deal with requests from officers to be moved from one part of the fleet to another. He wrote to a Member of Parliament who had asked for his nephew to be sent to a ship in the Mediterranean: 'It is no less remarkable than true that the officers serving in the Mediterranean are for the most part soliciting to be employed on the coasts of the United Kingdom, while those at home are wanting to go to the Mediterranean.'

To Lord Grey he wrote on 20 November: 'Your Lordship would feel for me if you were in possession of the powerful applications which I receive daily to remove ships from the defence of the coast to lucrative stations which in fact do not exist: but Prize Money is the order of the day and all other objects are secondary.'

It was still a problem to find enough men to commission the available ships. Prize money was the only incentive for many, the press-gang the only way to man ships short of complement, while mutiny and desertion were ever-present threats to captains and officers who were less than popular. In a letter to Sir Evan Nepean on 8 December, St Vincent discussed the case of a man who had been sentenced to death for desertion:

The unfortunate man under sentence of death, having committed the crime he was expressly stationed to prevent, appears to me much more guilty than the person who went off with him. It does not appear by the Minutes in what manner he was apprehended, but had there been anything favourable to him, he would no doubt have stated it in his defence. I am therefore of opinion that the pardoning him might have a bad effect in the present circumstances of the War. I wish however that each Member of the Board should be called upon for his Opinion, for I have known instances of the execution of men for deserting producing the very contrary effect intended and upon one occasion a whole Boat's crew sent to bury a man who was hanged for desertion, committing the same crime the instant they had performed this last office.

St Vincent was renowned for treating any officer who questioned orders with severity. Captain the Hon. Henry Blackwood was lucky. He had been unwise enough to question his orders from Lord Keith in a letter to the Admiralty, which was passed to the First Lord. St Vincent wrote to him:

Honble Captain Blackwood

Nothing can exceed the astonishment which the perusal of your letter of the 17th instant has excited. The doctrines contained in it are of the most dangerous and mischievous tendency and I feel that I am acting improperly in not immediately laying them before the Board; but as such a measure must be productive of the most serious consequence to you as an officer, I refrain from resorting to it in hopes that you will in future consider obedience to the Orders you receive as the only principle of your duty.

He wrote to the Prime Minister on the same subject: 'It is lamentable . . . that this disposition to discuss has taken place of the implicit obedience which once formed the character of a Sea Officer and if not put down will inevitably be the destruction of naval discipline.' Blackwood went on to command *Eurylus* at Trafalgar, so it seems he did take St Vincent's words to heart.

In March 1803, and again in May, St Vincent, wretchedly unwell, had asked Addington to be relieved, but each time the

Prime Minister had begged the 68-year old Admiral to stay. The volume of attacks on St Vincent and his dockyard reforms emanating from William Pitt's supporters grew steadily. Three streams of opposition were combining to create a current which would terminate Addington's government and St Vincent's tenure of the crucial office of First Lord of the Admiralty – a post which, in the government of a country dependent on sea power, was nearly as important as that of Prime Minister. The three streams were party politics, the anger of thwarted contractors and public fear induced by the inaccurate stories of naval weakness which had been propagated by Pitt and his supporters.

Initially, Pitt gave Addington half-hearted support, while gathering missiles to launch at St Vincent, who was both the keel and Achilles' heel of Addington's cabinet. In February 1804 Pitt launched his campaign. He acknowledged his ignorance of naval affairs before launching a volley of innuendos aimed at St Vincent's management record as First Lord. He attempted to demonstrate the Navy's deficiencies in numbers, state of unpreparedness and inadequate deployment, and returned to his personal nostrum: the need for flotillas of little gunboats to attack the expected French landing craft and barges. Even Wilberforce, Pitt's staunchest supporter, noted in his diary that 'Everybody blames Pitt as factious for his motion about the state of the Navy.'

Sir Edward Pellew, temporarily home from his blockading station off Ferrol, emphatically refuted the implications of Pitt's attack:

I know and can assert with confidence that our Navy was never better found, that it was never better supplied and that our men were never better fed or better clothed. Have we not all the enemy's ports blockaded from Toulon to Flushing? Are we not able to cope, anywhere, with any force the enemy dares to send out against us? And do we not even outnumber them at every one of those ports we have blockaded?

The Treasurer of the Navy, Mr Tierney, produced figures which did nothing to support Pitt's allegations: the Navy had 1,536 ships available and fit for service, varying in size and function from

205

line-of-battle ships and frigates to blockships and small craft. In answer to the charge that St Vincent's Admiralty had failed to have ships built in merchants' yards he gave an example of such a ship which had cost more in repairs in the first thee years afloat than it had cost to build. To the accusation that insufficient manpower had been recruited, he retorted that whereas the war in 1793 had begun with 16,000 seamen and ended with 76,000, at the start of the current war there had been 50,000, since augmented to 80,000.

Vice Admiral Sir Charles Pole defended the Admiralty's deployment of the fleet and pointed out that the French and Dutch coasts had been under close blockade within forty-eight hours of the declaration of war. In an ironic speech supporting St Vincent, the poet, dramatist and politician Richard Sheridan referred to a toast proposed by Pitt six months earlier: 'To the volunteers of England – and may we soon have a meeting with the enemy on our own shores'. This sentiment, Sheridan commented, might be much assisted by 'substituting the honourable gentleman's favourite gunboats for our ships of the line and frigates'.

It is interesting to note that Nelson had changed his mind about the need for flotillas of gunboats to defend the coast – a strategic policy of which he had previously been highly critical. He wrote to one of Pitt's colleagues at about this time:

> I have read with attention Mr Pitt's speech respecting the Admiralty. My mind has long been formed upon that subject and with all my personal regard for Lord St Vincent, I am sorry to see that he has been led astray by the opinion of ignorant people . . . I had wrote a Memoir, many months ago, upon the propriety of a Flotilla. I had that command at the end of the last war and I know the necessity of it.

Formerly Lord Nelson had expressed the view that 'our great reliance is on the vigilance and activity of our cruisers at sea, any reduction in the numbers of which, by applying them to guard our ports, inlets and beaches, would in my judgement tend to our destruction.'

When the vote was taken, Pitt was in a minority of seventy-one and when the news of his attack spread abroad, the public were simply incredulous or openly hostile, but Pitt was undeterred. He had abandoned his lukewarm support of Addington and was determined to return to power as Prime Minister. He told his nominee for First Lord of the Admiralty, Lord Melville, that he could form a government from among his own friends, 'united with the most capable and unexceptionable persons of the present government; but of course excluding many of them, and above all, Addington himself and Lord St Vincent.' Pitt's determination and mastery of parliamentary manoeuvring were unstoppable. It was just a matter of time.

When on 10 May Addington resigned and St Vincent was superseded by Lord Melville, the Board of Admiralty resigned as a body. Those who had enriched themselves by graft at the expense of the Navy and the nation, heaved a sigh of relief.

Many who had resented St Vincent's economies and his harsh treatment of incompetence were equally pleased at his demise, but the Earl would surely have been shocked to learn that Nelson wrote to Emma, Lady Hamilton:

I am sure that nine-tenths of those who now abuse the Earl and Trowbridge were, and would be again, their most abject flatterers were they again in office. For myself I feel above them in every way and they are below my abuse of them. Now no longer in power I care nothing about them and now they can do no harm to anyone, I shall no longer abuse them.

This was the man who had previously, on different occasions, written to Lord St Vincent, his patron:

I feel obligations to you on every occasion . . . you are ever adding to my obligations and I can only endeavour to repay you . . . all your favours are not thrown away on an ungrateful soil . . . I feel you are my friend and my heart yearns to you . . . you are everything which is great and good. Let me say so . . . we are low in spirits but all in this house love you . . . God bless you, my dear Lord, and be assured that all my actions are to do as I believe you would wish me

207

... I do not fail ever to speak of you ... as the best and truest friend that can be in this world ... we look up to you as we have always found you, as to our Father ... all of us caught our professional zeal and fire from the great and good Earl of St Vincent.

St Vincent's Board of Admiralty was not only attacked in Parliament, but by newspapers and pamphleteers. The Admiralty brought a libel case against the proprietors of the *True Briton* on 12 February 1805 – for libels in their edition of 17 December 1803 – and also took proceedings against the publishers of two pamphlets imputing incapacity and misconduct to the Admiralty. When a well-wisher offered money to suppress the pamphlets St Vincent responded, 'I would not give sixpence to suppress or stop the circulation of that, or of all the pamphlets in the world.' In each case, either the author or printer was convicted and imprisoned.

A committee of Friends of St Vincent would, at a later date, publish a Memoir which amounts to an exhaustively detailed summary of the graft and corruption discovered in the royal dock-yards by St Vincent's Board of Admiralty during his term of office as First Lord. It is a powerful, if tedious, defence of his conduct, methods and actions, and is published in full as an Appendix to Volume 2 of St Vincent's letters (Navy Records).

To the surprise of former members of the Board of Admiralty, when Lord Melville took office in May 1804, he treated both his predecessor and Rear Admiral Trowbridge with friendliness and respect. Trowbridge was offered a choice of stations and of ships in which to hoist his flag, choosing *Blenheim* as flagship of the East Indies station. St Vincent was earmarked for the crucial post of C-in-C Channel Fleet. Clearly Pitt's opinion of St Vincent as a fighting admiral differed from his assessment of his performance as First Lord. The Admiral meantime had been drawing up a *Memoire Justificatif* to make public the facts on which his administration had been based, with the aim of substituting facts and figures for the theories and innuendo which had clouded the whole controversy. He informed Addington in January 1805 that unless 'Mr Pitt explains satisfactorily in the House of Commons the gross mistakes under which he made false and unjust charges against me and the late Admiralty Board, out it must come, *coute que coute.*'

The old admiral refused the invitation to become C-in-C Channel Fleet with the words:

> Unless Mr Pitt unsaid all he had said in the House of Commons against me; and lest any unfavourable impression should be made upon the mind of the King, on this refusal, I asked an audience at Windsor and humbly submitted that though my life was at the disposal of His Majesty and my country, I was the guardian of my own honour and could not trust it in the hands of Mr Pitt, after the treatment I had received from him.

Pitt had no intention of making either a retraction or an apology. On 5 February, he stated that every opinion he had entertained of the previous naval administration when out of office 'had been confirmed by everything he had seen, or read, or heard, since his being in office'. St Vincent demanded to be told whether or not the government intended to institute an enquiry into his conduct as First Lord. He got no definitive answer, but at the end of the month everything changed overnight when the Tenth Report of the Commission of Enquiry was published. The report covered financial management during Pitt's previous administration, when Lord Melville was Treasurer of the Navy, and showed that there had been wide misuse of public money. Parliamentary opinion turned in St Vincent's favour, a vote of censure against the government was only defeated by the Speaker's casting vote and two days later Melville was forced to resign, to be replaced by Admiral Charles Middleton, Lord Barham.

St Vincent pressed again for an investigation into his own conduct, to be told that no such investigation was contemplated, but Pitt was obliged to introduce a bill enabling the Commission of Enquiry to continue.

The parliamentary furore persisted through the autumn. Even the news of the victory off Cape Trafalgar on 24 October failed to calm the troubled political waters although it removed the immediate threat of invasion. Only the death of William Pitt on

23 January 1806 allowed the political storm to abate. St Vincent never received the apology he was due although restitution was made by Lord Grenville, Pitt's successor.

The Battle of Trafalgar has become legend. It was the justification and climax of all that St Vincent had achieved in a career which was shaped and defined by selfless duty. To him must be attributed a major share in the victory. It was he who had done so much to place Nelson in a winning situation. Lord Nelson, the great tactician, died without publicly acknowledging his debt to the man who had been his faithful patron from the day they first met to the day when the fall of Addington's government resulted in the resignation of that great strategist, Admiral Lord St Vincent.

Chapter Eighteen

Home Strait

Napoleon's emphatic victory over Britain's allies, Russia and Austria, at Austerlitz meant that the Royal Navy's line-of-battle ships were the front line of defence between Napoleon and world domination. The king asked Lord Grenville to form a coalition government, with Lord Grey as First Lord of the Admiralty. The pressure on St Vincent personally was eased and his *Memoire Justificatif* remained unpublished. He was invited to take over from Cornwallis as Commander-in-Chief of the Channel fleet – mainly to bolster public confidence. The Member of Parliament for Poole had unwisely decided to adopt the lost cause of the late Prime Minister and brought a motion of censure against St Vincent, but it was decisively defeated and transformed into a vote of thanks to the veteran Admiral for a career embodying triple victories over the enemy, mutiny and corruption.

St Vincent's old friend and former personal secretary, Benjamin Tucker returned to the Admiralty as Second Secretary. The invitation to St Vincent came initially from Lord Moira, secretary to the monarch. The 71-year old Admiral did not immediately accept, replying early in January from Rochetts, emphasizing that he was 'disabled by the wretched state of my health . . . seriously deliberating whether I should not embark for a milder climate . . . nothing short of the calamitous state the country is brought into could have prevented it.'

In the end, since he respected Lord Grenville and was prepared to serve under his coalition government, he agreed to accept. On

6 February he wrote to Cornwallis:

My dear Admiral

I am now called upon again to serve and, in the state the empire is reduced to, I feel it an imperative duty to obey the call, with only one repugnance, which arises out of the high respect and esteem I have for you; and I beg you will rest assured that every possible delicacy will be paid to your zealous services, for no man regards you more sincerely than,
    Yours etc.

St Vincent hoisted his flag in *Hibernia* on 8 March 1806 and reported to Lord Grey that he liked what he had seen of the vessel, though complaining that the men seemed of 'mean stature and flimsy muscle, particularly the marines'. He planned to put to sea at the first favourable moment, though 'dirty' weather was expected. As time went on he became dissatisfied with his flag captain, Captain Western, whom he described as 'the worst qualified to command the ship bearing the union Flag of any captain I have ever met with.' Yet he was able to write later to the First Lord: 'We are on the very best terms and shall continue so to the end, for I have guarded against the natural quickness of my temper and by that means avoided everything querulous.'

While others had commented that St Vincent was 'far from always preserving an unruffled command of his temper or of himself', it had also been observed that 'On stirring occasions of unofficer- or unseaman-like conduct, or when retarded by laziness or factiousness, a torrent of impetuous reproof in unmeasured language would violently rush from his unguarded lips.' Clearly he was a man not to be trifled with.

For five months, from March to August 1806, Admiral Lord St Vincent maintained the blockade of the French coast, keeping in touch with the Admiralty by means of voluminous correspondence on numerous topics: the deployment of his squadrons; the effect of wind and tide in varying conditions; the greed of the Port Admiral in Plymouth who wished to issue the sailing orders to ships joining the Channel fleet so that he would be entitled to prize money if the ships concerned took prizes. He demonstrated his intimate knowledge of the French coast and made observations on the shortage of reliable petty officers, suggesting that unless the differential between officers' half pay and full pay was widened, they would not serve in time of peace. He complained that one of his ships was 'in want of everything' and that he had nothing to replace her. To this he added: 'I do not like to state this to the Board because it would have the appearance of complaining, which I have never done in the whole course of my service.'

In April 1806, St Vincent suggested that the seamen of the fleet were getting too much pork for the 'moderate exercise and labour they undergo'. He believed the pork had 'generated the dreadful infectious ulcers which have deprived so many men of their limbs and lives'. He also thought that the supplies of fresh beef had been too frequent but felt that a cut in the ration would cause trouble in the officers 'from whence all our evils have originated . . . you well know how soon seditious expressions are conveyed from the ward-room to the gundeck . . . A revival of economy, discipline and order is difficult enough, any act which might create murmur would be equally hazardous and unwise.'

The availability of timber for shipbuilding was of constant concern to St Vincent who bemoaned the fact that Napoleon – 'that extraordinary character who governs France' – could build 200 sail of the line in four years and had access to timber on the Adriatic coast which might, with better management on the part of the Navy Board, have been used by the British.

The Admiral continued to take an interest in the welfare of his men, both individually and as a group. He worried about Admiral Sir Edward Thornbrough, who he said was a fine and gallant fellow but liable to 'sink under responsibility'. He requested that Thornbrough be replaced because 'if he continues in this languid state it will be all over with him.' In the last week of July he was objecting to the newly introduced rank of sub lieutenant, stating that 'all the youth of the service will become contaminated. The commanders of gun-brigs lord it over them and they are soon driven out of his mess and mixed with the warrant-officers, by which means they become professed drunkards'. Not long after he was able to reassure the First Lord that 'We have just finished filling up the squadron with five months provisions and as much water as the ships can stow: the people are in high health and both they, the captains and officers improving in all things.'

Information was coming in that the French were about to make a move and St Vincent, now Acting Admiral of the Fleet, was ordered to take his fleet into the familiar anchorage in the estuary of the Tagus, where they anchored on 14 August 1806 and were warmly welcomed, their presence helping to sway Spain towards the British cause and against Napoleon. However the weak and corrupt Portuguese royal family vacillated and contributed to the state of revolution, anarchy and civil war which eventually engulfed most of the Iberian Peninsula. St Vincent embarked on six weeks of frustrating diplomatic activity and was able to report to Lord Grey: 'I have every reason to believe that we had the blessings of the whole country from the Prince Regent to the meanest peasant.'

The day before leaving the Tagus on 28 September to take up station again off Ushant, St Vincent wrote to the First Lord again:

Although I was prepared for the death of Mr Fox, the certainty of that mournful event having taken place has quite overset me. I feel it the more poignantly because of your probable removal from the Admiralty; a measure I foresaw and in consequence I desired Mr Tucker to prepare you for my retreat from the command of the fleet – a station nothing upon earth, but Mr Fox and yourself could have induced me to reassume. I will, however, do nothing rashly, and I will take no step until after my arrival in Cawsand Bay; and I entreat you to leave orders, to be immediately dispatched to the squadron off Ushant, for me to proceed thither the moment I join Sir Charles Cotton.

A fortnight later, at Ushant, he wrote again to Lord Grey:

I beg leave to assure you that I have long held your public and private character in the highest estimation; and that next to the anxious desire of serving my country, which has ever governed my conduct, the support of the present administration was the motive that induced me to venture again on this fickle element, which Lord Howick will bear testimony to; and that a condition was annexed that I should not be required to keep the sea between the autumnal and vernal equinox. I have in consequence, hired a house at Rame, very near Cawsand, for the express purpose of conducting the business of the fleet without interfering with Admiral Young in the duties of the port of Plymouth . . . I have suffered so much during several winters successively, that I cannot possibly stand the fag of this station; and whether I shall be able to endure the humid air of the west is very doubtful.

While ashore at Cawsand, Lord St Vincent spoke in the House of Lords against Grenville's Slave Abolition Bill. The report of the debate records that: 'He deprecated the measure which, if passed, would, he was satisfied, have the effect of transferring British capital to other countries, which would not be disposed to abandon such a productive branch of trade.' When the Bill reached its report stage, the old Admiral repeated his objections, despite being a dedicated Whig. He considered that:

It would prove fatal to the best interests of the country . . . as soon as France made peace with us (and she would hasten a pacification in consequence of the passing of this Bill) her first object would be to get complete possession of the slave trade; and if she succeeded in that point, it would soon appear that she had got possession of an engine that would work the downfall of the naval superiority of this country.

It is difficult, from the standpoint of the twenty-first century, to understand his reasoning or see any morality behind his argument.

St Vincent's health continued to deteriorate and on 26 March 1807 he wrote to the Secretary of the Admiralty asking to be relieved of his command. Receiving no immediate reply, he wrote again before the end of the month:

Sir,
    I desire you will convey to the lords commissioners of the admiralty the lively sense I feel of the approbation their

lordships have been pleased to express of the zeal with which I have endeavoured to serve my king and country, in carrying into execution the important duties of the station assigned me; and how much I lament that the frequent return of the complaint I have been for some time past affected with leaves me no hope of being able to perform the various services comprehended in the command of the Channel Fleet, with advantage to his Majesty's arms, and satisfaction to my own mind. I therefore am under the painful necessity of repeating the request I had the honour to make through you to their lordships in my letter of the 26th inst.

His appointment was finally terminated on 24 April, 1808.

With his naval career now finally over, Lord St Vincent returned to live full time at Rochetts. He took a great interest in the estate and garden, dabbled in agriculture and involved himself in local affairs, becoming a consistently generous benefactor to the poor and disadvantaged of the district. The gardener at Rochetts wanted permission to fell an old oak which he considered dangerous, but his employer would not allow it, saying, 'That tree and I have been long contemporaries. We have flourished together and together we will fall.'

There are several accounts of the old Admiral's generosity to both members of his own family and of the local community. He even took up the cause of Lady Nelson when her late husband's family attempted to take advantage of her, and wrote privately to a friend, revealing his long-concealed opinion of Emma, Lady Hamilton: 'The Will of Lord Nelson has thrown a shade upon the lustre of his services. That infernal bitch Lady Hamilton could have made him poison his wife or stab me, his best friend.'

Martha, Lady St Vincent, was not an easy companion, being in poor health, plaintive, and demanding. According to Sherrard, she suffered from neurasthaenia, defined in the dictionary as a neurosis characterized by extreme lassitude and inability to cope with any but the most trivial tasks. Fortunately a devoted and cheerful niece, Mrs Brenton, was engaged as a companion and proved to be a benign influence in the household and a buffer between two strong personalities.

St Vincent continued to attend the House of Lords for some years and made occasional speeches on subjects affecting naval affairs and British commitments abroad, whether military or mercantile. He violently opposed an unprovoked attack on Copenhagen and the sending of British troops to Portugal. He expressed contempt of the device of 'Councils of War' as a substitute for executive decision by the Commanding Officer, and criticized the Convention of Cintra whereby the French, twice defeated by Arthur Wellesley, the future Duke of Wellington, were allowed to evacuate Portugal unopposed. Speaking in the House of Lords after Sir John Moore's masterly retreat to Corunna in 1809, St Vincent maintained that the campaign had proved to be the greatest disgrace of the Peninsular War to date; that the transports had been misused ferrying Spanish troops to the battlefield, that the British Army should have been sent to northern Spain and not to Portugal and, somewhat bizarrely, that a member of the royal family should have been in command because 'they have made the science of war their study from childhood. If they are not to be employed I am at a loss to conjecture for what purpose they were bred to arms!'

St Vincent made his last speech in the House of Lords on 23 January 1810 at the age of seventy-five. It is a good illustration of his interests, attitudes and demeanour:

My Lords, when I addressed a few observations at the commencement of the last session of Parliament to your lord-ships, I thought my age and infirmities would preclude me from ever again presenting myself to your consideration; but, my lords, such have been the untoward and calamitous events which have occurred since that period that I am once more induced, if my strength will permit, to trouble your lordships with a few observations. Indeed we have wonderful and extra-ordinary men in these days; we have ingenuity enough to blazon with the finest colours; to sound with the trumpet and the drums; in fact to varnish over the greatest calamities of the country and endeavour to prove that our greatest misfortunes ought to be considered as our greatest blessings. Such was the course of proceeding after the disastrous Convention of Cintra; and now, in his Majesty's speech, they have converted

217

another disaster into a new triumph. They talk of the glorious victory of Talavera – a victory which led to no advantage and had the consequences of a defeat. The enemy took prisoners the sick and the wounded, and our own troops were obliged, finally, precipitately, to retreat. I do not mean to condemn the conduct of the officers employed either in Spain or Walcheren; I believe they did their duty. There is no occasion to wonder at the awful events which have occurred; they are caused by the weakness, infatuation and stupidity of ministers. I will maintain, my lords, that we owe all our disasters and disgrace to the ignorance and incapacity of his Majesty's ministers. But what could the nation expect from men who came into office under the mask of vile hypocrisy and have maintained their places by imposture and delusion? Look at the whole of their conduct. The first instance of the pernicious influence of their principles, was their treatment of a country at peace with us [Denmark]. In a state of profound peace they attacked her, unprepared, and brought her into a state of inveterate and open hostility. Their next achievement was to send one of the best men that ever commanded an army into the centre of Spain, unprovided with any requisite for such a dangerous march. If Sir John Moore had not acted according to his own judgement, in the perilous situation in which he had been wantonly exposed, every man of that army had been lost to the country: by his transcendent judgement, however, that army made one of the ablest retreats recorded in the pages of history and while he saved the remnant of his valiant troops, his own life was sacrificed in the cause of his country. And what tribute had his Majesty's ministers paid to his valued memory? What reward conferred for such eminent service? Why, my lords, even in this place, insidious aspersions were cast on his character; people were employed to calumniate his conduct. But, in spite of all the minions and dependents of administration, the character of that general will always be revered as one of the ablest men this country ever saw. After this abortive enterprise another, equally foolish, unsuccessful and ruinous, was carried into execution; another general was sent with troops into the heart of the peninsula, under similar circumstances and the glorious victory [of Talavera] was

218

purchased with our best blood and treasure. But what shall I say, my lords, when I come to mention the expedition to Walcheren? Why I think it almost useless to say one word on the subject: it was ill-advised, ill-planned; and even with partial successes, it was doubtful whether the ultimate object was not impracticable. It is high time the Parliament should adopt strong measures or the voice of the country will sound like thunder in their ears. The conduct of his Majesty's Government has led to the most frightful disasters, which are nowhere exceeded in the annals of history. The country is in that state which makes peace inevitable; it will be compelled to make peace, however disadvantageous, because it will be unable to maintain a war so shamefully misconducted and so disastrous in its consequences.

St Vincent's involvement in public life was virtually over. In February 1811, Lady St Vincent died after a long illness. Her modest fortune, the property she brought to the marriage, her secure status in society, her piety and blameless reputation had anchored her husband's life and career for more than three decades. In his memorial to her, St Vincent described her as 'eminently pious, virtuous and charitable'. A lot could be read between those lines. He continued to enjoy the attractively situated Rochetts estate and added an east wing to the house with a portico supported by sections of the masts of some of the ships he had served in. This east wing, seen in the photograph, was destroyed by fire in the following century. It accommodated an impressive dining room and drawing room with bedrooms above them. St Vincent also created a lake, extending to several acres with trees planted along one bank, in which he kept a small boat with four oars. Captain Brenton recorded that on one occasion his Lordship allowed four fellow admirals to venture onto the lake:

The Earl of Northesk, Griffiths Colpys, Matthew Scott and Lord Garlies. They proposed to take a row, and an admiral's secretary who happened to be present was appointed coxswain to this illustrious 'crew of jolly-boat boys'. The gallant officers, it must be owned, did not give entire satisfaction to the coxswain in their manner of handling their oars and he offered them the never failing stimulant on such occasions if they would exert themselves 'Give way and keep stroke, my lads, and I will give you a glass of grog each when you get on shore.' The application of such encouragement by a secretary, to four venerable flag-officers produced a great deal of mirth and I believe put a stop to further progress in the excursion.

Lord St Vincent had supported Catholic emancipation in Parliament, and it was rumoured at one time that he was a Roman Catholic. Attendance at Church of England services on board ship was unavoidable for somebody of flag rank, but St Vincent rarely went to church ashore.

Even at this stage of his life, St Vincent had strong views about his beloved Marines, to the point of prejudice against the Army. He wrote:

> It is of great importance to our country that the public should be kept alive upon the subject of our monstrous army . . . the marine corps is best adapted to the security of our dockyards . . . no soldier, of what is termed the line, should approach them. Our colonies ought to have no other infantry to protect them; and the corps of marine artillery should be substituted for the old artillery. The ordnance and appurtenances for His Majesty's fleet should be vested in the Admiralty and entirely taken away from what is termed the ordnance department.

For him, the Marines were above reproach. When they were awarded the 'Royal' by George III, St Vincent eulogized: 'There never was any appeal made to them for honour, courage or loyalty that they did not more than realise my expectations. If ever the hour of real danger should come to England, the Marines will be found the country's sheet anchor.'

Needing a change of climate, in 1818 St Vincent took a villa near Hyères on a part of the south coast of France with which he was familiar from his active service. During his stay of several months he was conducted around Toulon dockyard by a French admiral, reporting that he 'had never spent a more entertaining day'. Clearly his reputation with the French overcame any resentment they might feel about the defeat at Waterloo in 1815.

On the occasion of the coronation of King George IV on 19 July 1821, St Vincent received the ultimate accolade from a grateful sovereign, when he was promoted Admiral of the Fleet – the first officer ever to hold the rank other than a member of the royal family. St Vincent would have a last meeting with the King on 10 August 1822 when the latter embarked on his yacht *Royal George* for a voyage of exploration to Scotland. The 88-year-old Admiral was received on board the yacht when she was lying off the Royal Greenwich Hospital before her departure. The King took St Vincent by the arm and led him to the quarterdeck where they sat and conversed for some time. When St Vincent rose to depart, His Majesty insisted on descending the gangway with him, holding him by the arm to assist him into his boat.

Admiral of the Fleet Lord St Vincent died on 14 March 1823 of 'excessive weariness and unrest'. On his death bed he was visited, among others, by three old friends: Doctor Baird his physician of many years; Benjamin Tucker, his former private secretary, now a Commissioner of the Navy and Second Secretary of the Admiralty; and by his former flag captain Sir George Grey – son of his old friend Sir Charles.

St Vincent was buried in the family mausoleum in the church-yard of St Michael's at Stone, near his birthplace, Meaford. There is a monument to his memory in St Paul's Cathedral, though his achievements, correspondence and dictums are the real memorial.

Looking back at his career and acknowledging the debt Britannia owed him for his lifelong dedication to protecting her from invasion by Napoleon, there is still a measure of regret on two counts: that Nelson's debt to his patron has not been acknowledged, and that St Vincent himself sometimes failed to put merit above prejudice and humanity above discipline.

Bibliography

Bonner Smith, David, *The St Vincent Papers*, Navy Records Society, 1921, 1926.

Brenton, Captain E.P., *Life and Correspondence of John, Earl of St Vincent*, 2 vols, 1838.

Carter, George, *Outlines of English History*, Relfe Brothers, London, 1924.

Chronicle of Britain and Ireland, Chronicle Communications Ltd, Farnborough, 1992.

Cochrane, Thomas, Tenth Earl of Dundonald, *Autobiography of a Seaman*, Richard Bentley & Son, London, 1890.

Grimble, Ian, *The Sea Wolf*, Blond & Briggs, London, 1978.

Kennedy, Ludovic, *Nelson's Band of Brothers*, Odhams Press Limited, London, 1951.

Knox Laughton, Sir T., *British Sailor Heroes*, Bickers & Son Ltd, London, 1930.

Lewis, Michael, *England's Sea Officers*, George Allen and Unwin Ltd, London, 1939.

——, *The Navy of Britain*, George Allen and Unwin Ltd, London, 1948.

Lloyd, Christopher, *Lord Cochrane*, Henry Holt and Company, New York, 1948.

Masefield, John, *Sea Life in Nelson's Time*, Methuen & Co. Ltd, London, 1905.

Sherrard, O.H., *Life of Lord St Vincent*, 1933.

Southey, Robert, *Life of Lord Nelson*, 1813.

Tucker, *Memoirs of the Earl of St Vincent*, 2 vols, 1844.

Table of Rates

	No. of Guns	Weight of Broadsides	No. of Men	Tonnage	Length of Lower Gun Deck	Cost (without guns)
First-Rate	100 or more	2,500–2,550lb	850–950	2,000–2,600 tons	180ft	£70,000–100,000
Second-Rate	98 or 90	2,050–2,300lb	750	2,000 tons	170–180ft	£60,000
Third-Rate	80, 74 or 64	1,970, 1,764 or 1,200lb	720, 640, 490	2,000, 1,700, 1,300 tons	170–160ft	£54,000–36,000
Fourth-Rate	50	800lb	350	1,100 tons	150ft	£26,000
Fifth-Rate	44, 40, 38, 36 or 32	635–350lb	320, 300, 250, 215	900–799 tons	150–130ft	£21,500–15,000
Sixth-Rate	28, 24, 20	250–180lb	200–160	650–550 tons	130–120ft	£13,000–10,000

Index